IMAGINING SIAM

A TRAVELLERS' LITERARY
GUIDE TO THAILAND

IMAGINING SIAM

A TRAVELLERS' LITERARY
GUIDE TO THAILAND

CARON EASTGATE DANN

MONASH UNIVERSITY PRESS
CLAYTON

Monash University Press
Building 11
Monash University
Victoria 3800, Australia
www.monash.edu.au/mai

All Monash University Press publications are subject to double blind peer review

National Library of Australia Cataloguing-in-Publication entry

Author: Dann, Caron.

Title: Imagining Siam : a travellers' literary guide to Thailand /
          Caron Dann.

ISBN: 9781876924621 (pbk.)

Series: Monash papers on Southeast Asia ; no. 68.

Notes: Bibliography.

Subjects: Literary landmarks--Thailand.

          Authors, Thai--Homes and haunts--Thailand.

          Thailand--Guidebooks.

Other Authors/Contributors:

          Monash University. Monash Asia Institute.

Dewey Number: 895.9109

Cover design by Jenny Hall.

Printed by BPA Print Group, Melbourne, Australia - www.bpabooks.com

contents

About the author

Caron Eastgate Dann is a lecturer, journalist and writer. She lived in Thailand from 1990–1993 and from 1997–1999, where she worked as a teacher and journalist. She researched and wrote her novel *The Occidentals* (Asia Books, 1999) there, under the name Caron Eastgate James. The novel has been published in Germany in translation as *Das Erbe der Schwestern* (Nymphenburger 2003, Knaur 2005). She graduated from Monash University with a PhD in literary studies in 2007 and her thesis was the inspiration for this book. In 2008, she worked as a lecturer in Communications for Monash University. She has worked as a journalist in New Zealand, Australia and Thailand and is a regular contributor to the travel section of the *Sunday Herald Sun* and an occasional contributor to other publications including *The Australian Literary Review*. She is currently working on several upcoming books, including the sequel to *The Occidentals*, a biography of Louis Leonowens (son of Anna of *The King and I* fame), and a non-fiction work about friendship and social networking websites. She lives in Melbourne with her husband, journalist Gordon Dann.

List of illustrations

Preface

My first impressions of Thailand were formed not by a package-deal holiday to a coastal resort or to a jungle hideaway, but by a stage show in Auckland, New Zealand—a 1970s amateur production of *The King and I*. With a group of other Caucasian children, I was to play the part of an unnamed Siamese princess. The fair colouring of many in the group compromised the credibility of our characterisations, so the wardrobe assistant gave us Chinese-style wigs to wear with straight black hair—although 19th-century Thai children had top-knots. I refused to wear my wig, because the hair looked so unfamiliar to me, so the show had to go on with one blonde seven-year-old Thai princess. That was the extent of my knowledge of Thailand until I went to live there in 1990.

For most of the two-and-a-half years of my first stay, I was an 'expat wife'. I used that most luxurious of commodities, time, to research and write a novel set in 19th-century Siam, published in 1999 as *The Occidentals*.[1] Soon after arriving in Thailand, I joined the Siam Society, an association devoted to preserving Thai culture and history, with a library of 20,000 books. Until then, my knowledge of Thailand's history was confined to largely fictionalised images of 19th-century schoolteacher Anna Leonowens and her sometime employer, King Mongkut, from *The King and I*. The idea for a novel came as I read more about the controversy surrounding Leonowens and the coming of Westernisation to Thailand.

Research for *The Occidentals* led me to the intriguing mystery and the real story behind the fictionalised accounts of Leonowens and King Mongkut dramatised in *The King and I*, and from there to examine an entire body of Western representations of Thailand. I found that although primary source material was plentiful, comprehensive secondary material was rare. There was little critical discourse, no survey of writing by travellers about the kingdom, and it was ignored in most academic discussions of Orientalism. Widening my search, I discovered that although travellers had written about Thailand for centuries, their work was rarely included in critical examination of such writing.

This book aims to fill that void. It evolved from my PhD thesis, completed in November, 2006. Early in my research, I said to my supervisor, Associate

Professor Robin Gerster, at Monash University, Melbourne, that I wished there were a broad study of Western writing about Thailand. 'You're writing it,' he replied. And, so I was. The study covers all types of prose written in or translated to English. It is aimed not only at scholars but also at general readers and travellers who are interested in travel writing about Southeast Asia and Thailand, in film, colonial and postcolonial writing. I hope that it will clear the way for further studies of travellers' literature written about this intriguing part of the world.

Acknowledgments

This book evolved from my PhD thesis at the Department of English, Communications and Performance Studies, Monash University, Melbourne. I am indebted to my supervisor, Associate Professor Robin Gerster, for his invaluable guidance, particularly on theoretical aspects.

When the manuscript was accepted for publication by Monash Asia Institute, I was extremely fortunate that Professor David Chandler agreed to edit my work. Professor Chandler, renowned for his books about Cambodia, has a formidable knowledge of Southeast Asia and has lived in Thailand. He also appreciates what will make a good read, and helped me pare back and revise the manuscript to move away from its doctoral origins. I knew we would work together well when, at our first meeting, he said 'This is going to be fun!'

I was incredibly fortunate, also, that historian Tamara Loos of Cornell University in the US agreed to read and comment on a large chunk of the manuscript before publication. Associate Professor Loos is the author of the ground-breaking text *Subject Siam: Family, Law, and Colonial Modernity in Thailand* (Cornell University Press, Ithaca, 2006). Her enthusiasm for the project and constructive criticism were particularly welcome. 'It [*Imagining Siam*] offers the first thorough analysis of travelogues and travel literature about Siam/Thailand…There is no other work focused singularly on Thailand that covers such a broad chronological time period,' Associate Professor Loos said.

Many thanks to Jenny Hall of Monash Asia Institute for all her work and co-ordination in a multitude of areas leading to publication. Jenny had the happy task of officially confirming MAI's acceptance of the manuscript. I was on assignment for the *Sunday Herald Sun* in Bendigo that day and the sun seemed to shine brighter and the town clock chimes seemed to peal just for me after I received her email! Since then, Jenny has shown never-ending patience with me, even when I have missed deadlines. Jenny is a source of calm encouragement and terrific ideas to make this book the best it could be.

During the writing of the thesis and the book, many writers were happy to correspond with me by email about their work, among them Susan Fulop Kepner, Al Habegger, and Mary Bulkley Stanton in the US, Lois K Yorke in Canada, Andrew Hicks, Howard Richardson and Philip Cornwel-Smith in Thailand, Robert Brunton and Gerard Foley in Australia.

I was fortunate, when I visited the Louis T Leonowens Company in Bangkok, to meet the then managing director's executive secretary, Sireeyada Leewattanakit. She gave me an address for Anna Leonowens's great-great-granddaughter, Lucy Bahr, who passed on my letter to her father, Louis T Leonowens in Guatemala. He has corresponded courteously and with enthusiasm, and has been a source of some interesting information about his famous namesake…but that can wait for the novelised biography I am writing of his grandfather.

I would like to give heartfelt thanks to my husband, Gordon Dann, a fine journalist who spent many hours sub-editing drafts of the manuscript and who has been extremely supportive in all my endeavours. Not many men I know organise their own weddings: it's usually left to the bride. In our case, I submitted my PhD thesis on 28 November 2006 and we were married less than a week later on 4 December 2006. So, about 80% of the wedding arrangements were left to Gordon—and he did a spectacular job.

I would also like to thank my mother, Dr Sheila Eastgate, for invaluable support throughout the project and for meticulously proof-reading the bibliography. My father, Dr Harold Eastgate, passed away unexpectedly during the final year of my PhD and sometimes I wondered how I would have the strength to go on. But then I was reminded that during the final stages of my mother's PhD, she lost her son, my 17-year-old brother, Phillip, in a road accident. She still managed to finish her PhD—so, I decided, I would be like her. Success! As a consequence, after working as a journalist for 28 years, I now have a new career as a full-time university lecturer, starting this year in Communications at Monash University (which followed an enjoyable part-time stint teaching mostly international students at Monash College).

And then, of course, there is Thailand. It has been the subject of some of the Western world's blockbuster films and is one of the most popular destinations for tourists, backpackers and adventurers alike. It is a country of vast contrasts and an interesting mix of cultures to add to the dominant Thai-Buddhist, including Chinese, Indian, Muslim and Anglo-Western. Yes, it is superb beaches of white sand, fringed with palm trees; it is raunchy red-light districts that cater to almost every desire; it is glittering temples; it is elephant rides through jungle paths. It is all the tourist brochures say it is, but it is so much more than that as well. Above all, it is itself: beautiful, complex, and most importantly, unique.

Thailand's famed holiday playground of Phuket took just minutes to turn from paradise to hell.—Danny Butler (Butler 2004)

For some 10,000 British holidaymakers, the hot weather and the legendary atmosphere popularised in Alex Garland's novel *The Beach* had made the southeast Asia region enduringly attractive. Yesterday, the dream turned to horror as a tsunami swept across the region…—Helen Carter (Carter 2004)

Foreign media coverage of the tsunamis that swamped South and Southeast Asia on 26 December 2004, insisted that 'we' had 'lost' the popular Thai resort island of Phuket, and that some sort of dream was over. In the weeks after the disaster, print and broadcast media repeatedly used the trope 'paradise lost', derived, of course, from John Milton's canonical 17th-century poem about Man's loss of innocence in the Garden of Eden.

Yet Phuket was not lost at all; it still existed after the tsunami, albeit after much loss of life and destruction of property, and has been largely rebuilt. Unlike the tourists, the people who inhabit the island could not simply board a plane and resume their normal lives, lamenting the loss of Eden. When bemoaning Phuket as a 'paradise lost', commentators in the West were obliquely lamenting the island's fall from grace as a seductive option for those attracted by the lure of 'exotic' Thailand. A name on the itinerary had been washed away, at least temporarily; this was seen as a touristic, as well as a human, tragedy.

In discussing his classic 1978 study *Orientalism: Western conceptions of the Orient*, Edward W Said identifies an habitual pattern to the Western imaginative management of 'the East', an intersection of imagination and ideology in which the Orient is 'routinely described as feminine', its symbols the 'sensual woman', 'the harem', and 'the despotic—but curiously attractive—ruler' (Said 2000:357). Thailand does not appear on Said's map of theoretical inquiry. His focus in *Orientalism* is almost exclusively trained on European responses to the Middle

East and, even in the broader *Culture and imperialism* (1993), Thailand does not rate a mention, though Vietnam, Cambodia and Myanmar do. One of the purposes of this study is to examine how Thailand as a culturally determined Western construct might fit into the paradigm devised and described in *Orientalism*.

Western constructions of Thailand constitute an intriguing case study of Orientalist attitudes, particularly because the country was never officially colonised, maintaining its political independence.[2] Consequently, there is no historical basis for the construction of Thailand as a colonised territory in the Western imagination. Nonetheless, Thailand has been systematically transformed into a classic neocolonial object of Western desire, an easily penetrated erotic zone that caters to the appetites of Western interlopers, the worst of whom expect everyone to speak English and to be willing to serve them with a smile of welcome and tacit subservience.

The international press coverage of the tsunami was remarkable for exhibiting the Orientalist strategy of articulating Western values while purporting to speak on the Thais' behalf. Tourists were photographed lying on beach chairs as the clean-up operation proceeded behind them—and were criticised for doing so, for showing 'disrespect' for the victims of the disaster and for those in mourning. In an article published in the Australian *Herald Sun* newspaper and headed 'Paradise lost', Melbourne journalist Ross Brundrett (2005:1) noted that people who continued their holidays in the disaster zone were 'deemed callous, even inhuman, by a scolding media'. Brundrett commented that the residents of Phuket might not feel the same—in fact were asking for tourists to return immediately. He observes that the question tourists were asking themselves was 'whether to return to tsunami-ravaged resorts…or should they keep a respectful distance, at least for the short-term?'.

Nine weeks after the tsunami, I travelled as a journalist to Thailand on a Thai Government-sponsored media familiarisation trip to view reconstruction at Phuket and Krabi. Thais, both those in authority and ordinary working people, made it clear they were grateful to the tourists who had stayed or had arrived since, and that they desperately wanted other tourists back because their livelihoods depended on them.

At the Andaman Recovery Seminar on 5 March 2006, attended by some 600 international journalists at Karon Beach, Phuket, the then president of Thai Airways International, Kanok Abhiradee, remarked that, though Thais felt great grief after the tsunami, 'life has to go on…we have got to look into the future so that life can get back to normal'. Already, the Tourism Authority of Thailand had produced a glossy brochure called *Andaman today*, describing each beach resort post-tsunami and reassuring would-be tourists that all was well 'For that perfect holiday beside the beach.' The brochure adds: 'Thailand's Andaman Sea overflows with options'. While this may be an inadvertently ironic play on the tragic inundation that killed thousands, the island post-tsunami abounded with blithe references to the disaster. At Phuket International Airport, traders were selling T-shirts picturing a huge wave overwhelming two wooden fishing boats, and containing the words 'Tsunami, Phuket, December 26, 2004', printed across the front. On the back of the garment were the words 'Never again'. Meanwhile, in Bangkok, the Marriott Hotel had opened a sushi bar called Tsu and an adjoining teppanyaki room called Nami (Carbone & Money 2005:14). The power of the dollar—or in this case, the baht—takes precedence, it would seem, everywhere.

After the tsunami: foreign tourists walk past Thai workers at Patong Beach, Phuket, on 20 January 2005. The workers were part of the clean-up operation after the tsunami of 26 December 2004. Credit: AP Photo/Teh Eng Koon.

There has been lamentably little inquiry into Western writing about Thailand. Individual texts, such as the works by Anna Leonowens and Margaret Landon, on which *The King and I* was based, have been discussed by several critics, but there is no comprehensive critical study or even a survey of Western literature about Thailand. Notable critics of Orientalist discourse, such as Said, Rana Kabbani, Mary Louise Pratt and Christina Klein, do not discuss Thailand, though their theoretical principles about the relationship of power to representation have been useful in my critical inquiry into Western writing about Thailand. In what follows, I hope to provide a basis from which future studies of the topic may be launched. For this reason, it is necessarily broad, covering writing from 13th-century attempts to describe Siam, through the formative phase of Western engagement with Siam in the 16th century, to the various competing European imperialisms in the 19th century, to today's era of mass tourism and the global reach and influence of mobile, economically and culturally powerful 'First World' populations.

As representational concepts, the terms 'East' and 'West' are problematic. They assume the world is divided into two hemispheres in dialectical opposition to the other, with an attendant set of binaries: those of feminine/masculine, sensual/intellectual, mystical/scientific, civilised/barbarous, and so on. The terms 'East' and 'West' themselves are Eurocentric and evidence of an inherited world view removed from empirical geography, but revealing what Ali Behdad calls 'the imaginative geography that separates the Orient from the Occident, the black from the white' (Behdad 1994:6). Said describes Orientalism as 'a style of thought based upon an ontological and epistemological distinction between "the Orient" and (most of the time) "the Occident"', dealing with the East by 'making statements about it, authorizing views of it, describing it, by teaching it, settling it, ruling over it...' (Said 2003:1–3). This study aims to test if attitudes that have been identified as central to Said's theory of Orientalism apply to writing in English about Thailand.

Pratt observes that by the mid-18th century, European scientists had divided humans into six categories, claiming the superiority of their own race. 'Asiatics' were branded as 'sooty, melancholy, rigid...severe, haughty, covetous' (Pratt 1992:32). Pratt contends that this derogatory categorisation is still influential in Western writing about the non-Western—those who are described in much postcolonial discourse as 'the Other'. Pratt's work has been useful in assisting the formulation of several lines of inquiry this book will address. Fundamentally, the study investigates how writing in English has produced a commodified 'Thailand' and how that writing has revealed the West's conceptions of itself in relation to Thailand. It argues that the rhetoric of travel writing has often propagated colonial and neocolonial aspirations and ideologies and examines how these have revealed themselves in literature about an Asian country that has not been colonised.

Kristi Siegel and Toni B Wulff suggest that travel and travel writing today are paradoxically circumscribed activities whose motto may well be 'to seek what you already intend to find' (Siegel & Wulff 2002:112). It follows that many travel writers react largely to what they have read about a destination so that when they imagine Thailand, they see not so much a complex socio-political entity as a collection of clichés. In essence, they perceive not so much a country as a destination.

Chapter one

Amazing Thailand

Behind a bend of the Me-Nam (the mother of the waters), the entire town of Bangkok appeared in sight. I do not believe that there is a sight in the world more magnificent or more striking...The first general view of the Oriental Venice surpassed all that we could have hoped for in our travellers' dreams.—the Marquis de Beauvoir, 1870 (Beauvoir 1986).

Bangkok—the name explodes off the tongue, filling the mind with steamy images of the archetypal Southeast Asian metropolis. As you emerge from the air-conditioned airport, the thick, jasmine-scented air instantly envelops your body, while the oceanic reverberation of distant traffic fills your ears. Your heart beats perceptibly faster, sensing that Bangkok is a place you'll not easily forget.—Joe Cummings (Cummings & Williams 2004).

Though written more than a century apart, these images of Thailand through the eyes of two disparate Westerners—a 19th-century French nobleman and a 21st-century American travel guide writer—share a common epistemology. Both exemplify Edward Said's concept of Orientalism as a systematic nexus of 'knowing' and 'representing', as 'a way of coming to terms with the Orient that is based on the Orient's special place in European Western experience' (Said 2003:1). For the Marquis de Beauvoir, Bangkok appears before the tourist as if by magic, as if it does not exist independently. It is, as de Beauvoir says, the content of 'travellers' dreams' (Beauvoir 1986:11). Furthermore, its 'magnificent' impression is defined by its favourable identification with a European city. Similarly, in Cummings's description, Bangkok becomes a reality as the tourist leaves the familiarity of the airport and emerges into what, at first experience, seems to be a conglomeration of European images of the seductive East—steamy, scented, embracing. It is, in both quotations, the Western idea of 'Orient' as described by Said (2003:1): 'a place of romance, exotic beings, haunting memories and landscapes, remarkable experiences'.

De Beauvoir and Cummings are writing in different epochs and for different audiences. While de Beauvoir's audience would have believed in the 'civilising' mission of colonialism, a significant percentage of Cummings's audience reasonably can be assumed to be critical of 19th-century imperialism and many would be aware of its role in the unjust treatment of so-called 'subject' peoples.

Given the chasms that separate the texts, the similarities are startling. They reveal that an easy-going travel guide writer today can evoke destinational desire for the East in fundamentally similar ways to those used by a snobbish 19th-century traveller. The feminised image of the dream-like Orient awaiting penetration by the Western traveller who will 'discover' it, is as prevalent today as it was then, as is the romantic notion of the brave (white) adventurer in frontier land.[3] Yet, while there are many books, articles and studies examining how this occurs in relation to other Asian countries visited by Westerners, particularly China, India and Japan, there is little critical discourse on how this has occurred in relation to Thailand.

Losing paradise

The idea of 'paradise' and the desire to discover it are important ingredients in the quotidian language of travel literature, including advertising, brochures, guides, and journalism. It is the search for 'paradise lost', Eden before the fall. Like Eden, the imagined pristine, lush, fertile landscape of Thailand awaits the traveller. And, as in Eden, seductions and dangers await.

Reportage in Australian newspapers of the tsunami of 26 December 2004 illustrates the extent to which Thailand often has been constructed as paradisiacal. Acclaimed Australian cartoonist Mark Knight skilfully illuminated this construction in Melbourne's *Herald Sun* just a few days after the tsunami. His cartoon of 29 December features swaying palm trees, quaint huts (labelled 'human lives', 'economy' and 'tourism') and stick figures running in all directions. At the centre of the sketch, two perplexed locals stand with a motorbike; behind the scene is a massive green wave; the caption reads 'Paradise lost'.

This idea that certain areas of the world are paradise for Westerners is also common in references to Bali, and similar headlines about 'Paradise lost' appeared after the two lethal bombs exploded there in October 2002 at nightclubs frequented by tourists (but to a lesser extent when bombs exploded at Jimbaran and Kuta restaurants in 2005). The concept of paradise goes hand-in-hand with that of ownership, as evidenced in the title of a book examining the consequences of the Bali bombing, *Who did this to our Bali?* (Anggraeni 2003). Australian academic Adrian Vickers, who has examined the construction of Bali in Western imaginations, says early 20th-century colonial ideas of 'paradise' differ markedly from the Balinese image of itself (Vickers 1989:2–7). Interestingly, Pico Iyer describes southern Thailand's Koh Samui as a 'baby Bali' in an article titled

'Paradise found, paradise lost' (Iyer 1997:138–45), evidence that locations deemed to be 'paradise' become interchangeable.

Paradise lost: this cartoon by Mark Knight in the Herald Sun, 29 December 2004, parodies the way areas hit by the 26 December tsunami, including Phuket, were portrayed in the Western media. Credit: The Herald and Weekly Times Photographic Collection.

The language of tourism, combined with that of war reportage (a genre with links to travel writing), was popularly employed to describe South and Southeast Asia in the weeks immediately after the tsunami. 'Tanned bodies, bagged bodies: the extremes of a tourist haven' was the sub-heading on the front-page lead in *The Sunday Age* on 2 January 2005. Meanwhile, the *New Zealand Herald* on 3 January proclaimed that, while Phi Phi before the tsunami was an 'isolated island paradise' which 'found fame in the Hollywood movie *The beach*', after the disaster 'it resemble[d] a war zone'(Masters & Phibbs 2005). Weeks later, Australian journalist Paul Edwards wrote of the 'sands of death' and 'the fatal shores' among interviews from South Asia travel industry specialists in Australia, who nevertheless declared Thailand a place that 'still is the land of smiles' (Edwards, 2005:6–7). The Australian edition of Britain's *International Express* noted that the tsunami marked 'the biggest loss of British lives in a single incident since the Second World War' (Little & Pukas 2005:1). *Time Australia* magazine called the tsunami 'sea of sorrow' and used more than 20 pages of photographs of the disaster, including the destruction of a restaurant at Hat Surin, Phuket, submerged resorts at Phi Phi Island and tourists comforting each other at Phuket city hall. 'For thousands of holidaymakers on the Thai resort island, vacation in paradise turned into a brutal lesson on the fury of nature', the report said (*Time Australia* 2005:14–53). Similarly, in Australia's *Royal Auto* magazine's cover story, 'the sea curled into a fist and delivered its cruel Boxing Day blow…' (Gebicki 2005).

In an article titled 'In death, imperialism lives on' in *The Guardian*, Jeremy Seabrook (2004), author of *Consuming cultures: globalisation and local life*, pointed out that the tsunami was more important to the Western media than other disasters because of the large numbers of tourists involved. Seabrook found a correlation between the language of imperialism and that of tourism and reportage of areas popular with Western tourists:

> But when we distinguish between 'locals' who have died and westerners, 'locals' all too easily becomes a euphemism for what were once referred to as natives. Whatever tourism's merits, it risks reinforcing the imperial sensibility.

> For this sensibility has already been reawakened by all the human-made, preventable catastrophes. The ruins of Galle and Bandar Aceh called forth images of Falluja, Mosul and Gaza. Imperial powers, it seems, anticipate the destructive capacity of nature. A report on ITN news made this explicit, by referring to 'nature's shock and awe' (Seabrook 2004).

Only weeks after editorial content in Australian newspapers was declaring 'Paradise lost', advertising—in a desperate effort by the tourism industry to regain customers—told us we could 'Re-discover Phuket' (Thai Airways advertisement 2005)[4] and that Phuket was a 'Paradise found' (Harvey World Travel advertisement 2005). This indicates the idea of Thailand as always willing to be 'discovered' again by intrepid travellers following in the footsteps of the colonial trailblazers. Seth Mydans's later *New York Times* article quoted a relief worker as saying visitors should return to Phuket in order to 'watch an event in history, watching how a place picks itself up'. He said that by watching this event, a visitor would become 'a traveler, not a tourist' (Mydans 2005) thereby, presumably, gaining credibility.

In 'Profit$[sic] of doom', an article examining the effects of the tsunami on international relations, Naomi Klein maintained colonialism never disappears, it merely changes its form (Klein 2005). The new colonialism was masquerading in post-tsunami Asia as reconstruction, Klein claimed. She cited Thailand as an example, describing how the government was forbidding families from rebuilding along the ocean front, rehousing displaced people in 'prefab concrete boxes'. Instead of rebuilding coastal communities the way they were, 'governments, corporations and foreign donors are teaming up to rebuild it as they would like it to be: the beaches as playgrounds for tourists...' (Klein 2005:33). Klein quoted the Thailand Tsunami Survivors and Supporters group as saying that for business owners and politicians, the tsunami was advantageous because it 'wiped these coastal areas clean of the communities that had previously stood in the way of their plans for resorts, hotels, casinos and shrimp farms'.[5] An earlier article by Alisa Tang in the *Honolulu Advertiser*, published just nine days after the tsunami, quoted an American tourist in Phuket, Greg Ferrando, of Maui, who echoed that view in claiming the disaster's positive side was in 'washing away rampant development' from beaches that had been 'swamped by development'. The article also quoted an Israeli expatriate, Moriel Avital: 'Paradise should be paradise and should not become this civilized' (Tang 2005). Such a notion would never be expressed openly in the Western media if a disaster wiped out London or Tel Aviv, for example. When the World Trade Centre in New York was bombed on 11 September 2001, it would have been considered grossly insensitive to say, 'Oh well, we were better off without the Twin Towers anyway'.

The print media's portrayal of the tsunami could be criticised as Eurocentric, patronising or neocolonial, yet the Thai tourism industry and media's portrayal differed little from that of Australia, Britain and the US. A post-tsunami Thai Airways advertisement for Australian audiences reads, 'THAI's Royal Orchid Holidays welcomes you back to this island paradise...'. Over a picture of Phuket's Kata Beach with two Western couples walking along the sand, the headline is 'Re-discover Phuket' (Thai Airways advertisement 2005). This is an example of the way Thailand has used the West's portrayal of it to its own advantage, coming up with its own Orientalist/colonial perception of the country to entice tourists. In a post-tsunami edition of *Sawasdee*, the in-flight magazine of Thai Airways, the airline's president, Kanok, assured customers that 'Thailand remains a tourism paradise' (Kanok 2005).

Out of the blue (Lyall 2006), a compelling account by Australian foreign correspondent Kimina Lyall of what it was like to live through the tsunami—and at times a damning indictment of the way the press reports disasters—was published in December 2006. Lyall was working for the *Australian* newspaper at the time as its Southeast Asia correspondent and lived with her partner, JP, at Golden Buddha Beach on Koh Phra Thong off Thailand's west coast. The couple built a house among a small predominantly expatriate community there, and Lyall would spend all her days off there. Being the day after Christmas when the tsunami hit the island, Lyall and JP were in residence. The tsunami killed 13 members of the community. (Miraculously, Lyall and JP's house remained intact.) Lyall's story offers a raw look at the disaster from two opposing viewpoints: on one hand, she is a journalist doing a job; on the other, she is intimately involved in the tsunami, its destruction and its aftermath. Lyall

conveys how the disaster was unwittingly treated as just another story by the
press and as a chance to feel charitable by the public:

> One woman even said: 'Oh, I must invite my friends around for dinner and
> you can tell us the whole story.'

> Almost everyone we met felt some kind of ownership of the tsunami, as if it
> was their disaster, too. Perhaps it was because they had reached into their pockets,
> pulling out enough dollars to compensate for the hours they had sat in front of
> the television staring at scarred beaches (Lyall 2006:239).

Though of course, the post-tsunami aid from Western nations was mostly
well-intentioned, Lyall's experiences reveal that it still carries the weight of the
old 'white man's burden'. Six weeks after the tsunami, she meets a German aid
organisation worker at Kurabari who is desperate to find 'a school destroyed'
and asks for her help, to which she replies that there were many schools
destroyed:

> 'But they are all taken,' he said, crestfallen. 'We only just arrived, and we
> are too late.'

> 'I'm sure there's something else you can do with your money,' I said.

> 'No, it has to be a school. It has to be a school' (Lyall 2006:223).

Along the way, Lyall's comments on travel in Thailand also make a worthy
contribution to the discourse. In their search for 'that ideal isolated beach', she
and JP come across Pakarang Cape, north of Khao Lak: 'We were all but the only
farangs (foreigners) there. Here was Thailand enjoying its own paradise' (Lyall
2006:6). She is conscious of their feeling 'that urge of all privileged Westerners
on holiday, the endless search for the best it's-bound-to-be-just-around-the-next-
point beach' (2006:7). Ironically, of course, when she and JP do find that ideal
beach and settle there, it becomes with the tsunami the opposite of the idyllic
experience they had yearned for.

Early travel guides

Travel guides to Thailand did not emerge until the late 19th century and tended
to be written by people who were there for another reason—usually trade,
business, diplomacy or in a governmental advisory capacity. In those days, travel
to Siam was difficult and expensive, and in any case, there was little tourism
before the advent of accessible air travel. Although mass air tourism took off
in the 1970s, established travel guide publishers such as Baedeker ignored
Thailand until the 1980s.[6]

Historically, travel was difficult within Thailand because of the inaccessible
terrain and the lack of infrastructure. Travel was laborious, uncomfortable,

unpredictable and expensive. Above all, it was considered dangerous by Thais and foreigners alike—tigers, venomous snakes and bandits, as well as the possibility of contracting a potentially fatal illness such as malaria, were some of the perils awaiting the 19th-century traveller. Ironically, after many decades of relative safety in the 20th century, Thailand is again considered dangerous, with frequent Australian Government warnings against travelling there. Since 2001, the warnings have included possible terrorist attacks within the definition of the US-led 'war on terrorism', political disturbances in southern Thailand, the danger of contracting bird flu or SARS, geological instability after the 2004 tsunami, and the military coup of 2006.[7] All have had a negative impact on tourism, particularly in the months immediately after each event.

Siam in the 19th century was not a tour destination for Westerners in Asia as were Singapore or Hong Kong. Bangkok was not a port of call on Thomas Cook's tours—Japan, China, India, Burma and Ceylon were listed, however (see Swinglehurst 1982:68–87). Travellers to Siam in the 19th century were mainly missionaries, businessmen, diplomats, or experts appointed by the King and his advisers to government departments or teaching positions. Owing to this lack of travellers, particularly those on the move for its own sake or those travelling specifically to write about it, writing about Thailand at this time is limited in scope, volume and quality. Most of it centres on Bangkok and is compiled by visitors who were not professional writers. After only a week in the kingdom, for example, de Beauvoir felt qualified not only to include a substantial chapter on it in his 1870 book *Voyage autour du monde* (the Siam section was later excerpted and published separately as A Week in Siam 1867), but also to proclaim the Siamese a 'hideous' race whose king (Mongkut) was 'very like a monkey', whose country he insisted would be invaded by Europeans and would 'soon succumb to the influence of France and England' (Beauvoir 1986:14,53,82).

Most guidebooks to Thailand in the late 19th and early 20th centuries were published in Bangkok for the expatriate community. Cecil Carter's *The Kingdom of Siam 1904* (Carter, 1988), compiled to coincide with the Siamese exhibition at the Louisiana Purchase Exposition that year, was one of few guides published overseas. It was, however, aimed at traders, not tourists. The most comprehensive early guide to Thailand was *The 1904 traveller's guide to Bangkok and Siam,* by J Antonio (1997), a draughtsman working in Bangkok. Antonio was a long-time Bangkok resident and the guide is unusual for the time in that it covers travel outside the capital, to areas such as Lopburi and Korat, though he discourages travellers from going to northern Thailand unless they have to.

Late 19th-century and early 20th-century guides to Thailand were, for the most part, practical guides without much hyperbole, though permeated with colonialist attitudes, as shown, for example, in Antonio's description of Siam as 'a country emerging from the darkness of an ancient barbarism' (Antonio 1997:1). Antonio (1997:1–2) says, however, that despite modernisation, visitors are drawn to the country because of the 'relics of ancient barbarism and superstition' that exist side-by-side with 'progress'. Antonio recognises that travellers not only seek an East made accessible because of Western modernisation, but also want to experience what they imagine is the authentic East, which, as many critics have remarked, can be interpreted as a search for aspects of our own vanished past. As far back as 1955, the anthropologist Claude Lévi-Strauss commented in *Tristes Tropiques* that travel books and their 'deceptiveness' owed their popularity to their ability to 'create the illusion of something which no longer exists but still should exist…' (Levi-Strauss 1955, cited in Fussell 1987:777). Furthermore, Behdad's description of anthropologists' observation and classification of 'natives' in order to write 'an ethnography that denies the Other coevalness' can be applied to travel writing in general, and particularly to the travel guide, which, like the anthropologists' writings, uses maps and other graphics 'to visualize the Other's culture' (Behdad 1994:6). An example is Antonio's meticulously drawn scale plan of Bangkok, which is included in his guide. This is, of course, a rather cynical view and can result in overanalysing travel guides: they may also be seen simply as information to enable visitors to better visualise and traverse the country.[8]

Antonio is mentioned in *The 1894 directory for Bangkok and Siam* (Tips 1996:163,170) as a Bangkok resident at least a decade before his guide was published, so he would have been well-equipped to compile a guidebook. As he notes in the preface, his was the only 'real' travel guide to Thailand published at that time (Antonio 1997:xix). Of course, many expatriates then, as now, lived a cocooned and privileged existence, socialising with other expatriates and upper-class Thais. They had little access to ordinary Thai life, though, as a photographer, Antonio could be expected to have observed his subjects more closely than other visitors might have done. His photographs are used in his guide and in Charles Buls's *Siamese sketches* (Buls 1994), and are reproduced in many other publications, sometimes without credit.

For all his experience of living in Thailand, Antonio's views on the perceived superiority of Western culture resemble the views de Beauvoir formed in a week. Like most Europeans of his era, Antonio believed Thailand should emulate the West and that it was the West's duty to enlighten the East. In his conclusion, he praises Thailand for its 'progress', but asserts that, 'Much remains to be accomplished, no doubt, before Siam can consider herself on the same plane as the older nations of the West…' (Antonio 1997:90).

Western writers tend to describe sites in the East by comparing them with those in the West, while asserting the superiority of advanced Western civilisation. An example can be found in Lucien Fournereau's *Bangkok in 1892*, first written for readers of a popular French travel magazine of the time, *Le tour du monde*. Fournereau scoffs at comparisons of Bangkok with Venice, though he continues to use the analogy himself, referring to 'the two Venices' and Bangkok's 'Venetian canals' (Fournereau 1998:15,17). He criticises the Siamese capital for its dirtiness and smelliness (ironically, criticisms that are frequently made of Venice itself). It is true that Bangkok was dirty, but many Western writers use the state of the streets to infer that its people were not clean personally, either. The belief that Asians are not as clean as Europeans was so deeply ingrained that even travel writers in the 20th and 21st centuries still feel the need to address it. In *Phuket*, English photo-journalist Fiona Nichols assures us that 'Thais live in attractive homes...Homes are sparse and immaculate; cleanliness is very important to a good Buddhist' (Nichols 1985:19).

Following anthropological thinking of the time, Antonio stereotypes Thais by classifying them. They are, he says, lazy (a 'national failing'), gambling-addicted, and habitual liars (Antonio 1997:90–1). There are, however, rare instances of early travel guide writers refuting racist beliefs about Thais. One such writer is AW Graham, whose 1912 book, *Siam: a handbook of practical, commercial, and political information*, was aimed at foreigners wishing to do business with Siam. Graham says the reputation of Siam's 'lower classes' as 'thieves' is 'not supported by facts'. He rebukes 'foreign observers' for having 'almost unanimously condemned' the Siamese as lazy. If tourists bothered to travel to the rural areas, where most Siamese reside, Graham says, they would see the Siamese are clever farmers, diligent scholars and hard-working clerks, whereas those in Bangkok have usually come there for reasons other than to work, and are happy to let the Chinese immigrants do menial jobs such as pulling rickshaws (Graham 1912:139).

Discovering paradise

In the first sentence of *Bangkok in 1892*, Fournereau writes 'The kingdom of Siam is in general little known' (Fournereau 1998:1), thereby negating the millions of Siamese who reside there and know it very well.[9] The sense of discovery has continued to capture the imaginations of Westerners and has permeated Western travel and exploration writing. Today's disputed distinction between travellers and tourists is evidence of this mentality. Self-proclaimed travellers purport to shun mass tourism and places where 'everyone' goes, in favour of the less-travelled path. Travellers like to have the *feeling* of being the first visitor—they might not mind seeing fellow 'travellers' but would be horrified to see a tour bus draw up. A detailed account of this phenomenon can be found in Klaus Westerhausen's study of the drifters' subculture, *Beyond the beach* (2002), featuring interviews with 63 travellers, most aged under 30, in Asia—principally Thailand—from 1989 to 1995. Westerhausen himself participated in the subculture for 25 years and looks at backpacking in its modern context as a supposedly sustainable mode of travel.

US university professor David Davies's memoirs, *Thailand: the rice bowl of Asia*, first published in 1967, illustrate how some English-language writing continued to construct the politically uncolonised Thailand as a colonial domain long after the days of the Raj in India, which was the main South Asian locus of British identification with constructions of the East. Davies is described on the dust jacket as being 'a distinguished anthropologist and explorer' who has 'made a special study of deficiency diseases among primitive people' (Davies 1973). Yet he relies on claims, hearsay and rumours for much of his material. Davies measures knowledge of an area by the extent of its penetration by Europeans, and likes to imagine that he is the 'discoverer'. He describes the northeast as 'deserted, lonely and dusty…where no European had ever been before' (1973:12). In fact, as we shall see, a number of Europeans had explored the northeast extensively in the 19th century, including the cartographer James McCarthy and the soldier and merchant, Louis Leonowens, son of the famous Anna Leonowens.[10]

The West's desire for the East manifests itself in its clamour to map the East and map-making has been identified in this way as inherent to imperialism. Davies likes to associate himself with pioneering cartography; in the introduction, he claims that one of his friends, a Mr Gairdner, spent 54 years in Thailand and 'carried out the first original survey of Siam' (Davies 1973:11). Gairdner might well have been employed as a surveyor by the Thai government in the early 20th century, but the first survey of Siam is widely attributed to McCarthy in the 1880s.[11] What is more significant, Thongchai Winichakul's definitive history of the mapping of Thailand, *Siam mapped* (1997), does not mention Gairdner.

Davies goes on to observe that Siam is one of the few countries that still has 'big unexplored regions…No one knows what lies in these areas' (Davies 1973:30). Yet, in the next sentence, he notes that these areas are inhabited. In Davies's view, these inhabitants are desperate for foreigners to arrive—they 'struggle to get a peep at any foreigner' (1973:12). This is an example of what Karen Lawrence calls 'the search to make it new' in travel writing and then to claim the land: '[E]ven if the territory has not actually been colonized, it probably has been in the imagination of the explorer' (Lawrence 1994:24). Davies is anachronistic for the late 1960s, particularly when he suggests internment of humans for anthropological study. He refers to the 'people of the yellow leaves' tribe in Thailand's northeast, suggesting that, 'If one or two could be caught, we could know for certain if they do differ markedly from common human stock, as has been reported' (Davies 1973:17). He doesn't say who has reported this information.

Despite Davies's backward-looking alliance with imperialist and colonial ideologies, his descriptions of Thailand are in some ways similar to those found in travel guides today. He evokes exotic images of sensuous women, glittering temples and 'wild and fascinating music', and reassures the reader that, although Thailand has accepted many 'ideas of the new world', it has maintained its unique traditions (Davies 1973:29).

The 'mystical East'

One of the most enduring imaginative constructions propagated by Western travel writers is that of the 'mystical East'; the trope appears constantly in all genres and across the centuries. Fournereau, a French architect and author of books about Asian art in the late 19th century, employed typical Orientalist language in *Bangkok in 1892*, the least scholarly of his works. Fournereau writes that Bangkok's famous pagoda Wat Cheng (now known as Wat Arun, or the Temple of the Dawn) is a 'magical spectacle, more beautiful than nature, because it is the palpable realisation of the most extravagant visions which can haunt you after the troubling reading of *A thousand and one nights*' (Fournereau 1998:28).

Enduring city scape: a view across the Chao Phraya River in Bangkok from Wat Arun (Temple of the Dawn) to the spires of the Grand Palace temples. This picture was taken in 1950, and the temples look the same today (though the city scape is now also full of skyscrapers). Credit: AP Photo/Charles Gorry.

In *Orientalism*, Said discusses *The Arabian nights* as an Orientalist construction, particularly in Richard Burton's translation and 'Terminal essay' (Said 2003:193–4). Fournereau's application of the mystique of *The Arabian nights* to Wat Arun underlines Kabbani's point that the tales deeply penetrated European literature, becoming synonymous with the Orient generally (Kabbani 1994:22,29) and blurring fact with fiction. The literary tourism boom is evidence of this with, for example, tours marketed by travel agents to the location for the 1996 book and 2000 film of *The beach*. There is also James Bond Island, colloquially renamed by the Thai tourism industry as such after *The man with the golden gun* was filmed there in 1974.[12]

The way fiction and non-fiction are combined in both filmic and literary texts is illustrated poignantly by a bizarre book called *Walt Disney's Siam* (Boulle 1958). The book was written as a companion to Disney's Oscar-winning 1954 film of the same name in its *The world and its inhabitants* series. Ironically, it was written by Pierre Boulle, the French novelist who was then best-known for another work on Thailand, *The bridge on the River Kwai* (Boulle 1952). The Disney-ised version of Siam is, of course, diametrically opposed to Boulle's depiction of the squalour and brutality of the Japanese prisoner-of-war camps along the Burma-Siam Railway. *Walt Disney's Siam* is written as a guided tour in a fantasy-like style, much of it as a conversation between a foreigner who knows the country and one who does not. Some italicised sections are quotations from various publications, including earlier descriptions of Siam, but none is sourced.

> In this 'backward' kingdom, the traveller is welcomed with smiles. Let us follow this bus. It is taking tourists, through wide avenues, to an hotel which can vie with our finest palaces. Yes, there are nevertheless a few highways in Siam. *All roads lead to heaven*, even Western ones, and this 'backward' kingdom has since a long time taken to the latter at the same time following its traditional lanes (Boulle 1958:43).

Much is made of the Siamese being independent and, given the time of writing, the late 1950s when anxieties about communism were feverish in the US, the book appears to have a secondary purpose as a put-down of 'Red' China. The Chinese in Thailand are presented as living in 'smelly hovels' in 'dirty and narrow' alleys where they run 'miserable shops' (Boulle 1958:48). In comparison, the 'primitive' Siamese are presented as a happy, simple, yet clever people whose educated class speaks Western languages and wears European clothes. 'You now find the Siamese *too* civilized,' our guide says. 'Let us go elsewhere…Let us flee from this quarter which does not quench your thirst for exoticism' (Boulle 1958:44). The book, though intriguingly poetic, reads as if it were describing a mystical fantasyland.

Late-20th- and early-21st-century guides

> My own travelling days are over, and I do not expect to see many travel books in
> the near future. When I was a reviewer, they used, I remember, to appear in batches
> of four or five a week, cram-full of charm and wit and enlarged Leica snapshots.
> There is no room for tourists in a world of 'displaced persons'.—Evelyn Waugh,
> 1946 (Waugh 1959:9)

Contrary to what Evelyn Waugh predicted, travel literature has flourished
since the Second World War.[13] There were, however, comparatively few travel
books about Thailand—particularly guides—before the 1980s. Lonely Planet's
first Thailand-specific guidebook was published in 1982, though it had included
Thailand in its Southeast Asian guides since the early 1970s.

Antonio's 1904 guide, with sections on how to reach Bangkok from overseas,
on accommodation, amusements, sights and where and how to travel within
the country, foreshadows what travel guide publishers produce today. Antonio
assumes Western travellers will prefer to seek the company of other Westerners.
Today, this attitude can be seen everywhere among tourists in Thailand, who tend
to congregate at certain beaches, resorts, and events such as 'full moon' parties,
where Thais and other Asians are a small minority. Thus, Gerster's analogy of
the hotel as 'a kind of neo-imperial enclave' (Gerster 1995:17) can be widened
to include the whole gamut of tourist experiences in Thailand.

Gerster goes on to note that travellers, particularly those to Asia, who read
about their destination before departing, are often influenced more by that
literature than by the actual sights/sites (Gerster 1995:22). As Behdad (1994:43)
describes, they travel, guidebook in hand, in order to verify what they have
read. 'Above all, the tourist guide can be viewed as an ultimate instrument of
knowledge (and therefore, power) that mediates the relation of the traveler to
the sight' (Behdad 1994:50). By itinerising, mapping and describing a location,
guides are 'defining the desire for the Orient', he adds (1994:52). While
purporting to be factual and objective, travel guides are often the creations of
highly subjective writers whose job it is to evoke an emotional response in the
reader—namely, desire. Travellers' responses to a destination are, naturally,
influenced by what the travel guide has led them to expect. Although travel
guides are packed with facts, every guide in English I have examined for this
study also employs the language of Orientalism, particularly in its introduction,
as part of its push to make Thailand desirable and to convince the reader that
this guide, above all others, will best help the tourist become a 'traveller'. As
Behdad (1994:43) observes, travel guides are 'an exhaustive enumeration of
possible positions of the reader's desire'. As long ago as 1929, Evelyn Waugh

was sardonically noting the smugness with which 'Every Englishman abroad…
likes to consider himself a traveller and not a tourist' (Waugh1959:17).

Guides are purchased with a specific type of travel in mind—budget,
adventure (for example, jungle treks),[14] ecotourism, luxury, recreation and so
on. Guide publishers are in an awkward position: on the one hand, people often
buy guides hoping they will reveal destinations that are 'off the beaten track';
on the other, once the 'secret' destination is in a guidebook, thousands may
visit and the guidebook is blamed for 'ruining' the destination. Alex Garland's
protagonist, Richard, comments on this dichotomy in *The beach*:

> Set up in Bali, Ko Pha-Ngan, Ko Tao, Borocay, and the hordes are bound
> to follow. There's no way you can keep it out of Lonely Planet, and once that
> happens it's countdown to doomsday (Garland 1997:139).

The guidebook market is changing with the increasing popularity and reach
of new media such as the internet. Lonely Planet co-founder Tony Wheeler told
me in 2007 that backpackers and young travellers in general no longer took
guides with them but used internet cafés instead (Dann 2007:15). The future
of printed travel guides, he said, was limited and, increasingly, would be the
preserve of older customers, eventually shrinking to almost nothing.[15] This trend
is evident in publications such as the glossy, full-colour *National Geographic
Traveler Thailand* (Macdonald & Parkes 2001),[16] which uses its influential
name to appeal to travellers who aspire to a more luxurious travel experience.
'A century of travel experience in every guide', the cover proclaims. Meanwhile,
the British-produced *Eyewitness Travel Guides Thailand* appeals to travellers
interested in arts, food and cultural life (Thiro 2004).

Parkes's introduction in the 2000 Moon Travel handbook is starkly Orientalist
in its use of the imagery of colonial travel:

> In a world gone increasingly dull, Thailand and its capital city of Bangkok
> remain worlds of magic and mystery, adventure and romance, far-flung
> destinations still strange and exciting in a Westernized world (Parkes 2000:1),

Parkes uses Western writing about Thailand to explain the country's appeal
as a travel destination. Parkes credits early Western writers, from Marco Polo on,
with initiating Thailand's 'romantic image' and says the tradition is maintained
by today's writers and adventurers who 'continue to explore and interpret the
brave new world of Thailand and Southeast Asia' (Parkes 2000:1). The question
must be asked: whose new world? Archaeological digs in northeast Thailand
have found evidence of hierarchical societies dated between 1400 and 1000BC,
and inhabitants of Thailand had established trade networks with neighbouring
countries (and perhaps further afield) by 1000BC (Barwise & White 2002:29).
Parkes's term 'new world' refers to its comparatively late entry to the tourism

industry's itinerary—from the tourist's perspective it is a land waiting to be discovered and explored.

Parkes acknowledges that the country's reputation as an 'Eastern paradise' is due not only to popular Hollywood films such as *The beach* but to the Tourism Authority of Thailand itself, with its clever advertising campaigns aimed at capitalising on Western mythologies of seductive Thailand. Parkes maintains that the campaigns, however, reveal the 'real' Thailand, which is, in fact, everything a traveller to Asia could want. Employing a familiar device of colonial travel writers, he implies that the 'real' Thailand is in fact not quite real, but is a happy, if infantile, place full of strange sights, but safe and sanitised for Western consumption—a sort of Eastern theme park, as evidenced in his description of some of Thailand's 'mythological creatures' which 'appear inspired by Disney' (Parkes 2000:4).

Parkes tries to give a more balanced view of Thais than the Western travel industry's stereotype of them as ever-compliant hosts. But in so doing, he proceeds only to propound more stereotypical views. The Thais are not given a voice to describe themselves, but are described only by Westerners. While acknowledging stereotypes of Thais as carefree, happy and docile, he then tacks on an irrelevant 130-year-old quotation from Leonowens, who alleges Thais are lazy, greedy and mean (Leonowens 1988:25). He goes on to assure readers that the true Thai society is 'more complicated, enigmatic, and ambiguous than either of these viewpoints' (Parkes 2000:24).

Parkes then presents some sobering statistics on drug abuse, violent crime, fraud and looting of dead bodies. 'Thailand is, in fact, a very violent country', he says, where murder is 'commonplace', the rate being the same as in the US (Parkes 2000:24–5). However, he later, confusingly, contradicts himself, saying Thailand's crime rate is 'much lower than that of any Western nation' (Parkes 2000:60). In Thailand, he advises, tourists should not look for an 'unspoiled paradise forever lost', because Westernisation has reached every part of the country, and formerly 'unknown' and 'untouched' destinations such as Koh Samui are now overrun with tourists from Europe and Australia and 'marred by schlock shops, sacrificing their souls for economic reward' (Parkes 2000:4). Parkes buys in to the whole 'adventurer/explorer in paradise' construction—or at least encourages his readers to dream about it:

> Even as you read this paragraph, somewhere in Thailand an adventurous backpacker sits on a deserted beach on an untouched island, smiling at the villagers and believing himself or herself to be the luckiest person in the world (Parkes 2000:4).

Parkes closes his introduction with, 'Have a great adventure' (Parkes 2000:5), acknowledging that travellers still seek excitement to turn into anecdotes to tell the folks back home. It is necessary to continue a pretence of the unknown, apparently, if one is to have an adventure, because today's travellers have been just about 'everywhere'. Susan Bassnett's observation that travel writing has historical links with cartography (Bassnett 2002:230) is evidenced in every travel guide. Further illustrating Bassnett's point that mapping and naming locations are forms of marking intellectual as well as physical ownership, Parkes features a map showing Western colonial expansion—strange, given Thailand was not part of that enterprise (Parkes 2000:15).

Naturally, every travel guide to anywhere aims to sell its destination in the most effective way its readers will relate to, and this changes with market demand. Thailand guide market leaders Lonely Planet[17] initially aimed its product at backpackers and still includes information for low-budget travellers, also publishing *South East Asia on a shoestring* (Williams et al 2008). Lonely Planet is aimed at the go-it-alone traveller who uses public transport, rather than at the tourist on a group package deal whose transport is pre-booked. The Lonely Planet series has steadfastly aligned itself with the *modus operandi* of the 'traveller', not the 'tourist'. The story of how the first Lonely Planet book, *Across Asia on the cheap*, evolved is legendary: in the early 1970s, English backpackers Tony and Maureen Wheeler made their way across Asia to Australia, where they put together a hand-stapled guide passed around among travellers in Melbourne.

In their 2005 autobiography, *Once while travelling: The Lonely Planet story*, the Wheelers say their guide was the first of its kind to Asia. Travel guide writers' claims of being 'the first' today are reminiscent of 19th-century European travellers' claims of discovery or of being the first white man to see an area. The Wheelers' first experience of Koh Phi Phi is a good example:

> The villagers on the island crowded around us…and they were amazed and delighted with their peculiar visitors. Little did we know we had 'discovered' Ko Phi Phi, now one of the most popular tourist destinations in southern Thailand. If you've seen the movie of *The beach* you've seen Ko Phi Phi…(Wheeler & Wheeler 2005:68–69).

Joe Cummings, a long-time Thailand resident who has written many Lonely Planet guides, claims in a 2001 interview that his 1982 guide to Thailand was the first in English since Erik Seidenfaden's in the 1920s (Seidenfaden 1958). Cummings says 'There were a couple of French and German guides available in translation, but they were very much geared towards hiring your own car and driver and staying in first-class hotels all along the way—completely insulated travel' (Cummings 2001).[18] In fact, there had been several guides since Seidenfaden's. In the same year as Seidenfaden's guide was first published,

Friendly Siam: Thailand in the 1920s by Ebbe Kornerup was released, with a comprehensive section on southern Siam, including Hua Hin, Phuket, Krabi, Koh Samui and Pattani (Kornerup 1999). Kornerup's prose echoes the lavish descriptions of travel guides today in equating Thailand with paradise and with fairytales. *The thousand nights and a night* is yet again employed in describing the hills around Petchaburi as 'like walking in Aladdin's magic garden' (Kornerup 1999:139).

Kornerup's guide proves that as far back as 1928, Thailand was becoming known as a tourist destination. Kornerup, who walked into Siam via Burma, gives more positive promotion to the country's tourism infrastructure than do many others. 'Siam is the newest holiday land…and there are excellent hotels and good rest-houses everywhere,' Kornerup opens his preface with (Kornerup 1999:v).[19]

Cummings is correct that few guidebooks before Lonely Planet's were written for budget travellers. Previously, there would have been little need for a 'shoestring' guide to Southeast Asia, as travel had been traditionally the preserve of people 'of means'. The early Lonely Planet guides differed markedly from most other guides (*Student guide to Asia* being a notable exception) in their accessibility: Lonely Planet guides were simply and succinctly written in the idiom of young people who considered themselves to be adventurous travellers. The guides listed cheap hotels and prices, public transport details and hints for happy travelling. The 1975 edition of *South East Asia on a shoestring* is without the 'welcome to paradise' spin of most of today's guides. Because of its colloquial approach, though, much of the language sounds humorously dated today, with statements such as, 'the freaks have totally taken over the Malaysia [Hotel]' (Wheeler 1975:131).

Descriptions in the 1990 *Lonely Planet Thailand* guide are plain to the point of being perfunctory. It opens simply by stating the fact that 'Thailand, or Siam as it was called until the 1940s, has never been colonised by a foreign power…' (Cummings 1990:7). By the 2003 edition, the guide is packed with florid adjectives to entice the jaded traveller, beginning by saying the country is a 'virtually irresistible combination of breathtaking natural beauty, inspiring temples, the ruins of fabulous ancient kingdoms, renowned hospitality and robust cuisine' with something for every traveller, from 'the pulse-pounding dance clubs of Bangkok to the tranquil villages of the Mekong River' (Cummings 2003:11). The 2005 edition responds to a culturally aware customer who, nevertheless, still requires an exotic experience. It is sleeker, glossier, has more colour pictures and less up-front copy. Its introduction, 'Destination Thailand', even starts by denigrating typical tourism industry language. 'Forget about the sloganeering

"Land of Smiles"; welcome to the Kingdom of Pleasant Contradictions', it urges (Cummings et al 2005:4). It then uses that very analogy, noting that Thais do, in fact, smile 'all the while' (2005:4). The description goes on to present Thailand as a mystical enigma complete with 'post-Stone Age cultures', perfect beaches and 'tranquil' villages. Sexual imagery abounds with the incorporation of words such as 'lure', 'irresistible' and 'throbbing'. Thais seem incidental to the travel, as this quotation from the 2005 guide's description of Banglamphu reveals:

> As a rule you can arrive anytime [sic] at night and find a place to crash. And services abound: you can't swing a *túk túk* driver without hitting an inexpensive Internet shop, Beer Chang stall or pad Thai vendor (Cummings et al 2005:144).

The 2007 guide is almost the same, swapping the last line for 'without hitting an internet shop, travel agent or beer stall (Williams et al 2007:149). However, this edition tries to give a more rounded picture of Thailand and its people. Thais are 'generally friendly', it says, advising visitors that 'A smile goes a long way here, chitchat is more important than a to-do list and doling out compliments is a national sport' (2007:41). However, the guide reminds travellers that 'the demographics of this country are just as complex as those of your own' and that although Thais do smile often:

> That doesn't mean that every Thai is a cheery Pollyanna. So many foreigners pass through the country completely oblivious of the culture and customs that many Thais, especially in the tourist industry suffer from 'foreigner fatigue'. They have used up their patience on penny-pinchers, neocolonialists and paranoiacs (Williams et al 2007:41).

Although its introduction to Thailand is more balanced and realistic, it is top-heavy on information about the 2006 coup (which was, after all, bloodless), at the expense of other issues. Meanwhile, it retains the tourism-industry clichés of finding a generic paradise: 'If Eden had an ocean, it would look a little like this…Ao Phang Nga is one of the region's most spectacular great escapes and full of picture-postcard flavour' (Williams et al 2007:656). The clichés come naturally, so ingrained are they in our psyche, so this is not a direct criticism of Lonely Planet's writers, who are dedicated, seldom highly paid and who seem to have great regard for and knowledge of the areas they write about. After all, there is no escaping the fact that, for tourists, these areas really are a kind of paradise. Tony Wheeler denies Lonely Planet's guides today employ stereotypical rhetoric in order to promote destinations:

> Lonely Planet got to be No 1 in this region because we were irreverent—we reported about countries warts and all. Most of our competitors produced travel books about Asia describing 'beautiful scenery and happy smiling peasants.' You wonder if the writers ever got past the hotel lobby (Gluckman c1999).

The rise of the desire to be an independent traveller in the last 30 years as a reaction against mass tourism would appear to be at least partly responsible for a resurgence of the language of exploration and discovery. Though 'discovery' in the 19th-century context is almost impossible today, the virtual reality of the appearance of discovery is paramount. In an article in *The New Yorker*, 'The parachute artist. Have Tony Wheeler's guidebooks traveled too far?', US travel writer Tad Friend does not agree with Wheeler, saying that in order to entice travellers to sample the destinations it markets, Lonely Planet cannot resist using what he calls the 'impoverished language of travel writing':

> And so 'palm-fringed beaches' and 'lush rain forests' and other 'sleepy backwaters' are invariably counterpoised against 'teeming cities' with their 'bustling souks'. Every region has a 'colorful history' and a 'rich cultural tapestry' (Friend 2005).

Friend says Lonely Planet guides are significantly influential, and recalls his own experience as a young traveller as evidence. He cites the example of the travel writer Pico Iyer, who has used Lonely Planet guides as research for books and who believes the guides actually change the nature of travel:

> Lonely Planet created a floating fourth world of people who travelled full time…The guides encouraged a counter-Victorian way of life, in that they exactly reversed the old imperial assumptions. Now the other cultures are seen as the wise place, and we are taught to defer to them (Friend 2005).

Despite its clichéd title, *The magic of Bangkok* (Sheehan 2002), a coffee-table book of glossy pictures and essays, offers a more balanced exposition than most travel guides. Its author, Sean Sheehan, criticises travel guides and books that 'splash out with superlatives when describing noted buildings' which do not do justice to the real experience of seeing, for example, the Grand Palace (Sheehan 2002:9). 'Familiar media images of the city, from temples to strip clubs, are like travel clichés everywhere which tend to disguise as much as they reveal,' he says (Sheehan 2002:3). He examines what makes Bangkok a 'world city', saying that although it looks like a 'quintessentially Asian metropolis', it has an immanent uniqueness.

Though most guides subscribe to the stereotypes as the best way to sell dreams to customers, there is a rising awareness that travel guides present a particular view of Thailand as demanded by marketing departments and the tourism industry. As Jason Gagliardi says in the *South China Morning Post*:

> Glittering golden temples. Charming floating markets. Graceful doe-eyed dancers. Teeming streetscapes. White sand beaches. Chattering tuk-tuks. Colourful and spice-laden food. Swaying palm trees. Lumbering pachyderms. Riotous fleshy nightlife. Such is the stuff of dozens of guidebooks that shriek from sagging shelves, content to serve warmed-over helpings of 'Amazing Thailand',

feeding befuddled tourists the cliches they expect, and perpetuating a consensual hallucination that isn't Thailand (Gagliardi 2004).

Seeking the 'real' Thailand

It is easy to understand why in 1904 a European would have to have been employed to write an English guide to Thailand. At the time, there would have been few Thais with the requisite English level for such a task.[20] A century later, however, there are still few Thais employed to write English-language travel guides about their country. An exception is Chami Jotisalikorn. Bangkok-born but raised and educated overseas, principally in the US, Chami specialises in coffee-table books, such as *thailandchic: hotels restaurants shops spas* (Chami & Tan 2006). Though it does include the obligatory pictures of elephants, hill tribes and temples, the book, aimed at well-heeled international travellers, is devoted to lavish descriptions and pictures of hotel interiors, spas, expensive restaurants and luxury shops. While praising what many might see as the height of Western indulgence, Chami insists that these installations are perfect examples of traditional Thai hospitality. According to Chami and Tan (2006:72), the Oriental Hotel, for example—built in English colonial style, begun by Westerners for Westerners and which stakes its reputation on the number of famous English and American writers who have stayed there—'represents the grandeur of Thai hospitality'. Yet, the Oriental Hotel could not be further removed from everyday Thai life. It was always so; as Andreas Augustin and Andrew Williamson remark in their 2006 history of the hotel, *The Oriental Bangkok*, it was one of the many grand hotels 'along the shipping routes' of Asia in the late 19th century that 'became famous oases of luxury in a desert of poverty' (Augustin & Williamson 2006:32). Chami and Tan (2006:113) also cater to Western travellers' tastes for colonial-style 'discovery', recommending Koh Chang as an 'island hideaway' that 'remains largely undiscovered by international travel crowds'.

Before mainstream travel-guide-publishing houses became interested in Thailand in the 1970s, the few guides to the country were mostly published in Thailand itself, and several were written by Thais, including the aforementioned works by Thong-in Soonsawad, Kim Korwong and Jaivid Rangthong. Interestingly, Soonsawad's book, more than any guide written by a Westerner, uses frequent references to European and American places and literature in order to explain his home country to the tourist. Calling Thailand an 'exotic wonderland', Thong-in explains that he has used his Thai background and his 'occidental education' to 'bring together East and West in order to present a highlight or panorama of Thailand which best expresses its Oriental character' (Thong-in 1965:v). The guide is an incongruous mix of descriptions of sights in Bangkok and other centres, with the precepts of Buddhism and quotations from Western writers such as Mark Twain, Emily Dickinson, Edgar Allen Poe and Coleridge.

The Authors' Wing in the original section of The Mandarin Oriental Bangkok.
Credit: photo courtesy of Mandarin Oriental Hotel Group.

Like Lonely Planet's Cummings three decades later, Kim and Jaivid acknowledge the work of Seidenfaden in providing useful information. Kim and Jaivid claim that their 1950 guide is 'the only complete guide book available to those visiting Bangkok and Siam' (Kim & Jaivid 1950). In his preface to the first edition, Jaivid says the guide was published because steadily increasing numbers of travellers—made up of businessmen, government officials and sightseers—came to Thailand after the Second World War and found no contemporary guidebook available. While, today, this attractive book's guide to temples, palaces and the arts might seem predictable, in its time, it would have been ground-breaking. There is also a wealth of historical and anecdotal information that gives an alternative perspective to that normally presented in guides by Westerners. For example, in Western guides, King Mongkut is usually presented as being enamoured of all things Western and eager to bring them to Thailand. As Spurr observes in *The rhetoric of empire*, Westerners in postcolonial times look for 'signs among non-Western peoples of their sympathy and identification with the West' (Spurr 2001:34–5). Consequently, the media has become obsessed with documenting the spread of Western influence, the increasing consumption of Western goods, which it has seen as tantamount to desire and approval of Western culture.

In contrast to the way in which many Western writers have portrayed King Mongkut, Kim and Jaivid (1950:145) report that the King considered scientific knowledge 'the only thing worthy of interest in western civilization'. While this may be an exaggeration, Mongkut did have a strong interest in science, at the same time upholding Siamese traditions such as religion, dress, and social structure including polygamy. The authors criticise Westerners for their ignorance regarding Buddhism, claiming that they approach it 'either as outworn superstition, as metaphysics or as altogether inaccessible mysteries' (1950:145). There is no section in Kim and Jaivid's guide on the supposed generalised personality or traits of the Thais.

Of the guides published in Thailand today, most are written by foreigners. Asia Horizons Books, based in Bangkok, specialised from the 1990s to 2005 in guides and coffee-table books about the region; all the writers were European. There is also a sub-genre of guides on how to live in Thailand for expatriates. One of the best known and most useful is *The Bangkok Guide*, now in its 17th edition, which was my bible when I first lived in Thailand. It has chapters that at first might seem colonial or outmoded to Westerners, such as how to hire staff including nannies, maids, gardeners and drivers. However, expatriates soon realise that employing staff is normal in Thailand; the maids themselves often have maids (basically, anyone who can afford it has domestic staff).

The only English-language travel-guide publisher that consistently employs Thais as writers is Time Out, although the editor of *Time Out Bangkok* (Cornwel-Smith 2005a) is an expatriate Briton, Philip Cornwel-Smith, a long-time Bangkok resident who is also the author of a guide to Thai culture, *Very Thai* (Cornwel-Smith 2005b). In researching Thai culture, Cornwel-Smith travelled extensively through Thailand for his book, which traces the origins of Thai customs, modes of behaviour and items of popular culture. Cornwel-Smith refutes the suggestion that as a foreigner, he may not be qualified to examine Thai culture:

'Just the opposite,' he says. 'I don't think it's a credibility problem not being Thai—much of the best writing on Thailand has been done by foreigners. Sometimes you need that detachment, to be able to step outside the culture to really see it' (Gagliardi 2004). Cornwel-Smith makes a valuable contribution in describing customs that are part of folklore and oral history, some of which are disappearing. *Very Thai* is the most comprehensive and successful book in English about popular Thai culture and is one of the few to look beyond the stereotypes without sentimentality. Cornwel-Smith says that while glossy books and advertising literature promote Thailand as the home of 'dancers and temples, elephants and floating markets, with lots and lots of fruit carving', *Very Thai* delivers explanations for the everyday culture of the 'real' Thailand, as opposed to the 'Amazing Thailand' of the tourism industry (Cornwel-Smith 2005b:9). He says he realises that his book is 'a partial view drawn from an expatriate's experiences' (2005b:10). He agrees that the stereotypical promotion of Thailand is carried out partly by the Thais themselves, asserting that in 'presenting' Thailand to foreigners, they prefer to 'Impress with grand sights, staged spectaculars and souvenirised crafts' (2005b:9). There is much information in the book that Thais will not easily tell foreigners. For example, when I worked with Cornwel-Smith at *Bangkok Metro* magazine in 1998, we discussed the fact that no Thai could or would tell you why almost all the cats there—both stray and owned—appeared to have broken tails. When I interviewed a descendant of King Chulalongkorn for *Bangkok Metro* about his 'Siamese cat museum' near Bangkok (actually a breeding cattery for the prized royal-favoured *khao manee* cats of Thailand), he avoided the question and changed the subject. Cornwel-Smith examines the theories and concludes persuasively that the deformity is genetic (2005b:63).

Another book that aims to help dispel the 'endless clichés and over-exoticised imagery' is *Bangkok Inside Out* by Daniel Ziv and Guy Sharett.[21] It is largely successful in doing this and provides a view of Bangkok as a complex and surprising city. As the book says in 'Land of Smiles', Bangkok's colourful culture means it 'falls victim to a dazzling array of stomach-churning clichés' and its Land of Smiles marketing campaign is 'over-romanticized', while tourists often miss the 'real' Bangkok, 'more intriguing and beautiful on nearly every level than the exoticized City of Angels of tourism brochures' (Ziv & Sharett 2005:76).

Brochures, advertisements and journalism

Aimed at a collective popular market, brochures, newspaper and magazine advertisements transparently document the way consumers expect to experience Thailand and their demands regarding a holiday destination. Pratt's 'monolithic' voice of mass tourism and the 'disembodied fantasies of tourist propaganda' which in the 1960s and 1970s presented 'exoticist visions of plenitude and paradise' (Pratt 1992:221), have changed little, becoming, with the advent of internet-booked travel, even more ubiquitous. Destinations such as Thailand's beaches, for example, must be presented as a low-cost paradise.[22]

Editorial content about Thailand uses much the same language as that of its more commercial discursive cousins, travel guides and travel advertising. That there is little difference in the vernacular of these genres indicates that descriptions of Thailand have become automatic. A 12-page supplement on Thailand in the *Weekend Australian* newspaper (Kurosawa 2004), paid for by advertisers but with independent editorial content, offers an opportunity to examine this phenomenon as advertisements appear side-by-side with stories. A Singapore Airlines advertisement proclaims: 'Now's the time to discover Thailand...your next holiday escape' (Kurosawa 2004:5). Over the page, a story about Thailand's 'best holiday islands' advises tourists thinking of visiting Koh Chang to 'Go before it's discovered'. Koh Chang, John Borthwick says in 'Land of Smiles', is 'the place to get away from all the others who are getting away from it all' (Borthwick 2004:6). On the same page is a Tourism Authority of Thailand advertisement that is remarkably similar in tone to the editorial: 'Amazing escape', it offers, for tourists keen on 'exploring the unspoilt beauty' of Thailand, 'the perfect escape from the everyday grind' (Kurosawa 2004:6–7). The familiar 'Amazing Thailand' Tourism Authority of Thailand logo also contains the words 'Unseen Treasures' (Kurosawa 2004: 6–7), while above, in the editorial copy, Borthwick writes: 'Thailand continues to unpack its treasure trove of islands' (Borthwick 2004:7). So, like advertising, editorial considers Thailand a marketable commodity awaiting touristic discovery and exploration. Borthwick goes a step further to declare that 'Backpackers, those unwitting talent scouts of the mass-tourist industry, have been colonising new Thai islands for years' (Borthwick 2004:7). Meanwhile, Kurosawa uses a quotation from a work of fiction, *The beach*, to begin the supplement (Kurosawa 2004:2), thereby further underlining the construction of Thailand as a fanciful destination. Kurosawa astutely pinpoints the desire of Westerners for the Orient of their imagination, an 'exotic paradise' with the trappings of Western luxury: 'Now the quest is to find undiscovered islands—but nonetheless equipped with spas, villas with plunge pools and David Thompson on sabbatical from his Michelin-rated Nahm in London, running cooking classes' (Kurosawa 2004:3).

Kurosawa's comments echo those of an anecdote related by the travel writer Thomas O'Neill in 'The Mekong', when a European hotel manager in Thailand tells him: 'People think they're having an adventure, even if they are staying in a five-star hotel and riding in air-conditioned buses' (ONeill 1997:189). In other words, the desire for adventure is so strong that, as long as the customer is told he is having one, he will believe it, even with accompanying trappings of luxury tourism. Travel brochures mention the word 'adventure' constantly, as do travel guides. Handmade Holidays' 2004/2005 brochure has at least five 'adventures' to choose from among its many Thai tour options. Its 'Trails of the Khmer Empire' promises a 'fascinating adventure' to the north-east, replete with hotel accommodation and air-conditioned vehicle, just as O'Neill's hotelier described. At the end of the adventure lies paradise—the reward of the perfect beach, the unspoiled jungle, or the 'little known' hilltribe village. In 'Thai breakers', an article in *Good Weekend* magazine, journalist Mark Dapin's search for the perfect beach ends at Tham Phra Nang in Krabi Province: 'The sand is as white as a bridal gown, the sea as warm as an embrace,' he gushes (Dapin 2004:34).

Chapter two

Reinventing 'Venice'

It is a good country and a rich; and it has a king of its own. The people are Idolaters and have a peculiar language…[T]his a very wild region, visited by few people; nor does the king desire that any strangers should frequent the country, and so find out about his treasure and other resources.—Marco Polo, 1298.[23]

Kipling's adage 'East is East and West is West and never the twain shall meet' (1915:3) may seem today to be an almost risible reminder of a moribund colonial age. Nevertheless, literary evidence suggests that, in some contexts, the divide is as great now in the geography of the imagination as it was in colonial times, and that it has been kept alive—and in some cases replaced—by the rhetoric of travel literature. To discover why, it is interesting to examine Western writing about Thailand from its origins, before there was a substantial body of work for writers to identify with or to fall back on.

While critical inquiry today is interested in what the East says about itself and in interpreting the bias of Western constructions of the East, there was little choice in Siam's case but to use mostly European accounts for information before the 19th century. Because Ayutthaya, the capital of Siam from 1350 to 1767, and most of its written records were destroyed by Burmese forces, Thai historians have relied heavily on Western accounts of their country before that time. These records are generally written not by writers viewing the country from a neutral or, at least, ostensibly independent position, but by European diplomats, politicians, traders, missionaries and others who had an acute interest in cultivating influence with the Siamese.

There are several authoritative accounts of Siam's interaction with the West and the West's written accounts, but these examine the literature almost exclusively from the historians' point of view. There has been little attempt to examine writing as literature, in light of Western ideas of the time regarding race, travel and imperialism.

Before 1511

Siam has been known to the West, albeit vaguely, since ancient times. The Egyptian astronomer, geographer and mathematician, Ptolemy, may have been the first writer for a Western audience to note the existence of the country now known as Thailand, in his *Geographike hyphegesis* in the second century.[24] He mentions the 'Sinus Perimulicus' (thought to be the Gulf of Siam) but says little else. Europeans appear to have taken little interest in the country before the 16th century and Siam was not on the Silk Road, the ancient trading passage that linked the Roman Empire with India and China. Interestingly, traders or travellers must have passed through it—or Siamese traders must have travelled among them—as early as the third century, because a coin of the Roman Emperor Victorinus (who ruled from 268 to 270), minted in Cologne, has been found at U-Thong, in archeological digs of the original Dvaravati Civilisation in Thailand (Higham 2004:69). Siam continued to have diplomatic relations with China, from where the Tai[25] had come; also, the Indian emperor Asoka sent missionaries to Southeast Asia from the third century BC (Higham 2004:69). In Europe, however, Siam was little known, even in the 15th and 16th centuries. As Edward Farley Oaten says in *European travellers in India during the fifteenth, sixteenth and seventeenth centuries*, first published in 1909, travellers writing about the East had a very small audience and the European public knew little more about the East than it had 400 years before and less than it did in the year 100 (Oaten 1973:13).

At the close of the 13th century, Marco Polo's seminal travel book included a short chapter on territory that today is part of Thailand (variously spelt 'Locac', 'Lokak', 'Lochac' or 'Soucat' in English translations of Polo's work). In reality, Polo probably never visited the country. A map in Yule's translation (Polo 1975) shows he passed by the coast of Siam but did not travel within it and certainly would not have travelled to the capital, Sukothai, or met the King he writes of, probably Ramkamhaeng (who ascended the throne about 1279).[26] He writes also of 'Caugigu' or 'Cangigu', which is thought to refer to the Kingdom of Lanna, whose capital was Chiang Mai.[27] According to Thai historian Rong Syamananda in *A history of Thailand*, Polo gleaned his information about Siam from Chinese sources (Rong 1990:3), embellishing and Westernising them. It is conceivable, too, that he heard about the country in the lead-up to the arrival of a Thai embassy to China in 1292, the same year he claims to have left China.

Polo's brief account is notable because his description constructs Siam as remote, mysterious, exotic, insular and with its own unsullied culture. His work was written strictly for armchair travellers—Siam was not even included in Portuguese maps until the second half of the 16th century and was not well-established on European maps of Asia until a cartographer with the French envoy of 1686 produced a comprehensive map of Siam and its neighbours (Thongchai 1997:113). When Polo wrote of Siam, European people already had preconceived views of Asia as a vague conglomerate, informed, according to Larner, by religious teachings, classical literature (such as that by Ptolemy) and legends of Alexander's conquests, the mission of St Thomas to India and the tales of Prester John (Larner 1999:8–25).

One of the few other Western descriptions of Siam before the 16th century was that by Sir John Mandeville, who claimed to be a British knight but whose real identity has never been ascertained. Larner believes Mandeville's 1356 book, *The travels of Sir John Mandeville* (originally published in French), was compiled from earlier sources, including Polo (Larner 1999:106). Mandeville's description of 'Calanok' (which may have been his term for all of Indo-China, not just Siam) is highly fanciful with its tales of uninhibited sex, magical animals and barbarous customs (Moseley 1983:10). His story of the king who takes a new virgin every night then casts her aside (or kills her) is a familiar one in later Western writing of the East,[28] for example, of the fable of King Shahryar and his bride Shahrazad (or Sheherazade) in *The thousand nights and a night* (Burton 1885). Mandeville's book, however, predates Antoine Galland's first European edition (1704–14) of *The thousand nights and a night* by more than three centuries.

Dirk van der Cruysse (2002) ignores Polo and Mandeville. He claims that a later Venetian traveller, Nicolo di Conti, 'disclosed the existence of the kingdom of Siam' in memoirs of his 25 years in Asia which he dictated to Florentine humanist Poggio Bracciolini and published in 1447. Visiting Mergui and Tenasserim (now part of Burma), di Conti, like Polo, remarked on the abundance of sappanwood and, like the tourists of today, he was fascinated by elephants (Cruysse 2002:3–4).

Ayutthaya: 'Venice of the East'

In the 16th century, Europeans began travelling to Siam regularly, particularly Portuguese diplomats and traders from 1511. By 1540, there were 300 Portuguese traders in Siam and 120 mercenaries in the Siamese army. Missionaries inevitably followed, and Dutch, English, Danish and French trading began in earnest in the 1600s (Smithies 1997b:1). One of the most famous travellers to visit Siam was Abel Tasman in the early 1640s, who anchored off Ayutthaya for three months. He included in his memoirs a description of goods he would procure and a note of the ceremonial presentation of gifts to the King (Heeres & Coote 1965:121).

As in previous centuries, writing about Siam was mainly in the form of memoirs by diplomats and merchants. It was, therefore, concerned more with politics and trading matters than in narrating travellers' personal experiences. Early European descriptions of Ayutthaya are valuable to Westerners and Thais alike because most local records were destroyed when the Burmese sacked the city in 1767.[29] Sources from the 16th and 17th centuries are important as the origins of today's travel guidebook and travel writing attitudes.

Turning the camera on the tourist: the author at Ayutthaya in 1991, when farang visitors were few enough to make them a talking point (and photo opportunity) for Thai visitors. Credit: Ian James.

A time-honoured device of travel writing is to use the familiar to describe the unfamiliar. Both Ayutthaya and Bangkok have been commonly known as the 'Venice of the East' in Western writing. Anna Leonowens in *The romance of the harem* claims a 15th-century German traveller, whom she calls 'Mandelslohe', was the first Westerner to use the term 'Venice of the East' in writing about Siam (Leonowens 1991:3). She is most likely referring to 17th-century traveller Johann Albrecht von Mandelslo (also spelt Mandelsloh), whose account was published after Fernão Mendes Pinto's and who quotes Pinto in his work (Olearius 1662). As late as 1989, Australian historian BJ Terwiel was claiming, in *Through travellers' eyes*, that Gervaise, in 1688, was the first to compare Ayutthaya to Venice (Terwiel 1989:203).

Most other sources say Pinto was the first to call Ayutthaya the 'Venice of the East'. He lived in Asia from 1537 to 1558 and spent some years in Siam (sources vary from several to ten). He may be the earliest Western traveller who had actually travelled there to leave an account of Siam (Cruysse 2002:16), though he wrote about it only after his return to Portugal. Pinto's most often quoted description of Ayutthaya is found in a 1554 letter he wrote to Jesuits in Portugal while he was in Malacca (Collis 1990:210–1). Pinto compares Ayutthaya to Venice in the letter, but a new translation of the text, which I commissioned from the Institute of Languages at the University of New South Wales,[30] shows he has been misquoted through the centuries. What he actually says is: 'This city is *like* Venice because in most of the roads one goes about through water' (Pinto 1904:63).

In his memoirs, *Peregrinâçao* (published in 1614, 31 years after his death), Pinto included nine short chapters on 'Sornau', which he says was known 'in those parts' as Siam (Pinto 1989:399).[31] According to the most authoritative editor and translator of his work, Rebecca Catz, the book is a 'corrosive satire', in which Pinto lampoons the Portuguese religious and political systems and reveals himself as an anti-imperialist (Pinto 1989:xv). Though Pinto writes in the first person, he adopts a persona to narrate the story. He witnessed only some of the events he relates. Reginald le May asserts, for example, that Pinto never travelled to Chiang Mai as he claimed, but compiled his account from stories told by other Portuguese travellers (May 1999:42–3). Catz asserts that, though the book was wildly popular, its satirical nature was not widely recognised, and so it was mistakenly read by many as straight travelogue (Pinto 1989:xxvii).[32] In an article for the *Journal of the Siam Society* in 1926, WAR Wood discredited much of what Pinto had written about Siam (Wood 1926:28–32), though Joaquim de Campos later blamed bad translations for erroneous material in Pinto's work (Campos 1940:15–23).

Like Persia, Thailand had, by the 17th century, been constructed in the Western imagination as a location of romance, violence, seduction and splendour. Siam seemed interchangeable with Persia in Western imaginations, as evidenced by the title of a strange play 'written by a young lady', *The unnatural mother* (Anonymous 1698).[33] The play uses Siam as a conveniently remote setting, but the writer does not appear to know anything about the country, because she mentions nothing about Siam itself in the work. Instead, it was based in large part on an earlier play about Persia, Elkanah Settle's 1691 play, *Distress'd innocence: or, The Princess of Persia, a tragedy.*

Europeans frequently compared Ayutthaya with other European cities, a habit that Count Claude de Forbin in the 1680s found ludicrous:

Here I cannot help correcting a mistake of our writers of travels. They tell us every now and then of a pretended city, they call it the capital of Siam, which they make to be very near as big as Paris, and embellish after what manner they please. But 'tis very certain that such a city never had any existence but in their own imagination, that the kingdom of Siam has no other capital but Odia or Joudia, and that as to the size of it, 'tis hardly so big as our own towns in France of the fourth and fifth rate (Smithies 1997b:49).

Forbin's style, which relies on dispelling popular myths and lampooning the places he visits, is an early example of a strand of travel writing that is very popular today, seen in the work of authors such as Paul Theroux and Bill Bryson.

Late 16th-century and early 17th-century accounts of Siam were often part of larger travel accounts of the area then known as the East Indies. While many early travellers to Asia mention Siam in their travelogues, most of these accounts have little literary value. Accounts of travels including Siam by Ludovico di Varthema, published in 1510 (Varthema 1970), Antonio de Morga, published in 1609 (Morga 1868), and Jan Huygen van Linschoten's 1598 account (Linschoten 1995) are of more interest to historians and geographers than to literary specialists. In many cases, writers had not actually landed in Siam, or had spent only a brief time ashore along the coastline. Tomé Pires, a Portuguese apothecary who arrived in India in 1511 and was Portugal's first ambassador to China in 1517, felt qualified to label, in *The Suma Oriental*, the Siamese 'cunning' and 'great tyrants' who often cheated in business, (Lach & Flaumenhaft 1965:20–22).

Richard Hakluyt (circa 1552–1616) is credited with bringing the idea of a British empire to the forefront of English thought with his celebration of imperialism, colonisation and exploration in *The principal navigations, voyages, and discoveries of the English nation* (1589).[34] As Steve Clark observes in *Travel writing and empire*, at the time of publication of Hakluyt's treatise, Britain had no overseas territories and Western nations did not have a stranglehold on empire (Clark 1999:5). Travel, of course, led to the establishment of empire, so it is useful to look at the philosophy behind travel and the 'discoverers' of territory in an attempt to explain imperial and colonial attitudes to the rest of the world. According to TJ Cribb (1999:106), the very word 'discoverer' was used in this context for the first time by Hakluyt, allowing white travellers to 'speak of discovering whole peoples, as if they were unknown to themselves'. Hakluyt's presentation of travel accounts—written in a factual way by men who had undertaken the travels—strongly influenced the way later travel writing was structured. Notably, and significantly, Hakluyt was not well-travelled himself.

Cribb notes that early English travel writing, influenced by Hakluyt, aimed to promote a desire for expansion, a belief that English imperialism was right (1999:102). In this way, such 'scientific' travel writing was the forerunner to 20th- and 21st-century travel guides that aim to provide a practical basis on which to promote and justify the touristic 'discovery' of foreign lands. Hakluyt's work included an account by Ralph Fitch, who visited Chiang Mai in the 1580s when he lived in India and Burma. Smithies says Fitch did not keep a diary during his travels, but wrote his account more than a decade later, drawing on the writings of others (Smithies 2001a:66). Smithies also makes the interesting point that Fitch was known well enough to have been referred to by Shakespeare in *Macbeth*.[35]

Dutchman Pieter Floris's account of his voyage to Siam on the *Globe* (1612–13) is more detailed than many others of his era, but as editor WH Moreland says, part of it describes political upheavals before he arrived, as recollected by his business partner, Anetheunis (Floris 1934:xxviii–ix). Moreland adds that Floris 'possessed in some measure the national gift for elaborating details so as to present an artistic whole' (Floris 1934:xii). He could not be questioned about the contents of his journals, because he died two months after his return to England in 1615.[36] Floris does not differentiate Siam from other countries in the region—'It is as badde there for presents as any other place of the Indies', he writes (Floris 1934:45). In observing a storm, he assures his readers 'that olde folkes had never seen the lyke in that country'. He must have been told this by a third party, since none of the 'olde folkes' is likely to have spoken Dutch or English—or perhaps he simply imagined it (1934:45).

One of the most picturesque descriptions of Ayutthaya was written by Jeremias van Vliet (1602–1663), a Dutch merchant who lived there intermittently from 1633 to 1642. Between 1636 and 1640, he wrote four detailed accounts of Thailand (Baker et al 2005).[37] Van Vliet considered himself racially tolerant and open-minded, yet he took advantage of commonly held Western assumptions about Asians to present himself and his colleagues at the East India Company in a more favourable light and to excuse some of their less savoury actions. One example is in his 'Diary of the picnic incident 1636–7', in which he blames inept Siamese translators for some of his staff's boorish, drunken behaviour at a company picnic that resulted in the Dutch men's imprisonment (Baker et al 2005:34–88). He says the King 'persists in his anger and refuses to listen' and is stubborn and arbitrary, while his subjects fear him and pity the Dutch accused (Baker et al 2005:53–5). He manages to turn the incident from a shameful show of foreign arrogance to a means of pointing to perceived deficiencies of the Siamese. They are, he says, greedy, untrustworthy and vicious (Baker et al 2005:69–70). Though his staff members have clearly behaved badly, hitting people, stealing food and disturbing the peace at a temple, van Vliet calls their actions 'minor faults' and decries the 'harsh' treatment of them by the King (Baker et al 2005:65). By the end of the work, he is, extraordinarily, questioning whether the Dutch did anything wrong at all (Baker et al 2005:88). He uses what he sees as King Prasat Thong's unfair treatment of those involved in the incident to justify the idea of a forceful takeover of the country, citing the diminished friendship (and therefore trading opportunities) between the Netherlands and Siam as a result of the incident:

> And probably this friendship will not flourish again as before, unless this cowardly nation is brought to better sense, and unless the disgrace which we have suffered has been washed away by the sword, in which may God Almighty help (Baker et al 2005:143).

Van Vliet seems to have had an inflated view of his own importance, however. The picnic incident is not noted by Wyatt as an important event in the 'ups and downs' of the relationship between the Dutch and the Siamese (Wyatt 2003:97).

Baker says van Vliet's chief motive in writing the work was not to inform but 'to save his career' after the 1636 picnic incident and, perhaps, even to obtain a promotion (Baker et al 2005:143). Van Vliet's wording reveals a profound sense of righteousness in regard to Dutch imperialism. He relates tales of sexual debauchery, including stories of the King's supposed lascivious appetite and his abuse of women. He claims that the King is drunk 'three times a day' and that alcohol is to blame for many of his bloodthirsty actions (Baker et al 2005:114–6). These further illustrate van Vliet's tactic of justifying a Dutch invasion. Yet he admits that not all he relates is necessarily true and much of his material is as told to him, not as he has witnessed himself. Since the King was hardly ever seen in public and there is nothing on record by eyewitnesses to his personal life, van Vliet's descriptions cannot be taken seriously. Rong Syamananda says that, contrary to what van Vliet claims, his predecessor, Joost Schouten, praised the King 'as ruling with great reputation' (Rong 1990:68). Van Vliet absolves himself from inaccuracies by saying he agrees certain stories he relates 'may seem fabulous' and that the reader should 'believe as much of what has been told as he may judge in conformity with the truth' (Rong 1990:178).

Siam as spectacle

Descriptions of Siam in the 16th and 17th centuries invariably present it as a spectacle, observed by the male Western visitor who is barely involved in the scenario before him. There is a sense of unreality to the spectacle described, a sense that Siam is not the 'real' world. Bassnett connects fictional literary sagas such as *The odyssey* and travel narratives as 'myths of the heroic explorer', showing the 'heroic risk-taking traveller', a tradition which she notes continued into the 20th century (Bassnett 2002:225). In the 16th and 17th centuries, of course, most people never expected to travel and, of those who did, only a few would go as far as Asia, much less Siam. Thus, the reading of travel memoirs was very much like the reading of adventure fiction. The travel writer had *carte blanche* to invent events and locations because the geography of Asia was, for Western readers, largely that of an imaginative location, not a real place the reader could hope or expect to verify himself.

Writing about voyages to foreign lands in the 17th century can be linked in its depiction of the heroic and the spectacle to contemporary theatre of the Restoration. Allardyce Nicoll noted in his ground-breaking 1923 study that Restoration drama used heroic tragedy to comment on society, seemingly from afar:

> ...[I]n the heroic tragedy heroism is cast out of the world altogether and carried to an Eastern or an antique realm of exaggerated emotions, mythical and hopelessly ideal. The heroic play is like a Tale of a Land of No-where. We are interested in that land, but we do not hope ever to enter therein. The persons who move and speak there are not our equals, nor do they even draw the same breath as we do (Nicoll 1923:102).

In reaction to the constraints of Puritanism and the virtual banning of theatres in England in the 1640s and 1650s, huge spectacles were staged, with exotic settings and moveable machinery for many scene changes.[38] Travel writing carried further the desire for depiction of the heroic drama in a remote location; the author had purportedly actually been to the location he described, encapsulating the panorama for readers who could feel as if they, too, were looking on to the scene. Scenes of wealth, pomp, violence and derring-do are presented, with the narrator—like the audience observing a play—at a safe distance from the action, but nonetheless somehow the hero of the piece. Thus, for example, in *A new historical relation of the Kingdom of Siam*, first published in 1693, Loubère (1969:46) describes an elephant that 'tore in pieces in the Street the Brother of a young *Mandarin*'. Loubère is considered a reliable witness and he could well have witnessed such an event. However, he clearly delves into the world of fantasy in some descriptions, such as when he relates an incident of three elephants brought aboard his ship as presents from the King of Siam to the French royal family. He claims that he observed the Siamese whispering in the animals' ears, 'Go, depart cheerfully, you will be Slaves indeed, but you will be so to three of the greatest Princes of the World, whose Service is as moderate as it is glorious' (Loubère 1969:46). This must have been concocted by the author to make a good story, for it seems too far-fetched that he could even have heard the whispers, let alone translated them from Siamese.

Another example can be found in the Jesuit Marcel le Blanc's memoirs, in which he describes observing the training of rebel troops, how they would be brought into the city by night 'to get them accustomed to overcoming the respectful fear that all Orientals, and in particular the Siamese, have of approaching the royal palace'. He says he can verify these 'nocturnal assemblies' because he observed them from the cabin 'where I stayed alone at night among the priests of the idols of the palace (Blanc 2003:41). Behdad says this sort of writing enables the observer/narrator, and therefore the reader, to feel 'a sense of conquest and triumph' in which the 'passive experience of viewing the scenery' becomes an active one, even 'a heroic deed' (Behdad 1994:105). In 'The Grand Tour', Jeremy Black remarks on the propensity for travel writing to be composed as 'a form of fiction' and 'at times similar to picaresque novels', becoming for readers 'an heroic or mock-heroic journey' (Myers & Harris 1999:79).

On His (Christian) Majesty's service

French embassies to Siam occurred in 1685 and 1687, while Siamese embassies were sent to France to visit King Louis XIV in 1681 (sinking en route) and 1686. Diplomats sent to Siam by Louis XIV wrote many accounts of their travels. Some of these were translated into English soon after their French publication, but most were reprinted only recently. Until Smithies's edition in 1997 (Smithies 1997a), the Chevalier de Chaumont's work had not appeared in English since a poor translation of 1687, while the Abbé de Choisy's account was not published in English until 1993. Besides Chaumont and Choisy, Tachard published an account of the 1685 embassy and there are lesser-known works by Vachet, Forbin and Bouvet. As Smithies says, 'it is generally accepted that Choisy's version is the most readable, Chaumont's the dullest, and Tachard's the most vainglorious' (Choisy 1993:14–5).

In his comprehensive study of pre-18th-century Western contact with Siam, van der Cruysse says that because Thailand has never been colonised, it has not 'felt the need to define its cultural identity and determine its history in relation to former colonizers' (Cruysse 2002:78). He says another reason for the difference to linear, chronological Western representations of history is the Buddhist belief in reincarnation, so '[t]he concept of history is circular; events of the past are reproduced in the future and thus lose much of their interest' (Cruysse 2002:68). Most travellers before the 19th century looked at Buddhism only perfunctorily and never attempted to contemplate it seriously as a religion. Consequently, they never got beyond what they saw as peculiar, or even laughable, beliefs and rituals. Therefore, they could not understand the Siamese method of writing history and derided them for their approach to it.[39]

Accounts of the 17th century, written mostly by diplomats and missionaries with a political or religious agenda, are consistent in their assertion that the Siamese king should be persuaded to convert to Christianity, thus aligning himself with Christian Europeans and giving opportunities for favouritism in trade. It must be remembered, of course, that most of the writers were representatives of European governments or religious professionals and, as such, must be seen to be 'toeing the company line', so to speak. Heresy was still a capital offence in the 17th century, while apostasy was unthinkable—for Christians, that is; it was believed a Buddhist should convert for his own good.

With little understanding of Buddhism, the French were frustrated by their inability to persuade King Narai to convert to Christianity, just as missionaries struggled to convert any of the Thai populace. From here emerged another stereotype—that the Siamese were stubborn and of a lesser intelligence than Europeans and that this was the reason they refused to convert. Henri Chappoulie quotes a Jesuit as saying the Siamese people's 'extreme stupidity' and the beliefs their priests instil in them result in a lack of the desire to learn, no taste for the arts, no ability for mathematics, no desire for the precise instruments of 'civilised' countries, such as watches (Cruysse 2002:141). What started as an attempt to explain the perceived shortcomings of diplomats and missionaries eventually lost its context and became just another racist insult. King Mongkut in *The King and I* is seen as enlightened because he strives to be scientific, unlike his supposedly ignorant subjects.[40] Yet, going back to Chappoulie's quotation, it is clear the Jesuit's reason for complaining about the Siamese lack of interest in trinkets is that it was impossible, therefore, to use them as incentives for the Siamese to learn about Christianity.

The advent of tourism, as opposed to independent travel, is considered a relatively modern phenomenon. But, as Chaumont's description of his trip to Siam shows, it has existed since at least the 17th century, though obviously in a different form to today's mass movement. Chaumont's diary-like descriptions of his visit to Siam reveal him as, in today's terminology, a tourist rather than a traveller. His journey from ship to luxury boat to first-class accommodation furnished in European style familiar to him, to palace via palanquin carried by ten men, correlates with today's escorted package tours. Meals are all provided, transport is arranged and every need taken care of. This leaves Chaumont free to view the spectacle of the other country; although physically he is in Siam, his experience there is more one of passively observing scenes rather than participating in them—to the extent that he is carried between venues (much the same way as tourists are taken on itinerised sightseeing tours by luxury coaches today). As a result, his account is rather perfunctory. Far from marvelling at the wonders of his new surrounds, he seems jaded by them. He was there to do his duty on behalf of Louis XIV and to help smooth the process of the Siamese king's supposedly desired conversion to Christianity, all part of France's quest for the 'conquest of souls and markets in South-East Asia' (Cruysse 2002:207). Chaumont failed and was never again sent on a diplomatic mission. Yet, his memoirs of the embassy are arrogant, infused with a self-regarding solemn grandeur. He does not admit his failure, but merely repeats the King's platitudes at their final audience: 'He was pleased to say he was very well satisfied with me and with all my negotiation' (Smithies 1997a:65). As Cribb says, critics such as Mary Fuller point out that the writings of early imperialist voyagers 'are revealed not as natural but as highly artificial constructs' whose failure is 'recuperated by rhetoric' (Cribb 1999:101).

The reserved, conservative Chaumont travelled to Siam as Louis XIV's ambassador with the flamboyant Choisy, who had been a transvestite before he became a Jesuit. Choisy has a much more animated style than Chaumont, effectively using humour and even mischief, and revealing a degree of racial tolerance. However, while acknowledging that the Siamese have been wrongly branded in foreign minds as being dirty because they are 'swarthy' and 'almost entirely naked' (Smithies 1993:157–8), he nevertheless encourages another stereotype when he writes of 'the feeble divinities which are worshipped in the East' (Smithies 1993:157–8,162).

The definitive Siam?

Loubère's account of Thailand, where he spent three months from September 1687 on behalf of Louis XIV, is arguably the best known and most respected of early Western writing about Siam. Loubère, who had read many travellers' accounts of Asia, asserts that the reading of Western texts about the East makes up for his limited actual experience there and enables him to better understand Siam (Loubère 1969:2).

Largely because of his reading, Loubère could be expected to have had many preconceived notions of Siam; he had, for example, read Pinto's book. To a considerably greater extent than Pinto, Loubère writes of the Siamese in what would become a stereotypical representation that endured into the 20th century, particularly that Thais are lazy. 'He works not at all, when he works not for his King (6 months): he walks not abroad; he hunts not: he does nothing almost but continue sitting or lying, eating, playing, smoking, sleeping…' (Loubère 1969:50). Loubère believes that the Siamese, as well as being slothful and having traits of animality, are intellectually inferior to white people. Noting that the academic studies of Europe are unknown in Siam, he says of its people, 'it may be doubted whether they are fit for such'. He blames Siam's extreme heat, which, he says, causes 'sluggishness of Mind and Body', but again, he cites laziness as the reason they cannot become accomplished in the sciences (Loubère 1969:60). The Siamese do only what is absolutely necessary, he insists, 'and do not like us place merit in Action' (1969:76). He does concede, however, that the heat is so great 'that the very Europeans could hardly study there' (1969:74). Attempting to take an equitable stance, Loubère says the weather affects all similarly, whether black or white, born in such countries: 'Everyone born in the Indies is without Courage; although he be born of European Parents. And the Portugueses [sic] born in the Indies have been a real proof thereof' (1969:90). Surprisingly, he concedes that the Siamese are talented philosophers: 'I therefore willingly believe what the Ancients have reported, that Philosophy came from the Indies into Europe' (1969:76).

Loubère makes a comprehensive account of the Siamese judicial system, setting out the rules of crime and punishment in what is probably the first such detailed description by a Westerner. Although much of the account is made without comment, he also says the system is unjust, corrupt and based on pillaging, a description that is still applied today to Southeast Asian countries, particularly when one of 'our own' is in court on trial, for example.[41] Moreover, Loubère says, 'Vanity always inclines these people to lying' (Loubère 1969:89).

Typically, Loubère believed that non-Christians could not be trusted and lacked moral fortitude: 'Nevertheless as it is not possible to have true Vertue, but in the eternal prospects of Christianity, the Siameses [sic] do seldome as I may say refuse to steal whatever they meet with' (Loubère 1969:75). Loubère reiterates with a list of aspects of the Siamese character: when enraged 'they have perhaps less discretion than we have'; they need to be treated 'with rigour' and 'are subtile and variable, like all those that perceive their own weakness'. He says even that the Siamese drink each other's blood to attain 'eternal amity' (Loubère 1969:76). He has found a way with that phrase to ally the Siamese with cannibals, to somehow relate them to those most unsavoury of sub-humans, the uncivilised savages of myths, adventure tales and horror stories.

A benchmark of postcolonial criticism is that Westerners have habitually feminised the East, rendering it inferior in Western males' eyes by equating it with what used to be called 'the weaker sex'.[42] Loubère uses this feminisation to discredit the character of the Siamese: 'All these reasons do concur to effeminate the Courage of the Siameses, I mean the heat of the Climate, the flegmatick Aliments and the Despotick Government' (Loubère 1969:90). However, he also offers some philosophical observations, such as pondering why it is acceptable to view a Siamese person naked, while a white man in the same state would be considered shocking: 'As these people have their Body of another Colour than ours, it seems that our eyes do not think them Naked...' (1969:27). Loubère even manages to have the Siamese themselves authenticate his opinion of them as physically inferior to Europeans, when he notes that members of a Siamese delegation in France 'presently apprehended' that white French women were beautiful, while 'the Siameses [sic] were not' (1969:28).

Loubère says he writes only about what he has seen, exactly as he saw it. However, given he was in the country only a few months, it is unlikely that he could have learnt the language well enough to give firsthand reports in such detail of, for example, marriage customs (Loubère 1969:51). He obtained them from other sources, including various translators at the court. He admits he relies on hearsay when he writes of the king's relationship with his own daughter (by one of his wives who was also his sister), repeating foreign speculation that he had married her: 'I could not find out the truth, but this is the common Report: and I think it probably, in that her House is erected as unto a Queen; and the Europeans who have call'd her the Princess Queen, have made the same judgment thereof with me' (1969:52).

The Falcon

Perhaps the most widely written-about visitor to Siam of any time is the Greek traveller, Constantine Phaulkon, commonly referred to as 'The Falcon'. That Phaulkon was able in the 17th century to rise through court ranks to become a Siamese nobleman and, in effect if not name, King Narai's *Phra Klang* (minister for foreign affairs and trade) still captures the imagination of Westerners. This has been evidenced by at least four recent English-language novels and a biography, plus numerous journal and newspaper articles. There are several older books about him and he is mentioned by travellers who met him. Unfortunately, Phaulkon does not appear to have written anything himself about his experiences.

Phaulkon is the ultimate '*Boy's own*' traveller, his story akin to a classic heroic paradigm: the white man who journeys east and penetrates the fabric of the host country, 'going native' in dress and manners and even becoming a nobleman, only to be turned upon by the very people he has lived among. Western culture is peppered with such stories, many of them based on true-life characters, such as soldier and adventurer Lawrence of Arabia, and Kipling's *The man who would be king* (based on the adventures of American traveller and writer Josiah Harlan in Afghanistan in the 1820s and 1830s).

The real character of Phaulkon will probably never be known. Many accounts of him are skewed according to each author's point of view: some say he was a scheming climber who plotted to take over the kingship of Siam himself; others say he had no intention of trying to become the ruler but wished the best for his adopted country and was a faithful supporter of King Narai.

In the last two decades, four novels about Phaulkon have been published in English: *The Falcon of Siam* (1988), *The Falcon takes wing* (1991) and *The Falcon's last flight* (2006), by French-Canadian writer Axel Aylwen, who lived in Thailand for ten years and returned there in retirement; and *Falcon at the Court of Siam* (2002), by a long-time Bangkok resident, expatriate British journalist and travel guide writer John Hoskin. Aylwen and Hoskin have written screenplays, but Hoskin says there is little interest in his script in the US because Hollywood is 'not very interested in Thailand, certainly not historically'.[43] Phaulkon, Hoskin claims, is 'not proactive enough to make a movie hero' because he 'does not sacrifice anything for a worthy cause or the common good'. His comment about the Western film hub showing little interest in Thailand may at first seem surprising, given the success of *The King and I*, *The beach* and *The bridge on the River Kwai*. However, this demonstrates that it is not Thailand *per se* that is represented in these films. Thailand is an exotic background in which to place heroic tales of adventurous Westerners. It is an example of what Behdad identifies as the West's appropriation of the Orient's 'imaginative space' to become 'a decorative foil' (Behdad 1994:132). In the case of Phaulkon, it would have been necessary to weave into a film a significant amount of Thai historical matter, which Hoskin says is considered an unattractive prospect to Western audiences. Interestingly, though, it is deemed acceptable to fabricate events, as occurred in the latest film of Anna Leonowens, *Anna and the King*.

There is much non-fiction about Phaulkon, notably *Phaulkon, the Greek First Counsellor at the Court of Siam* by Greek diplomat George A Sioris (1998). The biography examines writing about Phaulkon in an attempt to give a more balanced account of Phaulkon's life and ambitions. Sioris succeeds, though the book does not spread much light on the motivations behind Phaulkon's actions. It is most interesting for its photographs of the ruins and contents of Phaulkon's mansion, Ban Wichayen, at Lopburi. Germaine Krull and Dorothea Melchers also write of these ruins—the mansion was a mix of Thai and European architecture—and, like many other writers, of the ill feeling of some Siamese towards Phaulkon for living in such luxury (Krull & Melchers 1966:128–9).[44]

There is still room for a definitive biography on Phaulkon. There is a plethora of sources for information about him, including the memoirs of his contemporary travellers who met him in 17th-century Siam. English-language publications include works by Chaumont, Choisy, Forbin, Loubère, Tachard and Marcel le Blanc. As could be expected, the themes and attitudes expressed in the writing follow shifting patterns of European thought on travel, empire and contact with foreigners. Phaulkon's contemporaries use his story more to reveal the tactics and ploys of their competitors for Siamese trade than to attempt to show him as an authentic, three-dimensional figure. An 1862 novel by William Dalton reveals its stance in its full title: *Phaulcon the adventurer: or The Europeans in the East. A romantic biography*. Even though Phaulkon met with a most unromantic end—he was beheaded—at a relatively young age, Dalton has not allowed the facts affect what 19th-century readers expected travel to be: romantic, exciting, exotic. And, of course, the traveller was doing his duty as a Christian to attempt to convert the King of Siam to the 'true faith'. In *Siamese white* (1936), Maurice Collis portrays the Greek as a great but dangerous adventurer taking part in the exciting rush to grab the East's riches and turn them over to the West. While writers such as Collis are fiercely critical of Phaulkon, accusing him of working for his own gain, others argue that he was loyal to the throne and would not have been so naive as to believe he could usurp it. But, as Walter Strach says in 'Constance Phaulkon: myth or reality?' (2000), Phaulkon already controlled the country and any title would have been 'merely cosmetic'. Krull and Melchers say there is no evidence Phaulkon wanted to become king, 'and indeed Phaulkon's personal devotion to King Narai seems to counter it'. They blame court jealousy for his downfall and add, 'But gossip spreads everywhere and nowhere more than in the East' (Krull & Melchers 1966:137).

Portraying the 'Oriental despot'

Rulers at this time throughout the world tended towards the despotic, but the image of the 'oriental despot' became a particularly well-recognised stock character in Western tales of the East and has endured through the centuries. As we shall see, the caricature is prominent in *The King and I* and in Anna Leonowens's memoirs. The term 'Oriental despot' conjures visions of glittering palaces, beautiful concubines and legions of servants, ruled over by a tyrant whose subjects' lives are at the mercy of his every whim.

When European diplomats started visiting Siam in the early 16th century, many would have had preconceived notions of Eastern court life from such sources as Marco Polo. But, before King Narai's policy of encouraging foreign visitors, they had had only a vague idea of Siam's king and often did not even name him. Pinto did use names when he told a detailed, romanticised story of Phra Chairacha (who reigned 1534–57) and how he was poisoned by his 'Queen' (Cruysse 2002:16). Pinto got many dates and facts wrong and his story of great battles, massacres, plundering, 'splendid pageantry' at court, deception and murder sounds almost generic and could be set in any Eastern country. Loubère repeats Pinto's story and adds information about the royal lineage as told by Gervaise and van Vliet and from his own research in Siam (Loubère 1969:9). He refers to Narai as 'the King that now reigns' and 'the King of Siam' rather than by name. In fact, he says the King's name is deliberately concealed 'for fear lest any Enchantment should be made on his Name' (1969:101).

Although Loubère does not dwell on descriptions of glittering temples bedecked with jewels and the like, he establishes the King as a distant and enigmatic figure, noting that his subjects see their ruler only a couple of times a year in splendid ceremonies. He describes the palace and its staff and guards, and gives tantalising information about 'the Women of the Palace'. He claims that one of the King's wives is also his sister, that no-one else is ever allowed to see his wives, and that he takes virgins from their homes by force and makes them his concubines—sometimes just to extort money from their parents for their return (Loubère 1969:101). He is presented as an absolute ruler who passes judgement according to his mood, and 'puts to death whom he pleases without any formality of Justice…and sometimes the Accuser with the Criminal, the Innocent with the Calumniator' (1969:104). The general impression is that of a cruel tyrant, remote from ordinary people and fabulously wealthy, with swarms of wives, concubines and servants who kowtow before him. While much of this may be true, there are few disparities between the portrayal of King Narai in the 1680s and King Mongkut in *The King and I* almost two centuries later. Edward Said names this type of racial stereotyping as a key concept of European constructions of the Orient: 'One could speak in Europe of an Oriental personality, an Oriental atmosphere, an Oriental tale, Oriental despotism, or an Oriental mode of production, and be understood' (Said 2003:31–2). He also mentions Oriental despotism as one of the 'essential aspects' of European notions of Oriental character (2003:203,205).

Chapter three

Patronising Thailand

Whatever be the ultimate fate of Siam, whether she remain a buffer state between the territories of two great European Powers or whether she be absorbed by one or the other of them, the inhabitants of the country will have every reason to bless the rational and enlightened rule of the present reigning Sovereign who has clearly indicated, in most unmistakable manner, that his heart lies in the prosperity and progress of the country with whose care and guardianship he has been entrusted.—J Antonio, 1904 (Antonio 1996)

Travel from Europe to the East in the 19th century can be seen as an attempt to revisit the past in search of an idealised Europe, as it was in the early 18th century before the industrial and agricultural revolutions. By the late 19th century, according to Behdad (1994:16), this search for a Utopian elsewhere had become 'crucially productive in the micropolitics of imperial quest'. Although Siam remained politically independent, it was forced to cede territory to Western powers and to change its entire infrastructure to take account of acceptable and accepted Western standards of living and commercial conduct. For example, in an extraordinary endeavour to impress European scientists and other visitors, King Mongkut set up a temporary city at Hua Wan (on the upper southern Gulf of Siam, near Hua Hin), from which to view an unusual eclipse in 1868. Many Western luxuries were provided, including ice—shipped at great expense from Singapore—to chill the French champagne.[45]

With the advent of Thomas Cook's package tours in the mid-19th century, the opportunity to travel was extended to the burgeoning middle class in England and was no longer the exclusive province of the landed gentry (Buzard 1993:18). Consequently, travel writing and travel guides became more popular. Cook himself became an agent to sell guides such as Baedecker's, and produced his own from 1874 to 1939 (Swinglehurst 1982:45). Although Siam was not on a Cook's itinerary, Europeans visited it as independent travellers and many wrote about it for an audience hungry for fabulous tales from the East. Buzard draws parallels between the development of Empire and tourism, saying both have been justified as purporting to be 'benevolent institutions' that aimed to promote international harmony. Buzard goes further, claiming the two movements became inseparable: 'So nearly automatic did the association of imperial and touristic structures and situations become that even topical commentary and satire on tourism could carry striking imperialist overtones...' (Buzard 1993:322). Tourism began to be criticised as a force bent on infiltrating and breaking down other cultures. Because there were no mass-market tours to Siam, it was seen as a more 'authentic' Oriental destination than colonised nations. And yet, Siam was constructed in the Western imagination little differently to, say, Singapore or Saigon, as memoirs by travellers in the early 18th to the early 20th centuries show.

The last foreign accounts of Ayutthaya

And the river abounds in many species of excellent fish, which plentifully indulge the inhabitants, and make them indolent and lazy, and consequently proud, superstitious and wanton...In Anno 1720 there were not above seventy Christians in and about Siam, and they the most dissolute, lazy, thievish rascals that were to be found in the country.—Alexander Hamilton, 1727 (Hamilton 1997)

Though it is implied by some historians that Siam was 'closed' to Westerners after 1688, this can wrongly suggest that the country operated in much the same way as Japan at that time and that foreigners were barred. Certainly, Western trade was discouraged, limited mainly to the Dutch and the Spanish, but historian Rong Syamananda says only the French were expelled from Siam, while other nations continued to trade, albeit in a reduced capacity (Rong 1990:91). This reduction, however, he attributes not primarily to political action by Siam but to Western powers such as Britain having the opportunity to make bigger profits in India and other Asian countries.

There are two notable accounts of Ayutthaya after the revolution: *A description of the Kingdom of Siam* by German doctor and traveller Engelbert Kaempfer and *A Scottish Sea Captain in South East Asia 1689–1723* by Alexander Hamilton, both published in 1727. Hamilton and Kaempfer, by their own descriptions, appear to have entered Siam at will, to have been welcomed and allowed to travel where they would. However, it later became more difficult for Westerners to visit Siam. JM Barwise and NJ White say Christianity was 'virtually outlawed' in 1733 and intimate that Siam was not 'opened' again to European trade until the Anglo–Siamese Treaty of 1826 (Barwise & White 2002:103,153).

Kaempfer visited Ayutthaya in 1690, but he did not write of his travels until many years later, and he gets some basic facts wrong, such as the date of Phaulkon's execution, which he says was in 1689 but actually happened in 1688

(Kaempfer 2003:32). Coming within two years of the revolution, his visit was too close to the events to allow him to view them at any distance, and he presents a one-sided, negative view of Phaulkon's actions and intentions. Kaempfer's chapters on Siam are most notable for his exceptionally detailed description of Ayutthaya and its infrastructure, its streets, river system and houses. He is unusual in that he included not only descriptions of palaces and grand residences, but also of the ordinary 'suburbs of Siam': 'The Houses in the common Villages, that stand upon firm Ground, are generally built of Bambous, reed, planks, and other ordinary stuff', he says, while 'The booth, or Shops of the town are low, and very ordinary, however they stand in good order, and in a straight line, as the Streets are' (Kaempfer 2003:44,49). He also describes the foreign groups living in Ayutthaya, including those of other Asian nations such as Japan, as well as of European lands.

Hamilton's book, like Kaempfer's, is valuable for its description of Ayutthaya (which he calls 'Odia'). At the time of Hamilton's visit, King Phumintharacha reigned (1709–1733) and concentrated on improving the country's water communications and foreign trade with countries such as India (Rong 1990:86). Hamilton's text is full of rollicking tales of his travels through Asia and, predictably, he gets dates and other facts wrong, repeats hearsay and gossip, and perpetuates outlandish myths. He even mistakes the year of his visit, saying it was 1720: it was actually 1718, according to Smithies (Hamilton 1997:151).

Though Hamilton's observations of Siamese people promote the stereotypical European views of Asians as 'indolent and lazy', he has also many positive things to say about them, remarking that 'They are well shaped in body and limbs, with a large forehead and a little nose, and handsome mouth with plump lips, and black sparkling eyes' (Hamilton 1997:151,170). He praises the education system—'it is rare to find a Siamese but who can write'—and says the Siamese are good parents (1997:183). His comments on Siamese women and their liaisons with foreigners are interesting because they foreshadow arrangements of today that are remarkably similar:

> And the Europeans that trade to Siam accommodate themselves as they do in Pegu, with temporary wives, almost on the same conditions too, and it is thought no disgrace to have had many temporary husbands, but rather an honour that they have been beloved by so many different men... [T]he Siamese wives generally prove the most obedient, loving, and chaste...' (Hamilton 1997:170–1).

Hamilton devotes several pages to describing Ayutthaya's foreign trade and relations. He reveals that Dutch, Portuguese and French residents remained in Ayutthaya, so it is strange that there are not more published memoirs of their time there. Hamilton, who met Phaulkon's widow, Maria Guyomar de Pinha, while he was in Ayutthaya, inflates the importance of the European's contribution, attributing Siam's rise to become 'the richest and powerfullest kingdom in that part of the world' to Phaulkon's efforts (Hamilton 1997:167,161).[46]

Though Hamilton's account is important because of the scarcity of other accounts of the time, his 1727 work, written at home in Scotland during his retirement, does not appear to have had a large impact in its time, though it was reprinted decades later and has recently come to light again.[47]

Bangkok, the new 'Venice of the East'

Ayutthaya was destroyed by the Burmese in 1767 and the capital was soon moved to Thonburi, then across the river to the present site of Bangkok. When Westerners again began to write about Siam in the early 19th century, they had to rely for background on much earlier travel writing, centred of course on Ayutthaya, not Bangkok. Though not every traveller could have been expected to read the older accounts, many had and there are frequent references to 16th- and 17th-century material in 19th-century memoirs. As Behdad (1994:23) notes, 'to write about the Orient inevitably involves an intertextual relation in which the "new" text necessarily depends for its representational economy on an earlier text'.

Bangkok had been modeled on Ayutthaya, so it was natural that it, too, would be called 'the Venice of the East'. In Prince Esper Esperovitch Uchtomskij of Russia's account of the visit of Czarevitch Nicolas (later Czar Nicolas II) to Siam in 1891, *Csarevitch Nicolas of Russia in Siam and Saigon* (Uchtomskij 1999:7), his description of arriving in Bangkok includes a reference to it as the 'Venice of the tropics'. He refers to the Chao Phraya River as 'the Nile of Siam'—Kaempfer before him had also likened the Chao Phraya to the Nile (Kaempfer 2003:75).

Similarly, de Beauvoir refers to Bangkok as 'this Asiatic Venice' and 'the Oriental Venice', adding that there is not 'a sight in the world more magnificent or more striking' (Beauvoir 1986:11). De Beauvoir seems to want to transport the European Venice to the Oriental Venice, saying he and his party 'longed to get into gondolas and go through the lively canals…where the bustle, animation and noise bewildered us' (1986:11–2). Charles Buls goes further in his description of 'this Asian Venice', saying 'they paddle like Venetian gondoliers' and that even the 'canopy resembles the Venetian *felsa*' (Buls 1994:23).

A rare female traveller to Siam in the early 20th century, Marthe Bassenne, labels Bangkok the 'Venice of the Far East' in *In Laos and Siam* (Bassenne 1995:132). Fournereau mentions the Venetian connection three times in one four-page chapter. He does not explain its origins, but says the term gives Bangkok more prestige (Fournereau 1998:15–8).[48]

This desire to find the familiar in the exotic is a common practice of travellers and tourists, even those who imagine they eschew their homeland in favour of immersing themselves in the visited culture. Today, many Western tourists may feel comforted by the sight of an outpost of the fast-food empire McDonald's, for example. In the 19th century, while in a Buddhist country, travellers felt comforted by their own contemporary bastion of civilisation, the Christian church. De Beauvoir's recounting of his first journey through Bangkok opens with a description of the Church of Assumption, in which he praises the missionaries who 'voluntarily exile themselves that they may spread the words of gentleness, temperance and love' (Beauvoir 1986:17). Such qualities, apparently, were not native to heathen Siam.

Western travel writing about Thailand today, whether in guides or memoirs, reiterates that it is the only Southeast Asian country never to have been colonised. Yet there is no doubt that Westernisation has had an enormous impact on Thailand's infrastructure, education, business and cultural spheres. 'Modernisation' was introduced by King Mongkut in the mid-19th century and further encouraged by his son, King Chulalongkorn, partly as a means of keeping would-be colonisers at bay. Yet this very Westernisation resulted to a certain extent in the existence of what Jürgen Osterhammel calls 'quasi-colonial control' (Osterhammel 1997:20), evidenced by treaties between Thailand and Western powers such as Britain and, particularly, by the advent of extraterritoriality.

Until the diplomat John Crawfurd's embassy to Siam in 1822, there had been no significant European missions there since the 17th century. Though Crawfurd's mission itself was largely unsuccessful, his memoirs of his visit (Crawfurd 1967), mark a new era of writing about Siam. In the 17th century, Western visitors sought economic gains from trade, whereas in the 19th century, they wanted political control of the region in order to obtain riches by exploiting natural resources. There was no question in the Western visitors' minds that they had a right to these resources.

Osterhammel (1997:21) observes that colonialism occurs first and that imperialism follows. The British Empire was well established in the 1820s when it started to expand its sphere of influence to Siam. There was little need to question the legitimacy of Empire because, according to the British, it was successful, necessary and right; the establishment of British sovereignty in India and parts of Africa from the 1780s were cases in point. The idea that Empire was crucial for the world's peace and prosperity became axiomatic. As late as 1966, David Wyatt's perception was that Crawfurd's writing about Siam was, for the most part, 'but slightly marred' by his prejudices (Crawfurd 1967:introduction). Yet Crawfurd's writing is obviously affected by his views of the Siamese as inferior to the British. He makes this point clear in his unfavourable comparison of Siamese with Indians, the latter of whom he points out as superior:

> A crowd of men, women, and children, were collected out of curiosity, the greatest share of which seemed to be directed towards our Indian servants, whose neat, gay, and clean attire, formed a striking contrast to their own rude and slovenly semi-nudity (Crawfurd 1967:73).

Indians, of course, were by then British subjects. Crawfurd says the Thais are 'short, squat and ill favoured' and that they 'paid small attention to cleanliness, either in their dress or habitations' (Crawfurd 1967:63). He adds that 'the ludicrous importance and vanity of the Siamese character was conspicuous, even among the lowest persons whom we encountered' (1967:116). He criticises the Foreign Minister for his 'sullenness' and for being 'nearly without dress' (1967:81). The King, he says, has 'more the appearance of a statue in a niche, than of a living human being' and features that are 'very ordinary, and appeared to bespeak the known indolence and imbecility of his character' (1967:94). Furthermore, he says the King and the Court in their actions are 'very ludicrous if not disgusting' (1967:136).

Typical of his nationality and era, Crawfurd's benchmark of civilised government and society is Britain and he decries the Siamese reluctance to agree to his request for extraterritoriality for British citizens in Siam. The British government is, he says, 'free and civilized', while the Siamese is 'barbaric and despotic', and the two nations are 'in opposite states of civilization' (Crawfurd 1967:133). At this stage, Crawfurd had become frustrated at his inability to persuade the Siamese to acquiesce to British desires regarding a treaty and resorted to racial insult in an attempt to hide his own diplomatic failings. He continues throughout the chapters on Siam to attack their physical appearance as he evaluates it:

> Upon the whole, although we often meet among the Siamese with countenances that are not disagreeable, and admit that they are certainly a handsomer people than either the Chinese or Indian islanders, beauty, according to our notions of it, is a stranger to them. The physiognomy of the Siamese, it may be added, conveys a rather gloomy, cheerless, and sullen air, and their gait is slow, sluggish, and ungraceful (Crawfurd 1967:311).

Crawfurd's disparagement of Siamese people is a tactic used routinely by European colonialists to justify oppression of non-white peoples. As Said asserts, from the early 19th century, 'second-order Darwinism' was used 'to accentuate the "scientific" validity of the division of races into advanced and backward, or European-Aryan and Oriental-African' (Said 2003:206). There is barely a writer before the 20th century who did not employ this method of suppression. However, Wyatt maintains that, despite its disparaging remarks, Crawfurd's journal is 'an indispensable handbook for those seriously interested in Thailand' (Crawfurd 1967:introduction). As he says, it remains one of the few extant English records of Bangkok during the reign of King Rama II (Wyatt 2003:328). Because of Crawfurd's frequent negative descriptions of Siam and its people, it is easy to be overly critical of him when examining his work with 21st-century sensibilities. He does, at times, exhibit some tolerance of the other culture. An example is when he is summing up the King's reign as a whole and concludes that, despite his power over the lives of five million people, to his credit 'the country prospered under his administration—that he was rarely guilty of acts of atrocity, and that upon the whole he was admitted to be one of the mildest sovereigns that had ruled Siam for at least a century and a half' (Crawfurd 1967:137).

Kabbani notes that the enforcement of racial stereotypes to emphasise the allegedly uncivilised nature of non-white peoples was a vital narrative tactic for the travel writer catering to a popular home readership (Kabbani 1994:3–4). By doing so, the traveller became part of the machinery of imperialism and its associated devices, such as conversion to Christianity (Kabbani 1994:3). As Said underlines, literature is pivotal in continuing the 'practice of empire' (Said 1994:14). Grewal explains how 19th-century scholarship associated dark skin with unsavoury morals: 'blackness as a racial category became associated with opacity, fear, and horror, and features could be read as analogous to moral characteristics' (Grewal 1996:27).

Part of the way non-white peoples are represented as inferior is in writers' comparisons of them with animals. In the case of the Siamese, this occurred in Western descriptions of every echelon of society, from the royal court and the king himself, to the peasants. De Beauvoir says the Siamese have 'fishy-looking eyes' (Beauvoir 1986:30). Fournereau at first appears to praise King Chulalongkorn's looks, but tempers that praise by saying that despite the monarch's 'elegant' appearance, his 'jutting cheekbones' and 'shiftiness in the eye' give him 'the feline and crafty appearance which is moreover the specific trait of the race' (Fournereau 1998:87). Moreover, the custom of the Siamese to crawl before superiors—horrific to the Western sensibility—made it easy to equate them with animals. In *The mission to Siam and Hue the Capital of Cochin China in the Years 1821–2*, George Finlayson twice says their 'grovelling' before superiors makes them 'beast-like' (Finlayson 1826:126–7). Edmund Roberts, one of the earliest US citizens to visit Siam on official business, similarly describes them as having a 'brute-like attitude' and as 'crawling like a dog on all fours', in *Embassy to the Eastern Courts of Cochin-China, Siam, and Muscat...1832–3–4*

(Roberts 1972:237,246).[49] Roberts is among the most scathing critics of the Siamese based on race, calling them 'excessively ugly', 'hideous', 'disingenuous' 'lascivious', 'immoral' and 'fickle-minded', and likening the courtiers to crabs and lobsters (1972:240–58). He adopts a superior tone and shows his prejudices on almost every page. This is not surprising, given the US still allowed slavery when Roberts was writing and would do so for another 30 years.

Linked to expatriates' and visitors' comparisons of Siamese to animals are frequent complaints that the Siamese are improperly dressed—that, like animals, they are naked (or at least 'half-naked'). This is documented with distaste by almost every 19th-century writer, including Leonowens, FA Neale and Crawfurd. The truth is, Europeans in the tropics would have done better to discard their heavy, restrictive clothing, which contributed to infection and conditions such as prickly heat. Yet that very clothing was, for them, the mark of 'civilisation' and they refused in most cases to change it or even to compromise. It was considered that anyone who did so had 'gone native'. JGD Campbell's views are an exception in *Siam in the twentieth century* (1902). He explains how suited to the climate the Siamese *panung* is and expresses his hope that European dress does not take over at court as it had in Japan by the turn of the 20th century.

Not every 19th-century Western writer dismissed other races as wholly inferior. Sir John Bowring, Queen Victoria's plenipotentiary in China, exhibits an extraordinary amount of tolerance for his time, as the journal of his successful diplomatic visit shows, published in 1857 as *The kingdom and people of Siam; with a narrative of the mission to that country in 1855*. Bowring's narrative reveals his keen eye for detail in meticulously recording court procedure. Rather than continuously comparing the scene with what he has seen elsewhere, he simply tells what he sees, for the most part without a judgemental commentary, as in the following:

> His Majesty then appears on a throne placed upon an elephant's back, surrounded by persons carrying parasols, and followed by the heir-apparent. His ladies follow upon elephants, but in closed chairs, which screen them from sight: six hundred men close the procession, which usually consists of fifteen or sixteen thousand (Bowring 1857:95).

When considering the moral character of the Siamese, Bowring gives the most balanced account of any of his era. He examines the work of earlier writers, such as Le Blanc, Loubère and Pallegoix, and considers them in light of events and circumstances and of his own experiences. In so doing, he makes some interesting remarks about writing by travellers:

> Generalizations as to national character are among the great defects of writers on foreign countries, and, when examined, will in most cases be discovered to be the result of impressions early and hastily formed, or of some solitary

examples of individual experience, from which all-embracing deductions are drawn (Bowring 1857:102).

Bowring's conclusions about the Siamese are favourable; he says most Siamese he met displayed 'unusual frankness', that 'Dishonesty...is repugnant to Siamese habits', although 'Lying, no doubt, is often resorted to as a protection against injustice and oppression' (Bowring 1857:106). Bowring had a deep regard for King Mongkut, who appointed him ambassador plenipotentiary in Europe in 1867.

Forty years later, another American writer, Frank Vincent, who travelled through Asia for 15 years from 1871, was also comparatively open-minded and less abusive than many others, in his descriptions in *The land of the white elephant* (1874). Nevertheless, he makes it obvious that he believes his own culture to be above that of the Siamese, for example when he describes some recent additions to the streets of Bangkok:

> And thus are some small transplanted shoots, taken from the great tree of western civilisation, with its wide-spreading branches of progressive thought and action, slowly but surely taking root in the receptive soil of Siam, once so vain and capricious (Vincent 1988:131–2).

One of the earliest to describe Siam in terms of being a playground for Westerners was Belgian traveller and former Brussels mayor Charles Buls, who called Bangkok an 'oriental toy shop' (Buls 1994:12).[50] He admits that someone who really knew Bangkok would realise the riches of the temples concealed the city's poverty, but that a tourist or newcomer would see only the 'mirage'—its 'fantastic palaces, its golden minarets, its perfumed gardens, concealing in their pavilions, that are inlaid with mother-of-pearl and precious stones, the mysteries of the harem' (Buls 1994:12). Even the sun is, apparently, not the same one seen in Europe, but has become the 'glorious oriental sun' (Buls 1994:4). Buls includes harsh criticisms of Buddhism and of the Siamese. While he concurs that the Buddhist moral code itself is not inferior to that of the Christian, he insists racial characteristics are responsible for the white man's elevated status. Christian priests are superior to Buddhist priests, he says, not because of religion, but because of the 'activity of their race', that is science and leadership, which are 'factors of pre-eminence of Western people over Asian people' (Buls 1994:4). According to Said, this was a typical method of subjugating non-white people, who were 'viewed in a framework constructed out of biological determinism and moral-political admonishment' (Said 2003:207).

De Beauvoir urged a French takeover of Siam for trade purposes, insisting it would be a 'commercial, peaceful and lawful conquest' (Beauvoir 1986:74). His last adjective, 'lawful', is important; for imperialists, it was crucial that they were seen to be doing what was intrinsically *right*. Fournereau exemplifies the Western imperialistic stance when he inexplicably refers to the city of Bangkok as a 'colony' and puts forward his plan for France to take over Siam. He justifies this plan by saying that Siam could 'stand up rich and powerful' if the Siamese were 'pulled out of the sleepy lethargy in which they vegetate'; that the conquest would be peaceful; that it would be 'a work of humanity' to bring the Siamese out of their state of suffering under a harsh regime; and that it would be a 'philanthropic mission' (Fournereau 1998:163). Fournereau's dream of a French-ruled Siam is an example of what Gerster calls 'imaginative possession' in travel writing, where the 19th-century writer typically presents the case for colonisation as a positive step for the subject (Gerster 1995:9). This 'philanthropic imperialism', as Leigh Dale calls it (Dale 2002:87) can be traced through to the present. It is employed in raising money for charities, for example, and to justify Western occupation of countries such as Afghanistan and Iraq under the guise of saving them from themselves. As Kabbani says, the demise of Empire did not banish imperial ideas, which she contends are used as political manipulation as much today as they were in the 19th century (Kabbani 1994:viii).

It is useful to compare 19th-century Western European views of Siam with the views expressed by Prince Esper of Russia in his account, commissioned by the Russian government, of Czarevitch Nicolas's 1891 visit. In describing King Chulalongkorn, Prince Esper assumes his readers will equate a Thai with a 'Turkmeni', when he says any suggestion that King Chulalongkorn resembles a central Asian is incorrect. Rather, he looks Malaysian or southern European, Esper claims, or even northern European—'He somewhat calls to mind Ludwig of Bavaria' (Uchtomskij 1999:9). The prince was, of course, writing for a Russian-speaking audience who would relate to Turkmen as uncivilised, wild, exotic and different—people from a region that Russia at that time was trying to colonise (and succeeded in doing so decades later).

Prince Esper comments on the lack of European literature about Siam, noting that the few works that do exist give only a peripheral idea of procedures such as the official welcoming of visitors to the Court. He notes also that much of what is written is incorrect: 'Indeed, the intelligent Siamese complain with reason about certain tourists who have neglected to do them justice' (Uchtomskij 1999:31). The prince cleverly allies Russia with Asia, and specifically with Siam, denying that other Europeans have an understanding of either region and implying that Russia is the natural leader of Asia (1999:44). Meanwhile, he artfully criticises what he sees as the 'dangerous covetousness' of 'the great European nations' (1999:46).

The desire for Orient

Though the desire for knowledge of the Orient was fashionable in 19th-century Europe, spurred by the lurid stereotypes offered by *The thousand nights and a night*, most people had not the remotest opportunity to visit Asia. Travel was still largely the preserve of the wealthy, with the exception of sailors, soldiers and missionaries. In addition, travel to Siam at this time remained very much that of 'travail'. A posting to Siam was considered a hardship and Westerners who went there were considered by those back home to be adventurous, eccentric and even foolhardy, given the hazards. In 1892, Fournereau notes the filth of the streets and the river, and the problems with disposing of dead bodies (Fournereau 1998:17,153–4). Doctor P Neis, travelling through the country in 1882, remarks that, although the town of Luang Prabang looks 'enchanting', during the wet season the traveller has to walk up to his knees in 'blackish, fetid mud' (Neis 1997:69). De Beauvoir says that, despite its glittering temples, Bangkok is, in reality, not as enchanting as it first appears. He visits a slum area not seen by most Western vistors and remarks on how it shows 'another side of the East' (Beauvoir 1986:25) to the stereotypical view substantiated by *The thousand nights and a night*. He then contradicts himself and cannot help falling into the familiar wonder at the supposed riches of the East —'…if one were only as rich as a Siamese!' He goes as far as to claim Siam has 'more gold and silver in circulation…than any other spot in the world' (1986:38).

Finlayson, a surgeon and naturalist on Crawfurd's mission, wrote in his journal what amounted to a praise of man's ascension from a 'naked and helpless' being to one who travels throughout the world and who, therefore, 'has risen superior to the contending elements'—and, it follows, superior therefore to people who have not travelled (Finlayson 1826:xxiv). He sees travel as the mark of civilisation, of advancement of the species and even of godliness.

Desire for Orient also involved the titillation of readers by alluding to the forbidden. Notoriously, Victorian England tended to repress sexuality, sensuality and eroticism, going so far as to rewrite the fairy stories of Hans Christian Andersen, for example, in a more 'suitable' style.[51] In contrast, reading tales of erotic delights among non-white people in a place far away from home was an acceptable way of feeding the desire for the forbidden. There is a fundamental difference between the outcome of desire for Siam and desire for other Southeast Asian nations. Siam remained independent but was receptive to Western ideas and influences. This led to the beginnings of Western imaginings of Siam as a 'paradise'. It would take a hundred years for this construction to become naturalised, but the transformation had its origin in European attempts of the 19th century to bring Siam under foreign control.

While the description of travel in Siam in the 19th century principally concerns difficult journeys, the foundation of the country's construction as an Eastern paradise for Westerners can be determined in the literature about it. There already existed the assumption of mystery, riches and exoticism, promulgated, as we have seen, since the 16th century and underlined particularly in British imaginations with the publication of Burton's *The thousand nights and a night* in the 1880s. For British people of the late 19th century, Siam was a wonderful example of all they knew of the East. To quote de Beauvoir: 'Certainly this is no longer Europe transported to the East; it is Asia itself…'(Beauvoir 1986:16). The fact that it had had few visitors in the 18th century made it more alluring, more exotic, more desirable in the imagination of foreigners. It offered the thrill of adventure and discovery and fulfilled the desire to be the first to explore an 'unknown' land.

Occupying Thailand

> I pictured another teak man, with his retinue, suddenly appearing round a bend, and I saw myself greeting him as Stanley greeted Livingstone. Curiously enough, these innocent expectations came remarkably close to the real thing, I was to discover.—Reginald Campbell (1937)

By the early 20th century, Siam had been established as a viable destination for the traveller for travel's sake alone. The existence of Antonio's *The 1904 traveller's guide to Bangkok and Siam* is evidence of this transformation. The book describes various trips out of Bangkok—made possible by the building of a rail system—to towns such as Lopburi and Korat, with travel hints including camping equipment required. Antonio advises the traveller to wear a 'pith sola topee', to hire a 'good boy' and to carry a gun for game shooting (Antonio 1997:61–2). Foreigners have rarely been allowed to own land in Thailand, except in the case of pieces of land gifted occasionally by the monarch before the 1930s. In the late 19th century, Louis Leonowens was probably the first white man to obtain the lease of a teak forest, when he was granted a concession in Tak (then Raheng) province, but he did not own the land (Bristowe 1976:72). This did not deter the imaginary assumption of ownership, however, and late 19th- and early 20th-century literature about Siam abounds with the language of colonialism as well as of Orientalism. As Brian Musgrove asserts, travel writing provides 'rich source material on the formations of Western subjectivities out of the encounter with imagined others' (Musgrove 1999:33).

Travel in Siam took longer to develop than in most of the Asian colonies, such as Hong Kong, Singapore and Malaya, partly because of the country's very independence. Infrastructures were not particularly accessible to Westerners and have been wholly controlled by Thai governments, although many concessions were made to European countries from the 1850s in the form of treaties. Many Europeans who lived in Thailand in the 19th century were employees of the King and government, including Anna Leonowens and, later, her son, Louis. In that way, they did not perform the stereotypical role of white man as 'boss', though most of them considered themselves superior in race and culture. While expatriates living in Thailand were not there under the auspices of a colonial project, they still attempted to construct 'little empires' for themselves. The advent of extraterritoriality, the processes of which are described at length by WAR Wood in his memoirs (Wood 1991:24–39), allowed segregated communities to exist apart from normal Thai society. Peter A Jackson (2004), says 19th-century Siam was a 'semi-colony' or 'informal empire' that was 'subordinated to Western imperial power' (Jackson 2004:219). He says this mostly affected economic and legal systems, whereas political regimes, education systems and cultural production were controlled by Thais. In a 2008 article, 'Thai semicolonial hybridities', Jackson acknowledges that studies from varying disciplines 'show that the empirical situation of Siam/Thailand is demonstrably comparable to that in former colonies' (Jackson 2008:147). Spurr says the tendency of expatriates to separate themselves from the indigenous community is seen by them as necessary to avoid 'contamination', the fear of which 'continually recurs as a theme in colonial discourse' (Spurr 2001:87). Thai historian Hong Lysa agrees with Jackson and spoke at length on the subject in a 2002 lecture entitled 'Extraterritoriality in semi-colonial Bangkok during the reign of King Chulalongkorn' (Lysa 2002).

Westerners' habit of separating their living quarters from those of local people was widespread in Asia and was considered absolutely necessary for health and, particularly, for hygiene. The novelist Kazuo Ishiguro captures the fear of the white man in Asia in *When we were orphans* (2000), set in early 20th-century Shanghai, which, like Siam, was not a British colony, but was controlled to a large extent by British imperialist demands. The protagonist, Christopher Banks, is typically both terrified by and attracted to the 'Chinese areas of the city', because 'Out there, we were told, lay all manner of ghastly diseases, filth and evil men' (Ishiguro 2000:54).

Buls was one of several Belgian advisers, including the jurist Gustave Rolin-Jaequemyns, employed by King Chulalongkorn to help ward off French colonial ambitions in Siam. At the time of Buls's writing, Belgium had been independent for only 70 years, so he could be expected to empathise with another small country threatened with foreign takeover. His views are a mixture of criticism of the colonial advances of France and Britain, of understanding of how countries can be enticed into being taken over, and of support for his own country's colonial regime in what was then known as the Belgian Congo (about which Buls also wrote). Buls reveals himself as politically motivated rather than demonstrating a genuine understanding of the oppression colonialism propagated. He criticises the French for being 'ever ready to seize the smallest pretext to justify an armed intervention and the theft of a few stretches of Siamese territory' and the English for offering seemingly glittering deals that hide their real intention of handing over the country to Queen Victoria (Buls 1994:xx). Yet, on the next page he lauds Belgium for its 'work of civilization' in the Congo, writing of 'the heroism displayed by our officers, the dedication of our judges and missionaries and the perseverance of our engineers and commercial agents' (1994:xxi). Buls does say that it is time to dispense with extraterritoriality in Siam, acknowledging that it curtails the King's powers of sovereignty (1994:xxi).

Wood's autobiography is valuable to any study of the application of the trappings of the British Empire—in the form of extraterritoriality—to an independent, non-European country. His title, *Consul in paradise*, seemingly alludes to a popular song of the 1950s, 'Stranger in paradise' from the musical *Kismet*, set in ancient Baghdad.[52] As well as being associated with the Middle East, Siam appears to have been equated with the Near East in English minds ('near' and 'middle' being nominal terms used to convey the distance from England and barely differentiated by Westerners in terms of culture). This is shown by a caption in *The Black and White Budget*, a weekly pictorial newspaper, in April 1901. The picture shows King Chulalongkorn riding a camel with an Arab, probably in Egypt during one of his trips, but the caption intimates that the picture is of the King at home in Bangkok 'taking his usual morning constitutional' (Beek 1999:69).

Wood's book and its observations are significant because he became the Registrar of the Bangkok Court (1903–05) and ran his own Consular Court (1908–09) at Songkhla (then known as Singora). He later spent many years as a consular adviser to International Courts in Siam, so was at the centre of extraterritoriality in practice. Wood describes the Siamese authorities' reception of the advent of special courts for foreigners as enthusiastic, a claim diametrically opposed to Hong's thinking on the matter now (Hong 2002). Wood's view was that, after the Siamese Government signed treaties with Britain in 1855 and, later, with the US and other European nations, they 'were probably rather glad to be rid of the responsibility of trying foreigners' (Wood 1991:24). He concedes that the Thais deserved to be 'masters in their own house', but believes this could come about only if they modify their system to align with Western ideas (1991:25). He maintains that the presence of a British Consul in Siamese International Courts was actually in the interests of racial equality and that the British officers were 'always looking forward when the British Government would feel justified in relinquishing all our powers of interference' (1991:47).

Wood underlines this philosophy by repeating that the consular officers did 'very good work for Siam' and that this work was 'at no cost to Siam', which made it akin to a charitable deed (1991:47–8). It is yet another reiteration of the 'white man's burden' philosophy, of the need for the West to guide the East for the East's own good.

The 'expat' experience

Expatriate life is seen historically and today as an exoticised experience, a way of life separate and distinct from the ordinariness of the 'home' culture. In literature it has come to have a circular interpretation—because it is presented in this way by writers, readers expect to receive an exoticised description, and because it is expected by readers, writers feel encouraged, and perhaps even obliged, to fabricate tales of the weird, the exotic and the erotic. In this way, travel writing has continued to follow the tradition of telling stories about grotesque races, as parodied by Swift in *Gulliver's travels*. Patrick Holland and Graham Huggan see the presentation of these 'exoticist perceptions of cultural difference' as one of the problems inherent to travel writing: 'Clearly, travel writing at its worst has helped support an imperialist perception by which the exciting 'otherness' of foreign, for the most part non-European, peoples and places is pressed into the service of rejuvenating a humdrum domestic culture' (Holland & Huggan 1998:48).

They argue that European travel writing promotes divisions between race and class, assumes travellers have a right to lambaste the country they are visiting and uses 'a nonspecialist genre to pass off personal opinions as sociological observations' (Holland & Huggan 1998:49). This is particularly evident in the writing of long-time residents of Siam, though it may be more subtly imposed than in the writing of tourists. The expatriate, by the very length of his or her stay, is assumed by the reader to be able to speak with authority about the country he is describing. An example may be found in the memoirs of FA Neale, who lived in Bangkok in 1840 and 1841 but did not publish his memoirs of it until a decade later. In *Narrative of a residence at the capital of the Kingdom of Siam* Neale claims that the only amusements for expatriates in Siam who 'take up their abode in these little civilized parts' are fishing and shooting (Neale 1999:16). He relates a story of extraordinary cultural disdain towards the Siamese of a long-time British resident of Bangkok, which he says was shown 'not many years' before his visit. The man, Mr Hunter,[53] and another Englishman sail to Paknam where they alight at a temple and take pot-shots with their rifles at wild pigeons nesting in the pagodas. They are outraged at being set upon by angry priests and residents, but are reportedly rescued from harm by some passing Portuguese. The hunters demand to see the King over what they deem to be unfair treatment and Neale claims that, as a result, the priests are removed from the temple and 'exiled as felons'. Neale then surmises that residents at Paknam must bear 'a grudge' toward all English people because of 'the sound example that has been made of them' (Neale 1999:16–7). That Neale sympathises with the British side of the story shows that he believes it acceptable for a European to disregard Siamese culture to pursue recreation. The Siamese are, he says, 'at the best semi-barbarous' (1999:viii).

Anyone moving to live in a foreign country has, of course, preconceived notions of what that country will be like, mostly based on perceptions propagated by popular culture, such as travel books and guides, films, the media and conversation with other travellers. Often, the descriptions of one country are applied generically, so that one non-white or 'Third World' country is seen to be much like another. Thus, while still at home in Scotland, Reginald Campbell imagines Siam based on this type of 'knowledge'. Not having read anything particularly about it, he can conjure up only a quasi-African image of himself as the great white explorer, as evidenced by the aforementioned quotation in which he imagines himself greeting another white man in the jungle 'as Stanley greeted Livingstone'. As well as putting himself in Stanley's place, he imagines he will be 'tramping between steaming walls of green, a solar topee on my head, sweat upon my brow, and a long line of carrier coolies behind me' (Campbell 1937:9). Through five years working in the teak forests of northern Siam in the 1920s, Campbell keeps this image alive. When he writes his memoirs 15 years after he first saw Siam, the imagined picture is the reality for Campbell and the actual experience has moulded itself to his preconceptions.

Though Campbell often uses Western caricatures of the 'native' to poke fun at himself, he is in this way continuing that stereotypical view. He presents himself as a bumbling Englishman and describes how he tries to communicate with the Siamese by 'shrieking in his own language at the top of his voice' in order to penetrate 'the thick skull of the native'. By including the very description of this type of occurrence, Campbell makes it clear that he considers himself the superior being. He is always the 'master', while the Thais depicted in the book are 'natives', 'boys', drivers or some other sort of service providers, often not named by Campbell. It is an example of how 'self-mockery is counterbalanced… by self-exoneration' as the writer turns his travels into 'a series of gentleman's adventures' (Holland & Huggan 2003:34). Campbell acknowledges Western nostalgia for a pre-industrial, pastoral idyll by imagining Siam is in a time-warp, complete in its otherness by not even existing in the same century as Europe. Traversing a territory without bridges, cars or hotels, he wonders if he is dreaming: '*Surely* I was no longer in the twentieth century!' he exclaims (Campbell 1937:31). This depiction of the East by the West as being the domicile of backward, uncivilised heathens—'in place of a hotel was not my resting-place a bed set in an Eastern temple beneath an Eastern image?' (1937:31)—is a typical imperialist construction in which the 'hero' (the Western male) endures all manner of hardships in order to bring civilisation to 'benighted' lands. The quest is acknowledged in a contemporary review from the *Observer* quoted on the book's dust jacket, which praises it for its drama and humour, saying Campbell has written one of the best books of its kind, while 'extenuating nothing of the "white man's burden"'.

In his narrative, Campbell builds his own little empire in an area his company allocates to him in the Siamese jungle. He describes it as 'the valley that was mine' and is ecstatic to have 'a real jungle valley to myself' (Campbell 1937:56–7). Of course, what he means is that he is the only white man in the area, for the area is inhabited and he has his own retinue of 'coolies' and other servants. He calls for dinner and is served four courses in the English style, even though he is 'miles and miles away from any kind of civilization', and, in stereotypical expatriate style, he whines about the toughness of the roast chicken (1937:61).

Surveying Siam

Traditional Siamese maps bore little resemblance to 19th-century European charts. The Siamese productions were principally concerned with making a political statement about the country's situation with regard to neighbouring countries such as Burma. As Suárez (199:27) observes, it was a Western idea that maps should be an analytical presentation of geographical data, though that idea was eventually adopted by Southeast Asian mapmakers.

As could be expected from a traveller who considered the Siamese inferior in all aspects to Europeans, Neale is scathing when describing a map of Siam and Burma shown to his party during an audience with the then monarch, King Nang Klao (Rama III). Neale puts himself doubly above the Siamese, because he and his party are 'Europeans, and more especially Englishmen' (Neale 1999:54), and rudely relates how they can hardly conceal their mirth at what the King believes to be a map worthy of praise. Neale's denigration of the King—the most revered person in Siamese society—is particularly spiteful when he says he believes 'any coolly [sic] picked out of the streets of Madras would have cut just as respectable a figure as his Majesty, and even perhaps have had more manners and politeness' (1999:57). Not surprisingly, he remarks that he was never invited back to the palace, so perhaps his nasty comments about the King were the result of his pique at being ignored by the ruler thenceforth.

Cartography is recognised as a textual instrument of imperialism that was necessary to define boundaries of newly acquired territories and to chart imperialistic progress in the name of 'marking ownership' (Bassnett 2002:231). As Thongchai (1997:114) says, 'the desire for geographical knowledge seemed to be an integral part of colonial expansion'. Edward Said criticises historians and literary scholars who have not satisfactorily addressed the way in which 'the theoretical mapping and charting of territory' has influenced Western writing, both fiction and non-fiction (Said 1994:69).

Cartography is particularly important to the independent traveller and forms a base on which much travel writing rests. Because the terrain was so difficult to access, maps of the interior of Siam were sketchy before the 1880s. Mapmakers faced many difficulties, including almost impenetrable jungle, lack of infrastructure, an abundance of wild animals and disease-carrying pests such as mosquitoes. The best-known Western mapmaker of 19th-century Siam, James McCarthy, in his memoirs of 12 years surveying the country, remarks on the strong resistance by the inhabitants of the interiors he is mapping. Thongchai observes that, until King Mongkut's reign and the modernisation he invoked, the Siamese court had had little need of surveys. The Siamese were suspicious of the work and noblemen were afraid their lands would be confiscated (Thongchai 1997:115,118).

McCarthy, who travelled for some time with Anna Leonowens's son, Louis, was employed by the Siamese Government to produce the first map to scale of Siam in 1887. McCarthy's writing is entertaining, unsentimental and anecdotal. It is amazing how matter-of-fact his narrative is concerning such complications as recurring malaria, lacerated feet, a tiger carrying off one of his men and so on. He is racially tolerant when it comes to the Siamese, acknowledging the fact that he is not the 'master', but is a public servant in the Siamese Government's employ. He says the Siamese officials sent with him to be 'practically in charge of the exhibitions' treated him as 'a superior sort of attendant', but caused him so much stress he became ill (McCarthy 1994:18). This is a notably different attitude to that shown by British advisers in colonised countries such as India.[54] He appears to have worked well with his Siamese assistants and held them in high esteem—evidence is found in the book's dedication, in which two out of three of those mentioned are Thais. Inconsistently, McCarthy casts aspersions against other Asians: Chinese, he says, 'seem to thrive' in streets with 'intolerable stenches', while Burmese traders are usually 'hopelessly in debt' (1994:3,5).

At home in Thailand

In describing their everyday life in Thailand, expatriates in the 19th and early-20th centuries seemed to want to show not how different it was, but in how many ways it was the same as life at 'home'. English people, for example, wrote about how 'British' their experience was—how their clothing, food and habits mirrored those of people at home. In reality, they were trying to show that they had not gone native and that they had, despite all, retained the trappings of 'civilisation'. They had, in their imaginations, brought Britain to Siam.

Two 19th-century accounts of Christmas dinner at royal palaces in Siam—one by Neale and one by a missionary wife, Fannie Roper Feudge (1876)—are examined by Thailand-based journalist Bonnie Davis (1989:329–32). Both remark at length on the sumptuous European-style food and table settings. However, Davis questions the validity of both accounts, saying Feudge probably copied her account from Neale, who in turn probably copied his from a third author.[55] Davis does not have any compelling evidence for her views, however, and it would not be unusual for Neale or Feudge to have attended such dinners. Feudge does perhaps exaggerate the extent of her input—she claims to have supervised food preparation and room decoration—given that such European-style celebrations had been held there for two decades.[56]

Observing the expatriates, Lucien Fournereau in 1892 complains that Bangkok is run along British standards, instead of taking an afternoon break as places more influenced by expatriates from continental Europe do:

> Always under the influence of this insupportable Anglomania which obsesses people everywhere, and to conform to British customs, the offices, shops and bazaars remain open from ten o-clock to four p.m., despite the scorching heat... then thirst makes itself imperiously felt...God knows how much they consume of this whiskey and soda in a day! (Fournereau 1998:46).

Interestingly, four decades earlier, Neale found Bangkok quite different, claiming that everyone in Bangkok, 'Even we Europeans', takes an 'oriental siesta' in the afternoon (Neale 1999:39).[57] Painting a picture of the languorous life of expatriates in the tropics waited on hand-and-foot by the 'natives', Fournereau goes on to describe aperitifs at the English Club, heavy drinking and eating at the German Club and the 'whiff of French air' provided by the French newspapers at the Oriental Hotel where, 'During dinner, if you are feeling uncomfortable by the heat, they set in motion the pankah...' (Fournereau 1998:47). It is as if European culture has been transplanted to Thailand. Of course, this practice of remaining immersed in a home culture is not limited to European expatriates and applies to a certain extent to expatriates anywhere. However, when this practice is combined with the legacy of colonialist views, it becomes an assumption of ownership. Andrea Feeser notes that critics acknowledge that travel writing 'share[s] an interest in encouraging readers to see themselves as individuals entitled to consume land (through labor or leisure) in foreign places' (Feeser 2002:103).

An editorial in the *Bangkok Times* in 1900 points out how little interest the expatriates in Siam had in the Siamese people or their culture. Interestingly, the editorial reveals that the Thais themselves promoted the transplantation of Western culture:

> Our own home ways we rigidly enforce in our own little circle till these have come to rigidly hedge us in. Of Siamese ways the ordinary *farang* knows really next to nothing. We get to elaborate Siamese entertainments given by one or other of the Government departments and there we find few Siamese while the whole entertainment is conducted on purely European lines (cited in Beek 1999:72).

Beek notes that most Europeans in Thailand around 1900 had to learn to speak some Thai in order to make themselves understood by their staff, but that most knew only enough to get by. As Neale says, '[W]ith the exception of Mr H, very few of us could ever attain anything approaching to an efficient knowledge of that most barbarous tongue' (Neale 1999:189).

When expatriates from Victorian England went to Bangkok and other areas of Thailand in the 19th century, they brought their inappropriate clothing, cultural and social habits, and the ideological baggage of their class system, which put non-white people at the bottom of the hierarchy. Exceptions are made in individual cases. Neale, for instance, separates Prince Chuthamani, who later became the Second King, from other Thais, whom he sees as inferior beings (not forgetting, of course, that there was a rigid class structure in Siam at the time, too). The ordinary Siamese are, Neale says, 'almost savages…in a land but little heard of or known' (Neale 1999:97). He remarks on a Siamese dance performed for the English visitors, 'resembling much in its uncouth gestures the savage war dance of the South Sea Islanders' (1999:94). In reality, of course, Siamese dancing in no way resembles, say, Maori or Hawai'ian dancing.

For many expatriates, the longer the residence, the more the shortcomings of that country or its people are magnified as dissatisfaction increases, promoting a heightened nostalgia for home. This dissatisfaction was particularly applicable before the advent of fast, affordable travel. In the 19th century, 'going home' was possible only once every three or four years, or longer.[58] The complaints of European expatriates were frequently based on their dependence on their preconceptions of Eastern people—that they were indolent, dishonest, uneducated, dirty and less intelligent.

One frequent complaint was the high incidence of crime such as burglary. It is almost invariably written about as if it were much more prevalent than that of the home community, though there are no statistics to verify this. Wood complains about the number of thieves in Bangkok, saying he has been burgled some twelve times. He relates what he says is a favourite ploy of burglars, which is to wait until they see the 'dining room punkah' moving and then, taking advantage of the household's involvement with serving dinner, to steal valuables from the upper storey of the house while it is unattended (Wood 1991:13). It is difficult to ascertain the crime rate, because though the Ministry of Justice, formed in 1892, kept records of court trials and convictions, there were no reliable population statistics. Buls notes that most prisoners in jail in Bangkok 'have been condemned for banditry committed in the countryside'. He claims, however, that violent crime is 'less frequent than in Europe' and that, while the Siamese are 'very gentle in their morals', the 'treacherous Chinese commit theft' and the 'vindictive Malays, murders' (Buls (1994:66–7).

Though expatriates in Siam were keen to show how well they had emulated life in Europe, their lifestyle was, in reality, quite different to that of home, as Beek describes:

> Aside from the privileges they enjoyed—luxurious homes, servants to cater to every need, lavish parties, etc.—foreigners' lives were far from idyllic. The torrid climate was quite unlike the frigid winters of their home countries. Expatriates dwelt far from relatives, aware that if anything adverse were to happen to loved ones at home, there was little they could do to help. When they waved goodbye from the decks of ships carrying them to Siam, they knew that they might be seeing friends and relations for the last time (Beek 1999:85).

Health was a real concern. Though hygiene standards in the 19th and early 20th centuries were not much higher in Europe than in Siam, tropical diseases were a major threat because little was known about how to treat them (Beek 1999:85). In 1903 Arnold Wright and Oliver Breakspear (1994) provided information for employers about the length of time an expatriate worker should stay in Siam, advising three years for women and five for men 'for a first spell' before nine months' leave (including three months' travel time), followed by further spells of up to three years each, broken by six months' leave in a temperate climate (cited in Beek 1999:115). Expatriates deplored the lack in Siam of the types of holiday resorts that had been developed for Europeans in India: 'Siam is still, unfortunately, most grievously deficient in hill stations or other health resorts', Wright and Breakspear complain (cited in Beek 1999:115). Six years earlier, JGD Campbell (1985) similarly complains that 'A great drawback to

Bangkok, too, is the fact that there is no place for the jaded European to go for a few days' change'. He adds that there are no hill stations and the only two seaside resorts have no hotels, meaning the tourist must cope with the inconvenience of taking not only the household effects necessary for a stay, but the household staff, too (presumably the staff took care of the luggage) (cited in Beek 1999: 63,115).

Chapter four

Teaching Thailand

The more I see the Siamese people, the happier I am to have been sent here. They appeal to one's heart as children do, and they earn one's respect because they make the most of the simple things their country yields, without feeling envious of people who have more.—Jessie MacKinnon Hartzell, missionary, in 1912 (2001) [59]

When I was teaching English to Thais on Saturday mornings in 1993 in Nonthaburi province, 30 kilometres north of Bangkok, there was a school rule that teachers were not to speak Thai to the children, only English. This was not, as I first thought, out of any belief on the American principal's part that English was a superior language or that Thai was not fit for our 'international' school. She herself spoke and read Thai fluently. The rule was, rather, in response to a request from the pupils' parents. These parents—professionals who were part of Bangkok's growing middle class—were paying for their children to learn English from native speakers and they complained if they heard Thai spoken. Moreover, they wanted their children to be taught by white teachers with Australasian, American or English accents, and so much the better if the teacher happened to have blonde hair and blue eyes. Indeed, the tri-lingual Indian teacher at the school was paid approximately half of what the *farang* teachers were paid. Thais were employed as assistants or maids.

From the late 19th century, Western educators, instructors, government advisers, military experts, diplomats and missionaries had a substantial presence in Thailand. Many wrote about Thailand, in memoirs, travelogues, travel guides and even novels. From the 19th century, many of these instructors considered their work part of the 'white man's burden'. Feeser acknowledges that missionaries and officials were among the colonials who 'were the primary architects of Victorian imperialism' (Feeser 2002:89–90). The term 'white man's burden' was invented by Rudyard Kipling in his 1899 poem of that name, referring specifically to the Indian Civil Service. The ideology that designated white people as innately superior to people of other races existed from the 16th century, when Iberian and English colonial theorists defined imperialism as 'the fulfillment of a universal mission: as a contribution to a divine plan for the salvation of the pagans, as a secular mandate to "civilize" the "barbarians" or "savages"' (Osterhammel 1997:16). Three centuries later, the plan was still being promoted in, for example, Lord Lugard's 'dual mandate' theory of 1922 which promoted the idea that the 'higher races' should have guardianship over the 'lower'. In the case of Asia, Lord Lugard said, the tradition of despotic rulers would have to be changed and the people would have to be taught to give up superstitions and behaviour that contradicted Christian morality (Osterhammel 1997:16). In return, they would receive the benefit of Western learning.

The importation of Western instructors has, of course, been largely at the behest of Thailand itself, notably with the employment of Leonowens as an English teacher. To a certain extent, Thailand takes what it wants of Western culture and dispenses with what it doesn't want. The Christianising mission, for example, has never been successful. In the words of King Mongkut to Anna Leonowens in her letter of appointment:

> And we hope that in doing your education on us and on our children (whom English call inhabitants of benighted land) you will do your best endeavor for knowledge of English language, science and literature, and not for conversion to Christianity (Leonowens 1988:vi).

Taking up the burden

In the 19th and early 20th centuries, Siam was still considered a 'hardship posting' by expatriates who lived there, desperately trying to maintain some vestige of life at 'home'. In the 19th century, the Western imagination had yet to mould Siam and its people into something approaching a Western idea of paradise. However, George Blagden Bacon shows in his 1881 book (Bacon 2005) that it was already gaining a reputation as an enchanting place to visit. For the expatriate, however, it was a different story. Bacon writes that, though the beauty and splendour of Siam may make the traveller blind to its difficulties, the life of a missionary there is far from idyllic. The missionaries' job is made more difficult by the seductive surroundings which, like a Garden of Eden, continuously offer temptation: 'And all the beautiful earth, and all the drowsy air, and all the soft blue sky invite to sloth and ease and luxury' (2005:118).

The role of the many advisers, teachers and missionaries was not only to teach Siam to become more Western, but to become the Siam of Western imaginings, whether commercially or recreationally oriented. This remaking of the country was to be facilitated by education, often by teacher-missionaries. The teaching of English and science was considered inseparable from the teaching of

Christianity, and Christian codes of living and worshipping were incorporated at every opportunity. As Said (2003:206) remarks, the Orient was viewed as a 'locale requiring Western attention, reconstruction, even redemption'.

Part of the white man's perceived duty was to ensure 'they' were shielded from the lure of immorality. Reginald le May, who worked as a government adviser in Siam from 1908 to 1932, claims that popular Western films are having a detrimental influence on 'thousands of uneducated Eastern folk' (May 1999:159). As Terwiel says in his foreword to the 1999 edition of le May's book, this claim is evidence that he had 'internalised the idea that the Europeans…were the sole carriers of "civilisation" and that it was the "White Man's Burden" to demonstrate his role as representative of this rare form of mankind' (May 1999:ix). Another important factor in the presentation of 'ridiculous and melodramatic films' in 1920s Bangkok cinemas, le May says, is that they may harm the reputation of Europeans in the eyes of Eastern people. While le May intends, by that comment, to criticise the West, he is, of course, revealing his opinion of Siamese people as inferior in intellect to British people. More enlightened is his next criticism of the West, in which he scolds the British press for lampooning in a cartoon the crime of elephant-stealing in Siam and then explains why it is not a joke for those who live in Siam (May 1999:159–60).

A fable intended to demonstrate to Westerners the possibility of instructing Easterners in 'right' morals is what is thought to be the earliest novel set in Thailand, Dan F Bradley's *Simo: the story of a boy of Siam* (1899). Bradley does not specify when the book is set, but it appears to be during the reign of Rama III (1824–1851) when Bradley's father, Dan Beach Bradley, was a missionary in Siam. Dan F Bradley could be expected to have been familiar with Leonowens's books of the 1870s and his story shows many similarities. Its subtitle on the title page is 'The story of a boy of Siam', but at the start of the first chapter, the book is titled *Simo: a romance of the Court of Siam*, reminiscent of Leonowens's titles *Romance of the harem* and *The English governess at the Siamese Court*. Bradley's slim book tells of a poor country boy, Simo, who does well, moves to Bangkok and falls in love with a rich man's daughter, Soot-chei. Her greedy father presents her to the King for his harem, but Simo eventually manages to escape with her and elope to England, with Captain Orton[60] marrying them in a Christian ceremony en route. Simo's employer, an important government minister, is killed for helping him but as he dies he becomes a Christian so, presumably, his soul is saved and all is well.

Bradley's depictions of the harem could well have been inspired by Leonowens, particularly the scene where noble princess Soot-chei intervenes to save a slave-girl from being whipped (Bradley 1899:22). Similar to the way

Leonowens portrayed herself, Soot-chei becomes the champion of the women in the harem: 'She tried to comfort them as they sobbed themselves to sleep in their loneliness and terror when they first came' (Bradley 1899:21). Soot-chei's fate is to be forced herself to join the harem of the King as one of his wives, but her reward for remaining pure and loyal to her one true love is a Christian marriage and escape to England.

Simo is a fable that warns against polygamy and shows how monogamy is aligned with Christianity and Western civilisation and, therefore, with goodness. Bradley, who was born and raised in Thailand, establishes Simo as 'other' from the first sentence: 'Simo was the eldest of five brown-skinned children' (Bradley 1899:3). According to Ronald D Renard, reviewing *Simo* in 2001, the book had been forgotten until he found it offered on the trading website ebay, and reviewed it 102 years after it was published: '[A] review of this book is equivalent to reporting a new archaeological find,' he says (Renard 2001:129).[61] Strangely, Renard says that Bradley 'avoids much of the racist rhetoric of his time' (Renard 2001:131). On the contrary, racist rhetoric is present or implied on almost every page. The Thais are depicted as heathens with a barbarous religion who can be saved only if they adopt Western beliefs. One of the story's heroes is Phya Pet, the government minister, whom Bradley describes as a man of high moral qualities because he has adopted Western ways:

> Unlike the other officials at the Siamese Court, he had but one wife. He had sent his oldest son to London to be educated, and he liked the western ways of thinking, and tried to make himself familiar with the institutions and laws of England and America (Bradley 1899:35).

Moreover, Phya Pet believes love between one man and one woman is possible 'even among the corrupt, polygamous people' for whom polygamy is a 'hideous institution' and a 'barbarous substitute' for monogamy (Bradley 1899:42).

The ongoing significance of the 'white man's burden' is nicely illustrated on the dust jacket of Margaret Landon's now largely-forgotten 1949 second novel about Thailand, *Never dies the dream*. The novel is about a missionary school in Bangkok employing European teachers. Its cover illustration depicts the grounds of the school. In the background is a white colonial-style building with a Western teacher standing outside, as if on guard. On the clipped lawn with a mauve-flowering tree and manicured gardens, the Thai pupils play, watched by the teacher. Another teacher, fair-skinned and blonde, escorts an errant child back to the others from the boundaries of the lawn. On the periphery are two Thai adults, one in a colonial-style white-buttoned jacket, the other, as is often described in travel memoirs, 'half-naked', wearing only shorts and walking away from the school into the shadows. The illustration closely resembles a picture of the missionary Wang Lang School in Bangkok in 1875 (reproduced in Wells 1958:37). As the head of a school in Thailand (Anakul Satri Girl's School) in the 1930s, Landon would have been familiar with Wang Lang.[62]

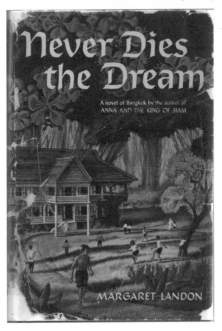

Never Dies the Dream dust jacket.

On Landon's cover, seemingly from out of the jungle that looms threateningly in the background, emerge large red orchid-like flowers. The jungle and the flowers represent the call of the wild—the lurking evil of the 'native' environment from which the English school has rescued the children. The depiction of the jungle as menacing yet enticing, as symbolising the savage and the uncivilised, is common to writing about non-Western countries, whether they be in Africa, South America or Asia. Similarly, the desert fulfils this function in narratives of the 'Middle East', Australia and North America. Harold Stephens, a self-styled modern-day explorer and long-term resident of Thailand, writes about the concept of 'jungle' in an article for Royal Orchid Holidays (Stephens 2005). As he notes, the romanticised 'Oriental jungle' as presented by Kipling and to a lesser extent Tarzan's creator, Edgar Rice Burroughs, bears little resemblance to the real thing. The very word 'jungle', he says, is a meaningless term applied by British hunters 'not out to study the rainforests, only to make use of them for their own purposes' (Stephens 2005).

Though most visitors to 19th-century Siam rarely saw the jungle, unless they were travelling merchants or missionaries, an image of it as being ready to overwhelm civilisation lurked in their imaginations. For those who did travel through it, the jungle became a metaphor for the unknown and for the 'hardship posting' they had accepted. It is the barrier between civilisation and the primitive. Yet it also represents excitement and adventure, the white man's quest to be a pioneer in 'frontier-land', something that home could not offer. As Jessie MacKinnon Hartzell says in 1912: 'the thought of the long trip to Nan—six days through the jungle, with nary a village—thrills me and frightens me' (Hartzell 2001:14). There is the assumption that because the jungle is seen as wild, untamed and uncivilised, it is not owned and, therefore, exists for the taking, as in Campbell's claim to have 'a real jungle valley to myself' and, once he is there, to have become 'a little king' (Campbell 1937:57,215).

Like many other Western travellers in Thailand before and since, Hartzell remarks on the durian fruit, reviled for its pungent odour. 'I shall not try,' she determines (Hartzell 2001:15). She is, otherwise, an adventurous woman who has left her comfortable life in the US to marry a man she barely knows and to travel with him to rural Siam. Yet it is typical of Westerners' fear of 'going native'. The vestiges of civilisation must be maintained—that means Western attire, food as far as possible, religion and literature. Interestingly, Hartzell describes the smell of the durian as being 'like asafetida'—as has been shown repeatedly, the Western imagination readily links Siam with Persia and Mesopotamia (2001:15).

Hartzell's description of the jungle could have been inspired by readings of Kipling or Burroughs. Bamboo forests, she says, 'look centuries old, with great vines draped from one to the next'. Hartzell (2001:18) says that, compared with the jungle of Thailand, 'all that I have seen before appears man-made and commonplace'. Significantly, when she emerges from the jungle and arrives at Nan, she is met by 'a huge delegation of native Christians headed by Dr Hugh Taylor' (rather optimistic of her as it is well documented that there were barely any conversions) (2001:18). Though Hartzell comes across as kind, intelligent and brave, she held the Eurocentric views of her time which dictate that Westernisation and, most importantly, Christianisation, are to be the salvation of the heathen and that it is the duty of Christians to save them. 'A clean, nice-looking native man has told Dr Taylor that he would like to work as my cook', she says of one of the supposed converts (2001:18). In a portrait of Hartzell, her granddaughter, Joan Acocella, concedes that Hartzell goes along with the Western political ideologies of the day, seeing 'nothing wrong with colonialism, let alone with missionaries, and at points—lovingly, no doubt, in her mind—she compares the Thai people to children' (Hartzell 2001:xxxiii).

The association of children with being endangered by 'savage' influences was a driving force in the colonial urge to take up the 'burden' and save them from themselves. This perception was extended to non-white adults, too, who were depicted as simple, naive and in need of instruction and salvation. This was justification for the white man's right to spread Christianity and Westernisation, even in countries, such as Siam, that had not been officially colonised. Bacon in the 1880s, recollecting his visit of 1857, says the Siamese 'have, of course, the defects and vices which are to be expected in a half savage people' governed by 'the capricious tyranny of an Oriental despotism' (Bacon 2005:234). The climate makes them lazy, he adds, and they indulge in 'animal passions'.

In *Land of the moon flower*, Gerald Sparrow, who spent 25 years in Thailand from 1930 as a judicial adviser to the Thai government, exemplifies the British conception of Thais as child-like and not part of the real world when he explains the opinion of Siam held in London: 'In Whitehall and the State Department it was possible to speak of Siam lightly as a toy kingdom in a gracious never-never world…' (Sparrow 1955:63). Sparrow goes on to acknowledge that the reality is something quite different. Considering he was writing in the 1950s, he has a particularly enlightened view of East-West relations, revealed in the opening chapter of his memoirs when he comments on a stage production of *The King and I* at Drury Lane, London:

> As we left the theatre it struck me that this play was typical of a tendency in Britain and in America to assume that Western culture is innately superior to that of the East, and that developments in the Eastern hemisphere are profoundly influenced by British diplomats, American teachers and Russian political philosophers. I believe this to be a great delusion (Sparrow 1955:17).

Sparrow acknowledges that spreading the culture, technology and ideology of the West may not be as well received by Eastern people as Westerners believe. He continues to attempt to dispel Western images of superiority throughout the book. Interestingly, the chapter which describes Sparrow's arrival in Thailand is titled 'Last paradise'. Five decades before Sparrow, missionary Mary Bulkley Stanton was writing in her diary, which was not published until 2003, that Bangkok was a 'Shangri-La of peace and plenty', though she concedes that the tropical climate 'could be downright cruel to the Westerner' (Stanton 2003:75). They were early references to Thailand as paradisal; today, barely a guidebook, travel article or brochure fails to inform us that Thailand is such.

Spreading the word

> It is said by Mr Gutzlaff, that they are in expectation of the coming of the Saviour of mankind, and that the people who are to effect a change in their religion, are to come from the West.—Edmund Roberts, 1837 (Roberts 1972:248) [63]

Roberts's statement regarding Western hopes that the Thais would become Christians seems as bizarre and misplaced as the French misapprehension in the 17th century that King Narai would convert. German missionary Karl Gutzlaff is not alone in his assertion. His associate, Jacob Tomlin, insists a young Thai man has told him of an 80-year-old sage who has predicted the coming of a 'Redeemer or Saviour of his nation' and points to the missionaries as 'the forerunners of Him that I spoke of' (Farrington 2001:50).[64] Bacon, too, claims people in northern Thailand believe they will one day 'receive a religion from the West' (Bacon 2005:219). It was probably, however, not as strange an assumption as it may be thought today; many populations throughout the world were converted—almost 100% of Polynesians, for example. Yet the Siamese remained faithful to Buddhism and many of the few Siamese converts to Christianity reverted to Buddhism after a short time. Wells notes that from 1831 to 1849 the 22 Congregational, or American Board, missionaries in Siam did not make one Thai convert; the missionaries of the Presbyterian Board worked from the 1840s to 1859 before making their first convert, while the American Baptists made only 45 converts from 1833 to 1863 (Wells 1958:3). Vincent, on visiting the American Presbyterian Rev SG McFarland in Pechaburi in the 1870s, said the missionary claimed only 20 converts, one of whom had since reverted to Buddhism (Vincent 1988:140).

Remarking that McFarland spoke fluent Siamese and Lao, Vincent also made the broad claim that McFarland, therefore, 'thoroughly understands the people and their country after so long a residence' (Vincent 1988:140). This is an assumption made throughout history: that length of stay and language skills somehow automatically give the foreigner an understanding of the other culture. American missionary David Abeel points out that short-term visitors lack a knowledge of the language and culture of the visited country and cannot, therefore, possibly comprehend its society, so they imagine the Siamese are happy with their lot. He goes on, however, to say they need Westernisation, including Christianity, to 'improve their condition' (Farrington 2001:124).

Disguised, it might be said, as doctors, teachers and other useful professionals, missionaries had much more opportunity to interact with Thais than other expatriates and tended to have superior Thai language skills because preaching to the 'natives' in their own language was essential to catch their attention. It would seem reasonable to assume that missionaries would, with widening experience and knowledge, lose some of the prejudiced views of their compatriots. Yet, a reading of texts by missionaries in Siam in the 19th and early 20th centuries shows this was not the case in the work of most of them. Perhaps it was the customary expatriate dissatisfaction, coupled with their failure to convert the populace to Christianity, that increased their sense of condescension. In his

1902 book, missionary JDG Campbell, later a British politician, says among the 'defects' of the Siamese are that

> ...they are little more than a nation of full-grown children. The serious business of life is quite beyond them; what appeals to them are its show, its scenic effects, and its pageantries...Few Siamese seem really capable of grasping the serious nature of work. A Cabinet Council will break off suddenly in the midst of a discussion to admire some new European toy brought in by one of its members. For, like children, the Siamese have a passion for novelty... (Campbell 1902:126).

Campbell asserts that what he views as the simple lifestyle of the Siamese ensures they are happy and carefree, while the Westerner, being part of a 'complex civilisation', must suffer 'the weariness, the fever, and the fret of Western life' (1902:126).

Landon's aforementioned *Never dies the dream* is fictional, but it provides an interesting insight into her imaginative construction of Thais in particular and Asians in general. Notably, Landon is often scathing toward the Chinese (other than those who are Christians), while she is merely patronising toward the Thais. All the stereotypical devices used in her earlier book, *Anna and the King of Siam*, are reproduced in *Never dies the dream*, and a reading of the latter explains much of her process of interpretation of Leonowens's story.

Landon lived in Bangkok from 1927 to 1937 with her minister husband, Kenneth Perry Landon, also an author. She makes no comment on life in Bangkok as a missionary in her preface to *Anna and the King of Siam*, instead describing how she came to uncover the then obscure story of Anna Leonowens. However, she reveals her bitterness about missionary life in *Never dies the dream*, through a comment made early in the narrative by her protagonist:

> India Severn had long ago accepted the fact that to be a missionary was to be considered queer, to be herded into a kind of ghetto that was no less real for the circumstance that its walls existed only in people's minds. This was true in America even among church people, and it was true in Bangkok. Missionaries were regarded as *déclassé* not only by businessmen, whose instinct to profit found altruism suspect, but also by their country's official representatives (Landon 1949:2).

Through the character of India, Landon writes of 'the deviousness of the Eurasian'and reveals her acquiescence with the then widely held view that racial intermarriage was inadvisable. She tells of an English major who never allows his Siamese wife to sit at the dining table with him (Landon 1949:5), the cautionary tale of an American woman unhappily married to a Siamese prince (1949:12) and of a Siamese who 'was an ignorant woman of the sort that attached themselves to white men' (1949:13). The offspring of 'mixed' marriages are often sullied, too, in Landon's view: she tells of one who is 'a pretty girl, but dark with the blood of her Siamese mother' (1949:60), of another with skin a 'dusky off-white' and 'sultry like an August day', but who has a propensity for violence and brings shame on the school when she runs away with a classmate's brother (1949:53,79). Of the American woman, Angela, married to the prince, Charoon ('Jerry'), the lesson is clear: marry a Siamese and you will eventually become part of a harem. It is understandable, Landon says, that Angela falls for the Siamese man at first. After all, he acts like an American and is tall and good-looking, 'more like a Spaniard in appearance than the conventional idea of an Oriental' (1949:176). But when the couple come to Siam to live, the real Jerry is revealed:

> With time Angela felt a change in Jerry that frightened her. Imperceptibly he became a Siamese. In America he had been one of her own kind, and she had loved him deeply. Now among his own people he took on their coloration of thought and action until to Angela he seemed almost alien (Landon 1949:177).

Landon is issuing a warning: 'They' may look westernised, but, underneath, the savage is just waiting to break out. After all, she seems to be saying, 'they' are not like 'us'. Nor should 'they' be permitted to become too much like 'us'. Interestingly, Landon's story of Charoon and Angela in some ways is similar to the later memoirs of Prince Bira's English wife, Ceril Heycock, of marriage to a Siamese royal in the 1930s and 1940s, although not published until the 1990s (Birabongse 1992).[65]

Landon gives another example of Europeans' disapproval of what today is called multiculturalism and of their need to assert their cultural superiority. Miss Cole ensures, Landon says, that the pupils 'remain Siamese' and are 'not allowed to adopt European manners, as they understood them, which was imperfectly' (Landon 1949:273). Bizarrely, Miss Cole sets herself up as the caretaker of Siamese culture, admonishing the girls when they make mistakes. While the Siamese are 'aping everything European', Miss Cole becomes 'more Siamese than the Siamese' (1949:273). So, in Landon's view, Westerners are needed even to teach the Siamese how to be themselves.

Though it purports to be a moralistic story about a straight-laced missionary woman, the narrative reverberates with repressed sexuality. There is a reference, for example, to men being seduced by 'succulent little brown girls' (Landon 1949:11) and a description of the 'silken docility' of Siamese girls. Particularly erotic is a scene in which India bathes in rain water, 'plunging her head up and down in it' and watching it 'overflowing voluptuously through the drain' (1949:19). There are also obvious homosexual connotations,[66] for example, when India finds herself mesmerised by the 'breathtaking beauty' of the '(s)lender and yet ripe' girl, Angela, who 'seems to have been carved of gold' (1949:12–3).

Another character, Grace, later accuses India of having an unnatural interest in the girl and the two have an extraordinary conversation (for the time) about the nature of the relationship (1949:135).

Margaret and Kenneth Landon on their 50th wedding anniversary, 1976.
Credit: Landon Collection Wheaton College (IL) Special Collections.

The novel abounds with descriptions of the selfless hard work of the missionary teachers and with stories of children left in their care as boarders because, according to Landon, the children's English or Chinese Christian fathers do not trust their Siamese wives to adequately care for the children while they are away (Landon 1949:44–5). Landon frequently mentions skin colour and her protagonist, India, imagines that children not used to interacting with white people would find 'her fair colouring abnormal, grotesque, even a little repulsive' (1949:49). This would have had the effect, of course, of making the unwesternised Thais, not the fair-skinned teacher, appear grotesque in the minds of Eurocentric readers of the day. One of the girls, Ploy, is described in a particularly unpleasant way. For example, she is described as 'squatting on her haunches like a toad' (1949:55). The novel is a hotch-potch of biased information about Siam and claims about the Siamese character. Thais are, according to Landon, 'often vengeful' (1949:70). Landon cannot disguise her view of Asians as simple beings in need of instruction. Even when she tries to debunk myths, she succeeds only in further ingraining herself in a stereotypical presentation of Asians. For example, when Grace warns India that 'Orientals' seem to have a sixth sense when 'reading character', India replies: 'They're no more infallible than dogs or children. You're too easily impressed by clichés, Grace' (1949:134).

There are many books containing the memoirs and journals of 19th- and early 20th-century missionaries in Siam. Some were first published by their churches and circulated among congregations and among children at church schools. Nevertheless, as Christina Klein (2003) points out, the contribution of missionaries to perceived knowledge about Asia was important and influential: 'missionaries effectively "produced" China, Japan, India, and other parts of Asia at a time when few Americans had direct contact', she says (Klein 2003:30). The White Lotus publishing company in Bangkok has recently reprinted many of these volumes, including those of the pioneering Protestant missionaries, Tomlin, Gutzlaff and Abeel (Farrington 2001). Meanwhile, the descendants of some missionaries have collated and edited memoirs to produce new books from previously unpublished material, including the aforementioned early 20th-century diaries of Edna Bruner Bulkley (Stanton 2003) and Jessie MacKinnon Hartzell (2001).

Protestant missionaries in Bangkok in the 1820s and 1830s seemed by their own descriptions in journals to have dealt mainly with the city's Chinese population. Contrary to later 19th-century descriptions, they regarded the Chinese as more 'civilised' than the Thais, whom they saw as 'natives' in the colonial interpretation of the word. This seems to be merely because there was a much more extensive history of contact with Chinese people and many of the missionaries could speak their language. In fact, as Anthony Farrington observes in his introduction to missionaries Tomlin's, Gutzlaff's and Abeel's 1828–1832 journals, they did not aim to convert the Siamese, but went to Siam expressly to work among the Chinese immigrants and to distribute Christian literature to junks in the port of Bangkok that would travel back to China (Farrington 2001:vii).

Later missionaries went to Siam with the purpose of Christianising the indigenous population. Many, such as American Daniel McGilvary, went to northern Thailand to work among the 'Lao', as they called the people of that area. McGilvary spent 50 years in and around Chiang Mai in what turned out to be a largely fruitless endeavour to convert the population. From his memoirs, *A half century among the Siamese and the Lao*, first published in 1912, however, the reader may be left with the impression from McGilvary's zealous descriptions that there were many thousands of converts—he claims in 1911 that the church in northern Thailand has 4000 members (McGilvary 2002:413). He speaks of Christianity as 'the new religion' of the country (2002:105), intimating throughout the book that a mass conversion is not far away, though ultimately admitting that the missionaries had been disappointed in their endeavours. McGilvary blames the Catholics (particularly the French), Thai authorities and, to a lesser extent, the failures of the Presbyterian Mission itself, for the lack of conversions. In a 2002 edition of McGilvary's book, Herbert R Swanson of the Office of History, Church of Christ in Thailand, attributes the lack of conversions mainly to the missionaries themselves. He says they refused to make adjustments to allow for local beliefs or customs or to listen to 'local wisdom' and insisted on emphasising the evils of a 'heathen' religion such as Buddhism (McGilvary 2002:xxiv–v).

McGilvary himself unwittingly reveals part of the source of the limited conversion rate when describing his visit to the home of a local ruler: 'At the door, the officer suggested that we pull off our shoes. We replied that it was not our custom, and was unnecessary' (McGilvary 2002:357). This incident occurred in 1893 when McGilvary had been in Siam 35 years; he never made allowances for local culture and insistently retained Western customs to make his point about the superiority of Western civilisation, even if it meant being rude to his hosts. As Osterhammel points out, the majority of missionaries 'shared the cultural arrogance of their secular compatriots' (Osterhammel 1997:96). McGilvary's belief in the rectitude of his exertions extends to a sweeping judgement he makes on behalf of all the world. He follows the correct religion at a fundamental level, he believes, because while 'Catholicism and Protestantism had alike produced great nations, Buddhism never had' (McGilvary 2002:390).

Before McGilvary wrote his memoirs, those of missionary Lillian Johnson Curtis were published in 1903 as *The Laos of North Siam* (Curtis 1998). Curtis's recollections covered much the same ground as McGilvary's, though her experience was more limited in time and scope. In fact, McGilvary felt compelled to comment on Curtis's book, praising it for its 'accuracy and its valuable information', yet tempering that praise when he added, 'especially in view of the author's short stay in the field' (McGilvary 2002:13).

Curtis was travelling with and assisting her husband, the Reverend LW Curtis, spending four years in the north of Thailand. Curtis hardly mentions her husband and then only by his initials and surname once, followed by a few references to 'W—'. She divulges few personal details of her circumstances, family or marriage; she presumably had no children, since she does not mention any. In her descriptions of Eastern culture, of Buddhism and the need to 'Christianise and civilise' the Siamese, Curtis is as zealous as the male missionaries:

> We have seen that the Laos, though a simple, comparatively happy people in their social lives, are pitifully helpless and sinful spiritually...What they need is a Saviour from sin, a Power to keep from sin...To the Christian there can be no doubt that the Laos need Christ (Curtis 1998:244).

Curtis discusses the work of Leonowens and is familiar enough with her writing to quote it (Curtis 1998:137–9,250). It is strange that neither Curtis nor McGilvary mentions Louis Leonowens, who was well known in the north of Thailand when they were carrying out their missions there. Louis was, however, probably someone the missionaries would rather have forgotten, with his un-Christian, 'gone native' lifestyle. Dr Cheek, a sometime business partner of Louis, is mentioned by Curtis and McGilvary, but only during the time of his missionary service. Both Curtis and McGilvary mention in passing that Cheek resigned from the missionary service to pursue his own business interests (Curtis 1998:289; McGilvary 2002:283). In reality, Cheek must have been a disappointment and an embarrassment to the other missionaries as he became notorious in Chiang Mai for indulging in what they saw as hedonism and for maintaining a harem, to which his former-missionary wife apparently turned a blind eye (Bristowe 1976:82–3). According to Bristowe, bawdy popular rhymes were even sung by local people in Chiang Mai, Lampang and Phrae well into the 20th century about the shenanigans of Cheek and Leonowens (Bristowe 1976:83).[67]

Curtis's work is notable for its recognition of Thailand as more than a hardship posting or a 'civilising' work in progress. She, more extensively than other missionary writers of her time, constructs Thailand as an idyllic landscape. While the male missionaries seem wholly concerned with their work and its success or otherwise, Curtis appears to have taken time to enjoy the land she was travelling through. She employs a touch of dark exoticism in her descriptions, though it is usually used to point out the dangers of non-Christianised territory. She ends her introduction with: '...[W]e will turn to Laos-land with all its witchery of tropical splendor, and with all its darkness of demon worship' (Curtis 1998:xi). Later she says that despite the difficulties of the trip to northern Thailand, well documented by other writers, 'the journey will be rich in adventure and full of the charms of a tropical land and a strange people' (Curtis 1998:29). In recognising the travail of travel and its strangeness as adding to its charms, Curtis pre-empts travel literature of today, with its great number of writers seeking 'untouched' yet visually beautiful, even paradisal, scenery.

The landscape Curtis travels through enables her to indulge in an apparent nostalgia for childhood. There is, she insists, 'around palace life in Siam as much splendor and picturesqueness as we read of in the *Arabian Nights*' and she claims that King Chulalongkorn liked the tales so much, he had them translated into Siamese (Curtis 1998:12). She doesn't say how she has come across this knowledge and it may be hearsay, or wholly fanciful. She reveals a desire to conjure an exotic image for her readers, when only one page later she laments the lack of an important visitor or festival day to turn the Grand Palace in Bangkok into 'a fairyland of outward spendor and beauty'. In reality, it is disappointingly dusty, full of cobwebs and has 'a general look of disorder and stagnation', she says (1998:13).

This harks back to material on the linking of 'squalor' with moral and spiritual emptiness—with, in effect, Eastern savagery as opposed to Western refinement. Early missionaries such as Englishman Jacob Tomlin left no doubt in their writing that they equated 'savagery' with responsibility for the lack of medical knowledge in Siam: the patients crowding their clinic are 'poor wretched heathen', many of whom 'by the most ordinary means, under His blessing' are miraculously cured 'from the most inveterate diseases' (Farrington 2001:61). He suggests that if 'savages' or 'natives' can be Christianised, it demonstrates their acquiescence with Westernisation—their agreement, in essence, with colonisation and the place of the West as teacher and guide. This illustrates an edict of colonial discourse, according to Spurr, that 'a colonized people is morally improved and edified by virtue of its participation in the colonial system' and by its 'identification with the basic values of Western civilization' (Spurr 1993:32–3). Spurr notes that 19th-century Darwinism supports the eradication of 'savagery', which, it dictates, belongs to beings of lesser advancement (1993:82). Interestingly, given fierce debate at the time on Darwin's theory of evolution, both secular and religious representatives agreed on this point. As Spurr says, 'This rhetorical trope—the warning against the seductive dangers of the savage— surfaces throughout the colonial world in every form of writing: journalism, fiction, missionary narratives, and administrative reports' (1993:83).

Although Catholic missionaries have had a longer residence in Thailand than their Protestant counterparts, most of the Catholics were French and there is no work of note published for general readership in English in the 19th century. In the 20th century, there have been only a few memoirs by Catholic missionaries. One of them is *Teresa of Siam*, by Teresa Lightwood, an English nun, which was published in 1960 and tells of her time as a missionary in Thailand from the 1920s. On her arrival in Bangkok in 1928, she is, she admits, 'outraged' by the sight of a woman in traditional dress 'naked to the waist' on the street (Lightwood 1960:28). Her reaction is much stronger than that of Protestant missionaries, men or women, even of the century before her. But then, as she says, her own 'rigid code of convent modesty', in which she was not permitted even to undress in sight of another sister, was responsible for her reaction (1960:27–8). Ironically, given her initial reaction to the national dress, she writes with nostalgia about the way Thai women looked before they adopted Western dress, which she says saw their shift from 'bodies that moved without artiface' to the adoption of 'a far more conventional, stereotyped outlook on clothes (1960:28).

The history of female Catholic religious in Siam is short, starting in 1924, only four years before Teresa Lightwood arrived, according to her calculation (Lightwood 1960:30). Male Catholic religious had a long history of being in Siam, but, of course, following the principles of their faith, did not have wives to accompany them. Though the impoverished nuns seem more involved in charity work than in 'spreading the word', their attitudes towards Buddhism are negative, similar to those of the Protestant missionaries. Lightwood even blames Buddhism and its emphasis on merit-making for driving a young orphan 'from Indo-China' to attempt suicide at her convent in Chiang Mai (1960:42–3).

Lightwood's book was written more than three decades later, long after she had renounced her vows. She had continued her association with Thailand and adopted twin girls there. Lightwood effectively employs much of the usual rhetoric of travel writing in her attempt to present an interesting travelogue to her readers. Chiang Mai, she says, is like 'stepping back a hundred years by comparison with Bangkok' and she goes on to describe the idyllic countryside (Lightwood 1960:44). Her description of 'glamorous' Bangkok after dark, where 'the reflection of lamps caused a magic glistening across the muddy waters of the *klongs*' would not be out of place in a 21st-century travel guide (1960:34).

The work of today's missionaries, such as Father Joseph Maier, demonstrates the radical change in attitude from working in the 19th century to convert the indigenous people, to working *with* them in the 20th and 21st centuries for positive change seen as promoting human dignity, not necessarily Christianity. 'Father Joe' has worked to help the poor in Laos and Thailand since 1967, settling in the notorious Bangkok slum neighbourhood of Klong Toey in the 1970s. In his book, *Welcome to the Bangkok slaughterhouse* (Maier 2006b), Father Joe never mentions his desire to save souls by showing them what he believes to be the true religion. The improving results of the work itself whether medical, educational or social, today seem to be at the centre of the missionary's campaign, with Christianising a coveted but unlikely ideal. Father Joe and his Mercy Centre in Klong Toey even support devotion to Buddhism, as evidenced in both his book and in a recent article he wrote on the Mercy Centre's website. 'Entering the monkhood is a glorious experience for these kids…' as well as a way of making merit and showing respect for family, King and country, Father Joe says in his 2006 'Easter letter' on his website, www.mercycentre.org (Maier 2006a).

Demonstrating how far missionaries have come since the 19th century (remembering McGilvary who refused to remove his shoes to step inside a

Thai house), Father Joe even moved the date of the 2006 celebration of Easter festivities so it did not clash with Thai New Year celebrations. Pre-empting criticism of his arrangements as being untrue to the Catholic faith, Father Joe says: 'You can't ask Buddhist, Muslim or Christian kids not to party...So...we try to give them the best of both worlds' (Maier 2006a). Like Teresa Lightwood, Father Joe does have some criticisms of the effects of Thai beliefs, though he does not directly target Buddhism. Commenting on the belief that ailments or afflictions are the results of sins committed in a previous life, Father Joe maintains that, 'Brainwashed in this way, you become—and remain—always fragile' (Maier 2006a:147).

Speak English

Very few Thais spoke English until after King Mongkut's reign (1851–1868). Westerners had to learn Thai or conduct business through interpreters, often using a third language such as Malay. As Thai historian Rong Syamananda notes, Crawfurd's negotiations in 1822 were complicated because 'there were no Thais who could speak English any more than there were any Englishmen who could speak Thai' (Rong 1990:114). Thais rarely travelled, except for occasional diplomatic journeys to Europe from 1684 and the first full embassy led by Kosa Pan to France in 1686. The Thais travelled with an interpreter, though Kosa Pan reportedly spoke some French (Farrington 2001:132).

Contrary to many reports, King Mongkut was not the first Thai to learn English. Abeel, for example, mentions several upper-class Thais who could speak some English (Farrington 2001:132) and observes that even a 'heathen boy' assisting on a river boat knows an English phrase, though it is an offensive sentence and probably the only English the boy knows (2001:150). However, King Mongkut and his brother, the Second King, Prince Itsaret, were rare for their times in that they spoke English fluently. Much merriment has been made by Westerners of King Mongkut's unique style—as seen in the film *The King and I*—yet his vocabulary was astonishingly broad and he wrote English better than many contemporary English people.

Osterhammel notes that the Christianising mission had 'unintended side effects' in that 'secular western cultural values', through education and social work intended to facilitate conversion, 'developed their own dynamics' (Osterhammel 1997:97). This was particularly true in Thailand, where conversion numbers were so small. Social work and education, by default, became the primary work of missionaries. Osterhammel's assertion that 'colonial regimes and missionaries acted to undermine native cults and religious convictions' (1997:97) is demonstrated in the memoirs of Jane Hays McFarland, who compares British students and education systems with those of the Siamese:

> A teacher of a Siamese school need have little trouble with its government if it were not so impossible ever to be sure of the truth. When a boy gets into mischief, he always plans to tell a lie about it; and he can do it with such an air of candour that he will make the teacher almost disbelieve his own senses. But this fault is doubtless largely owing to the early training in heathen homes and in the old-fashioned 'wat schools' of the country (McFarland 1884:75).[68]

According to Wyatt (2002:71), literacy in some areas of Thailand in the 1890s was much higher than it was in Europe or the US. Yet McFarland goes on to disparage not only Siamese parenting skills and the Siamese education system, but its literature as a whole. Any indigenously produced writing will not have a positive effect on the student reader, she says, and will be neither truthful nor capable of improving the reader, 'for the literature of Siam has nothing of that kind' (McFarland 1884:75). Moreover, the local schoolrooms, she says, are 'filthy' and 'cheerless' places where students and teachers sit on the floor, and the syllabus is at the whim of each teacher (1884:75). In addition, she claims that 'the Oriental mind' stops growing after childhood, so the Church, she says, must start with the children in order to 'Christianize and civilize such a people' (1884:77).

Mrs McFarland's most salient point is that religion and education are inseparable: 'Christianity implies knowledge, and missionaries believe in schools', she says (McFarland 1884:77). Her simple statement reveals the extent of 19th-century Western reflection upon its culture as the true, right and, in fact, only path for all people to follow. The missionaries' objective in providing education was not to enable their subjects to think for themselves, to observe and question, but only to be brought 'into the fold' of the Western, Christian, and 'civilised' world.

Since about the 1950s, most foreigners teaching English in Thailand have not been missionaries. They are now largely a mixture of academics intrigued by the East, young travellers trading promises of Westernisation for an exotic expatriate experience, misfits who have opted out of what they see as the 'rat race' of the West, partners (usually wives) of foreign men working in Thailand who want something to do and Western men married to Thai women (and, less frequently, Western women married to Thai men).

An interesting case study is that of John Quincannon, in Jerry Hopkins's 2005 book, *Bangkok Babylon*—a title that illustrates Thailand's continuing connection with the Middle East in Western imaginations. Quincannon sells all his possessions in the US and leaves his university lecturing job to move to

Thailand in 1987 because he wants 'something different' (Hopkins 2005:192). Quincannon drifts for five years, 'ticking off Thai provinces on a map' (2005:192) as he visits them, rather like the conventional package tourist. This reconstitutes the question of whether there is any difference between the traveller, the tourist and the long-term expatriate. Quincannon's experience of 'ticking off' the areas he has visited is similar to Davies's anthropological account several decades earlier.

Significantly, Hopkins says English teaching is seen as a necessary evil—both by foreign teachers who do it to make a living and stay in Thailand, and by students who learn English because they feel they should. As he says, it is 'a sort of shotgun wedding between East and West' (Hopkins 2005:196). Today, English is taught because Thais demand it and are prepared to pay for it, seeking personal economic and social benefits. Interestingly, in the 19th century, some Thais were paid by missionaries to learn English.[69]

By the second half of the 20th century, teachers seemed to have more appreciation for the validity of Thai culture. Despite that, some, such as Davies, still lamented the failure of the Christian mission. He says Thailand is in most ways not inferior to the West, yet contradicts himself by adding: 'we surpass them only in technology, and in Christian concern for humanity' (Davies 1973:14).

Some studies suggest teachers in Thailand have not succeeded in teaching a passable standard of English; in 2005, Thailand was named eighth out of nine Southeast Asian countries (just in front of Cambodia) in terms of English standards in the Test of English as a Foreign Language (TOEFL).[70] It should be remembered, however, that these figures included Thais teaching English as well as native English speakers teaching English. Except for the minority of Thai students wealthy enough to employ native English speakers as tutors, the standard of English among the general Thai populace remains rudimentary. The desire of wealthy Thais to employ a native English teacher for their children started with King Mongkut and arguably the most famous English teacher in modern history, Anna Leonowens. (It is not so well known that Leonowens was not the first English teacher of the royal children—a number of missionary women had preceded her but had angered the King when they insisted on teaching religion as well.) A photographic still from the 1956 film is an apt illustration of the white teacher informing the Asian pupils about 'the world'.[71] The scene erupts in consternation when Leonowens pins up a new map on which Siam is very small—though, as she points out, not as small as England—and when the children then refuse to believe in the concept of snow. Yet Leonowens retains control, particularly when the King/parent sides with her and tells the children they must not contradict her.

Governing Thailand

While some government advisers undoubtedly had ulterior motives to infiltrate the Thai Government and, thereby, provide trading opportunities for their home countries, most were there to further their own careers. Adventurers such as Louis Leonowens started on the King's staff (in his case, as an army officer) and used the contacts and experience to graduate to private business. Unfortunately, Leonowens left behind no memoirs and only a few letters.

The history of foreigners being employed as government advisers in Siam began with Phaulkon. No individual foreigner since has been allowed to obtain such extensive influence or position within the royal court or the Government. Foreign advisers have remained just that, employees of the Thai Government, with limited powers beyond their areas of expertise. Their chief duties have been to assist in developing the country's infrastructure—bridges, railways, expressways and, late last century, the Bangkok Skytrain. As this book has shown, Western literature has been peppered with references to the cultural and social sophistication of Westerners. Writers are also concerned that Thais are seen to acquiesce with this notion. Abeel, for example, claims requests by Thais for Western accessories such as items of clothing, 'shows us their idea of the superiority of foreigners in some respects at least' and will make 'them' more readily able to accept the religion and 'sentiments of more polished nations' (Farrington 2001:131).

Many of the government advisers who worked in Thailand in the 19th and 20th centuries published their memoirs, often based on the detailed journals they customarily kept during their stay. But perhaps because they were the employees of Thais, and not 'in charge', government advisers seemed to adopt less superiority than did other expatriates in Siam. An important example is a conversation Gerald Sparrow reports between himself and his wife, Barbara, who asks him if he will mind 'working under the Siamese' (Sparrow 1955:37). The question, he says, 'means a lot if you ask it in England, but not very much here. These people have always been their own masters and have no inferiority complex' (1955:37). Sparrow seems to abhor racism and the assumption by the West that it is in an authoritative position above the East, even though he himself was involved in the judicial practice of extraterritoriality for part of his stay. His decades in Thailand from 1930 to the 1950s and his friendships with numerous Thais seem to have prompted him to maintain a stance in which he admonishes the West (specifically England) for misunderstanding Asians' attitudes to the West. English gentlemen, even the most sophisticated, he explains, do not realise that Asia does not want to be treated like a vassal or an adopted child of the West, but as an equal with something to contribute to world civilisation. Instead, the English talk of the East 'as if it was an inferior garden suburb, referring in tones of kindly patronage to its standard of living and its slow political development' (1955:120).

Sparrow takes issue with many stereotypical descriptions of Asians. They are neither filthy nor inscrutable, he says (Sparrow 1955:205). He uses his experiences in Thailand to underline his political beliefs about the world in general. Unlike, say, Leonowens, he is frank about what he means, directly criticising the colour bars then in place in South Africa and the US and the handling of diplomatic incidents with the Maori King, Koroki, of New Zealand and others. He does not become embroiled in Western fears that Communism would take over Asia. Yet even Sparrow, enlightened as he is, cannot avoid falling for what is held in the West to be common knowledge but is actually not based on fact. For example, he claims that 'The field of vision of Asiatics is markedly wider than that of Europeans' (1955:155).

Sparrow's tolerance has its limits and he retained his belief in the rightful place of men as leaders in society at large (Sparrow 1955:84, 152). After his separation from his English wife, Sparrow chooses certain Thai customs to justify 'keeping' two Thai women as partners concurrently. Most significantly, like 19th-century Western visitors before him (including British consul Knox), when he retires and returns to England, he goes alone. It appears he does not even contemplate taking his Thai de facto wife of many years with him—instead, in the end, he treats her as an employee: 'Chaluey was well provided for. After all those years of loyalty, she would have her own house and income' (1955:237).

One of the better-known memoirs from the late 19th century is Ernest Young's *The kingdom of the yellow robe* (1986). Young lived in Bangkok for several years and worked for the Education Department of Siam. The tone is authoritative, that of the expert, yet much of the book is based on hearsay, outsiders' observations of the culture and flagrant surmising. Young makes sweeping statements that he admits are based only on observations: 'As far as the casual observer can judge, in this capital of Siam there are no Siamese engaged in any hard manual labour at all' (Young 1986:9). Young has the attitude of a kindly patriarch toward the Siamese. He points out childish behaviour, chuckles over what he describes as their 'amusing errors' and nostalgically describes times past when 'the word of a native was as good as his bond' before 'civilisation' ruined things so that '[t]oday the dwellers in the city are never to be trusted' (1986:139).

Young's claims are often far-fetched in his effort to illustrate the Siamese as naive 'natives'. For example, he says that a group of Siamese watching an artist at work outdoors could not tell the difference between paint being brushed on canvas and the operation of a camera. This is highly unlikely, particularly as the Thais themselves have a long history of art and craft expertise, and cameras were known in Siam. (King Chulalongkorn was an enthusiast.) For the traveller, he paints a picture of harmless 'natives' who sometimes like to play tricks on visitors but who know their place when dealing with white people. He relates an anecdote in which a European traveller figures out a fisherman's scam. The fisherman, according to Young, 'exclaimed in the vernacular, "Master very clever, very clever!"'(1986:193–4). The anecdote could have come from any colonial writer describing travel within the empire. Ironically, of course, Siam was not a colony, nor were the white visitors in any way 'Master' to the Siamese. Yet the impression from Young is that white visitors are, in fact, the masters. The comments of George Bacon in 1881 on the Westernisation of Siam are a prime example of the way Westerners regarded the East in the 19th century and of their sense of total and unquestioned superiority:

> There are two tides—one is going out, the ebb-tide of ignorance, of darkness, of despotic power; and one is coming in—the flood-tide of knowledge and liberty and all Christian grace…sometimes the drift of things is backward toward the Orient, and sometimes forward, westward, as the "star of empire" moves (Bacon 2005:92).

Chapter five

Locating Leonowens: Anna Leonowens, Margaret Landon and *The King and I*

We advanced through the noiseless oval door, and entered the dim, cool pavilion, in the centre of which the tables were arranged for school...It was not long before my scholars were ranged in chairs around the long table, with Webster's far-famed spelling books before them, repeating audibly after me the letters of the alphabet.—Anna Leonowens, 1870 (Leonowens 1988:85)

In the dim cool pavilion the chairs were arranged as before, at the centre of the hall...The youngest of the royal children was only five, the oldest ten. It was not long before they were ranged around the long table with a Webster before each one, open at the first page...Anna said the letters of the alphabet and the children recited them after her.—Margaret Landon, 1943 (Landon 2000:101-2)

Another highlight was visiting Anna's classroom: a small porch of one of the Royal Palaces where her blackboard is still part of the wall!—Lucy Leonowens Bahr (Bahr 2001).

When Lucy Leonowens Bahr visited the Grand Palace in Bangkok in 1997, she was thrilled to be shown the porch of a palace building with an old blackboard that her great-great-grandmother, Anna Leonowens, had purportedly used as her classroom in the 1860s. The pavilion where Leonowens taught the royal wives and children of King Mongkut is not pointed out in any guide or map to the Grand Palace. The classroom was in the Inner Palace area known as the *Nang Harm*, where the King's consorts, wives and children resided. Leonowens herself says it was in an area known as the 'Temple of the Mothers of the Free' (Leonowens 1988:83), though official English maps of the Palace today do not mark this temple as such, if it still exists. No-one has lived in the *Nang Harm* for many decades and it is closed to the public, so Bahr was privileged to see the porch with the blackboard, which, of course, may or may not have been at the site of Leonowens's classroom, for there have been many schools at the palace before and since her time. Material about the Grand Palace barely mentions Leonowens; she is officially *persona non grata* in Thailand because of the unflattering portrait she painted of one of the country's most revered kings and, rather unfairly to Leonowens, because of the way her story was dealt with in film and popular fiction in the 20th century.

Siam on stage: Yul Brynner and Deborah Kerr are photographed on the set of the Broadway production of The King and I on March 13, 1957. Brynner made a career out of playing King Mongkut, performing the stage show thousands of times between 1951 and 1985 (the year he died) and winning an Academy Award for the 1956 film. Credit: AP Photo.

The story of Anna Leonowens's five years in Thailand is perhaps the most renowned of travellers' tales of that country. Leonowens is not, however, known principally for what she did or wrote, but for what others portrayed her as doing and writing during a small proportion of her life. Many seem not to know or care that she went on to be a champion of human rights in Canada and was well respected for her decades of work there. Instead, she has been subjected internationally to a barrage of criticism, much of it by commentators who have not bothered to read her original works. Her story became internationally famous through one of the West's most successful stage and screen musicals, *The King and I* (1951 and 1956 respectively). It is this musical, based only loosely on the schoolteacher's memoirs but more closely on a later novel by Margaret Landon, that has been Leonowens's undoing. The 1956 film *The King and I,* which purports to be based on the true story of Leonowens, has influenced the way Westerners have viewed Thailand, its monarch and its people, for more than 50 years. There are several other films: John Cromwell's 1946 film *Anna and the King of Siam*, Richard Rich's 1999 animation *The King and I* and Andy Tennant's *Anna and the King*, also released in 1999. There is also a 1972 American television comedy series of 30 episodes, titled *Anna and the King*, in which Yul Brynner reprised his role of King Mongkut and Samantha Eggar played 'Anna Owens'.[72] The first episode of the series and a documentary about its making were included on the 50-year anniversary DVD of *The King and I* released in 2006. The series is described as having 'fallen through a time warp from the late 1950s' and, strangely, the reviewer seems to think China and Siam are the same, commenting that the series is '*Family Affair* with foot binding' (Reed 1999).

Like all adaptations for the screen and stage, the story in *The King and I* takes extensive liberties, becoming a highly romanticised version of Leonowens's work—which itself did not always adhere to the facts as we know them. Naturally, the Thai authorities were not impressed with the film's presentation of King Mongkut as a caricature who could fall in love with a Western widow; both *The King and I* and the more recent Jodie Foster film *Anna and the King* were banned from screening in Thailand. It is, however, Leonowens's reputation that has suffered most, despite the fact that she never hinted at any sort of romance between herself and the King and had many positive things to say about him, as well as negative observations. It is only comparatively recently that some critics have re-read Leonowens's original works and have realised they have some value, despite their considerable flaws. Among those finding new value in Leonowens's writing are women, including US academic Susan Morgan, whose powerful feminist argument for Leonowens as a champion of women's rights features in the Introduction to a new edition of *The romance of the harem* (Leonowens 1991) and whose biography of Leonowens, *Bombay Anna* (Morgan 2008) has shed new light on the true story behind all the fiction, fabrication and fantasy.

The original: Anna Leonowens

When they were published, Leonowens's stories of living and working in Siam, where she instilled Western learning and morality into the royal family, caused a sensation. Effectively cut off from Western trade for 150 years, from the late 17th to the early 19th centuries, Siam was considered mysterious and exotic—that is, if Westerners had heard of it at all. People were, therefore, prepared to believe the most fantastic stories about it. Leonowens lived and worked in Siam as a teacher to the royal children from March 1862 to July 1867, gaining a rare intimate knowledge of the daily life in what the West called the 'harem'. Her books about her time in Siam, *The English governess at the Siamese Court* (1870) and *The romance of the harem* (1873), established her as a writer and adventurer and she was able to make a living on the speaking circuit. Audiences were captivated by her titillating tales of life within the King's extensive Inner Palace of women, but also by her picturesque portrait of Bangkok, a city most of her readers and listeners would never see themselves.

In *The English governess*, Leonowens's descriptions of activity on the Chao Phraya River, then the main highway of the city, are vivid and still recognisable by today's visitors:

> Here were the strange floating city, with its stranger people on all the open porches, quays, and jetties; the innumerable rafts and boats, canoes and gondolas, junks, and ships; the pall of black smoke from the steamer, the burly roar of the engine, and the murmur and the jar; the bewildering cries of men, women, and children, the shouting of the Chinamen, and the barking of the dogs...In the distance were several hulks of Siamese men-of-war, seemingly as old as the flood; and on the right towered, tier over tier, the broad roofs of the grand Royal Palace of Bangkok,—my future 'home' and the scene of my future labors (Leonowens 1988:8).

In *Subject Siam*, historian Tamara Loos says Leonowens was 'required reading' for Western women going to Siam in the 19th century, including Mary Backus, Florence Caddy, Mary Lovina Cort and Katherine Grindrod (Loos 2006:118).[73] However, most texts written by male contemporaries of Leonowens ignore her. By the 1940s, and probably even earlier, it seemed hardly anyone had read or even knew of Leonowens's original books about life in the *Nang Harm*. As the Australian historian Monica Anderson maintains, women's travel writing in the 19th century was deemed by men to be 'partial, low in "geographical knowledge" and high in emotion' (Anderson 2006:22). Though Leonowens writes much about domestic matters inside the women's quarters, she writes also of the culture, language, religion and society of Siam—not always successfully, but to the best of her ability, considering the few resources available to her (Kepner 1996a:25). It is, however, the domestic matters she writes of that are her chief strength and which are the subject of a text no man could have written.

Leonowens's principal influence was to bind the practices of slavery and polygyny as mutually exclusive, Loos says, with monogamy the solution to freeing women from becoming effectively enslaved as minor wives (Loos 2006:118). As Loos says, Western writers' 'narrow castigation of polygyny as a sexual perversion, an injustice to women, and a sign of an uncivilised nation' fails to take into account its historical perspective (2006:119). However, Leonowens's memoirs are believed to be the only comprehensive eyewitness accounts in existence of life in the *Nang Harm* and, as such, cannot be bypassed.

Margaret Landon came across copies of Leonowens's books when she was living in Thailand and used them as the basis for her fanciful 1943 novel *Anna and the King of Siam*. The novel was adapted for Broadway and Hollywood with little deference to factual events, yet the 'based on a true story' line had audiences fooled that the story happened just as it was depicted. Through the productions, Leonowens became an almost legendary figure who supposedly changed the future of a remote kingdom. Few knew, or cared, that *The King and I* was (and still is) banned in Thailand because of its historical and cultural inaccuracies, although Leonowens's first book, *The English governess at the Siamese Court*, is readily available at Bangkok's English-language bookshops.

Ironically, the Broadway stage show, though never produced in Thailand, was partly responsible for a resurgence of the Thai silk-weaving industry, through the endeavours and vision of long-time Bangkok resident and American expatriate, Jim Thompson.[74] Thompson inspired one of the 'non-ugly' characters in the film *The ugly American*, set in a fictitious Southeast Asian country (Klein 2003:220).[75]

The silk king: Jim Thompson at his house in Bangkok in 1966, where he had a large Southeast Asian art and artifacts collection. He disappeared in the Cameron Highlands of central Malaysia in 1967, and was never found. Thompson's Thai Silk Company still exists, with many outlets in Thailand and abroad. Credit: AP Photo.

At the time of their publication, Leonowens's books were read as the memoirs they are, not as histories. Leonowens had written a book of 'recollections', not 'diaries', as some have called them (Donaldson 1992:35), and a 'romance' highlighting the evils of slavery and championing the emancipation of women. Somehow, the books came to be thought of as a sort of history of life in 19th-century Bangkok and a biography of King Mongkut and his wives. When it was discovered that not everything in the books was, strictly speaking, the 'truth', Leonowens was discredited.

A similar development accompanied Baron de Montesquieu's 1721 novel *Persian letters* which, according to Robin W Winks and James R Rush (1990:7) was 'understood as a commentary on the West using a fictional Persia' when it was published, yet a century later was considered 'a true source for information about the Middle East'. Later still, the work was 'exposed' as not being based on any reality of Persia—yet the book was never intended as such. However, Montesquieu's works were highly influential in the 18th and 19th centuries on Western thinking about the East, so it was likely that Leonowens was familiar with *Persian letters* and its stories of the seraglio and the evils of despotism. Montesquieu also promoted the idea that the climate and geography of Asia predisposed it to despotic leaders more so than the climate and geography of Europe (Bok 2003).

Leonowens has been criticised by almost every male historian writing about 19th-century Siam for her unflattering portrait of the King. Leonowens did write negative descriptions of King Mongkut, casting aspersions on his character and accusing him of abusing his power (Leonowens 1988:109,264). Yet she also wrote much about his nobleness of spirit, high standard of education and desire to rule his nation well. While she describes King Mongkut as prone to sudden rages, she also reveals him to be a scholar and a doting father, as well as a man who 'really had a conscience' and who had a 'remarkable' mind (1988:159,109,264). In fact, a re-reading of Leonowens's work reveals that she presents a more extensive and rounded picture of King Mongkut than many other Western sources of the time. She was one of the few to see him in his domestic capacity as husband and father, rather than solely in his official role as ruler, and describes several scenes of family life, such as this one in the 'breakfast-room' during an afternoon meal: 'Here he chatted with his favourites among the wives and concubines, and caressed his children, taking them in his arms, embracing them, plying them with puzzling or funny questions, and making droll faces at the babies' (1988:99).

Despite Leonowens's disapproval of King Mongkut's practice of polygyny, *The English governess* contains information, not available in any other primary document, about court life of the time and this should attest to its value. She includes an hourly account of the King's day, even about how he chose the wife or concubine whose presence he required and the games he played with his children. Most of her negative statements about Siam concern the King and his behaviour, particularly towards women. Of Thais in general, she is, for her time, quite enlightened and finds many qualities among them to admire, noting, for example, that they are 'neither bigoted nor shallow' (Leonowens 1988:78).

Instead of concentrating on the most interesting parts of her book, namely her stories of teaching the children and living in the *Nang Harm* before moving to a house in Bangkok, critics have quibbled over whether she really undertook a trip to Cambodia's ruins of Angkor Wat, the 12th-century temples that were uncovered in the jungle in 1860 by Henri Mouhot and are today a popular tourist destination.[76] Her detractors, including Warren (2000), doubt she ever went there, but say she copied her account from others, mainly Mouhot's *Travels in Siam, Cambodia and Laos, 1858–1860* (1989). Morgan says Leonowens claimed in a letter to a newspaper editor in 1873 to have kept hundreds of pages of notes about her controversial journey to Cambodia (Leonowens 1991:x), but Kepner doubts there were ever any diaries or notes.[77] She must have kept some sort of account of her school and lessons, however, as she does mention writing the names of the palace women she taught in a 'book of my own' (Leonowens 1988:86), which, sadly, most probably no longer exists.

Regarding the Angkor Wat trip, described in a chapter towards the end of *The English governess*, David Chandler, author of *A history of Cambodia* and many other books about Cambodia, says Leonowens's extensive plagiarism of Mouhot and minimal input of her own observations make a strong case for her critics.[78] Despite this, I think it is likely that Leonowens did actually make the trip, simply because she had no compelling reason to make up her account of it. Her journey to Angkor Wat is included in *The English governess* almost as a diversion—if it were not there, the book would not suffer. Though it was rare for a single woman to travel beyond Bangkok, it was not impossible. Leonowens was used to tropical climates, had lived most of her life in Asia and had travelled extensively in 'difficult' lands. She had lived in or travelled to the Middle East, India, Australia, Singapore and Malaysia. Going to Angkor Wat was just the sort of trip she would have been likely to have undertaken. Obviously, she has plagiarised, though in her preface to *The English governess*, Leonowens (1988:vii) does credit Mouhot and several others as sources. Travel writers frequently use the ideas and words of others in their own writing and Leonowens is no exception, as Smithies (1995:124) points out. It is possible, of course, that Leonowens did not make the trip—Morgan in the new biography has found nothing to support Leonowens's claims. Morgan does, however, show that Anna and Louis Leonowens went with members of the Court to the ruins of Ayutthaya in 1863 (Morgan 2008:148–149), so perhaps that trip was the inspiration for her Angkor Wat description.

There is no doubt that some of what Leonowens wrote is offensive to Thais. However, it is no more so than what was written in most other travel books of the time. Critical discourse about Leonowens should more correctly place her as a product of her age. Edward Said (2003:206) asserts that *all* 19th-century Western writers write about Asia as a place needing Western salvation and, while this is too sweeping a statement, it demonstrates that Leonowens was certainly not alone in her disparaging comments.

The very critics who discredit Leonowens praise the works of male writers, despite their flaws. The works of Loubère and van Vliet in the 17th century, Crawfurd, Bowring, McCarthy, de Beauvoir and McGilvary in the 19th century and many others, are considered authoritative and valuable, despite their errors and embellishments. Numerous writers fill their accounts of Siam with Christian righteousness, scathing criticisms and erroneous descriptions of Buddhism, slurs on the Thai monarchy and the people themselves, generic and racist descriptions of 'Orientals' and constant references to the superiority of the European race. And yet, their writings are considered in context of the time they were written and are valued for their historical and social detail—so why not give Leonowens the same consideration?

Other Western writers besides Leonowens portray Thai kings in an offensive manner. Neale, for example, describes the appearance of King Nangklao (Rama III) as 'ludicrous'. Furthermore, he continues: '[He] had very much the appearance of an old over-bloated Brahmin priest…At length, after puffing and blowing like a porpoise, he managed with an evident effort to press into the service his very wheezing and wretchedly cracked voice'. He goes on to describe Rama III as 'His corpulent Majesty', as having 'fishy-looking eyes' and as asking 'many trivial and ridiculous questions' (Neale 1999:53–5).

Also insulting is the Marquis de Beauvoir's description of King Mongkut: 'His Siamese majesty…is perfectly hideous, and very like a monkey. But King Mongkut piques himself upon talking English, and we understood nearly one word in ten' (Beauvoir 1986:53). Similarly, diplomat John Crawfurd (1967) in his 1828 memoirs criticises the King's physical appearance. Yet Crawfurd is lauded as an important chronicler of his time by highly respected historians such as David K Wyatt.

Before it became fashionable to dismiss Leonowens, her books were valued for the opportunity they gave readers to glimpse what none of them would or could have access to. Bacon (2005:119–20) praises Leonowens's work for its 'entertaining' presentation of court life. Like Leonowens and more recently, Susan Morgan (2008:152), he criticises King Mongkut's use of power, for 'his free share of the faults and vices to which his savage nature and his position as an Oriental despot, with almost unlimited wealth and power, gave easy opportunity' (2001:120). He calls the Siamese 'heathens' and praises the work of the European missionaries in bringing Christianity to 'this benighted people' (2001:118). In contrast, Leonowens exhibited a broad mind regarding religion and made many positive comments about Buddhism—for example:

> We are prone to ignore or to condemn that which we do not clearly understand; and thus it is, and on no better ground, that we deny that there are influences in the religions of the East to render their followers wiser, nobler, purer (Leonowens 1988:184).

Written histories are, of course, subject to political, social and cultural biases, as any other writing is. The work of William L Bradley, descendant of 19th-century missionary Dan Beach Bradley, is an example. His book *Siam then—the foreign colony in Bangkok before and after Anna* (1981) is a mixture of fiction and non-fiction, told in the first person of his ancestor, Dan Beach Bradley. Despite the title, William Bradley's aim is to diminish the influence of Leonowens. He does this by barely mentioning her (though he uses her name in the title to attract readers). He refers to her in his Cast of Characters, under 'Other foreigners' as 'teacher in the Royal Palace and amanuensis of King Mongkut' (Bradley 1981:xv,xix). In his opinion, Dan Beach Bradley was 'the Western foreigner (*farang*) who did the most to smooth the way for Siam's transition from a traditional to a modern state' (1981:xvi). Funnily enough, Leonowens herself credits Dan Beach Bradley and several of his fellow missionaries as being of most help to Siam: 'To their united influence Siam unquestionably owes much, if not all, of her present advancement and prosperity' (Leonowens 1988:242).

Leonowens has been disregarded partly because of what was made of her work by others—to the point that 20th- and 21st-century critics of Victorian travel writing often omit her from their books. Anderson's *Women and the politics of travel* (2006) is a case in point. The book focuses on the writing of Isabella Bird, Florence Dixie and Kate Marsden, but a great many other women travel writers are mentioned. Leonowens, however, whose work caused such a stir when it was published, is not. A review of *The English governess at the Siamese Court* noted that Leonowens's experience was unique for a foreigner, giving the only insight available to the royal family of Siam (Anonymous 1871:293). A review of *The romance of the harem* went further, demonstrating that Leonowens had indeed successfully achieved her aim of exposing the plight of women dominated by men: 'No recent book gives so vivid a description of the interior life, customs, forms and usages of an Oriental Court; of the degradation of women and the tyranny of man' (Anonymous 1873:378). However, though many reviews praised Leonowens's writing, Susan Brown (1995) observes that the praise was not unanimous. Brown cites an 1873 review of *The romance of the harem* in the *Athenaeum* questioning the authenticity of the tales—probably the first to do so. (The journal had also questioned the authenticity of her trip to Cambodia in *The English governess.*).

In his 1972 biography of King Monkut, John Blofeld (1987) extracts Leonowens's most unflattering descriptions of Mongkut, which he counters with stories to show she was wrong on each point. Blofeld devotes extensive passages to discussing Leonowens as an important, yet flawed, influence. In his Introduction to the 1987 edition, Michael Smithies questions the need to include Leonowens at all: 'She does not deserve to be taken seriously...Had there been time to revise his book, John would certainly have given Anna a lower profile' (Blofeld 1987:iii), he presumes. In his determination to discredit Leonowens, Smithies blames the popularity of *The King and I* musical and film for inflating Leonowens's importance in Blofeld's mind (Blofeld 1987:ii). As many others have done, Smithies links Leonowens's work with what is portrayed in films, failing to distinguish between the two. Blofeld mentions *Anna and the King of Siam*, but does not name Landon as the author, leaving the later book vaguely and erroneously connected with Leonowens as author, then describes Leonowens's own books (Blofeld 1987:68–9). In contrast to many others, Blofeld does have some positive thoughts on the effect of Leonowens's books:

> By a stroke of irony, they did King Mongkut no great harm and even a certain amount of good in the eyes of posterity, as he emerged from the books, plays and films based on those works as a rather pleasant, if whimsical and unpredictable personage. But for Anna, he would scarcely be known to the world outside Siam (Blofeld 1987:69).

Blofeld claims much of Leonowens's material was plagiarised from 'old periodicals' (though he does not name these sources) and accuses her of 'malicious fabrication'. Yet he goes on to repeat 'a story'—that is, an unsubstantiated piece of hearsay—that Leonowens's books were written out of scorn when King Mongkut did not meet her demands for a hefty severance pay (Blofeld 1987:69). Morgan's new biography chronicles well the events that led to Leonowens's departure from Siam, at first on furlough but then permanently when the King died and her former student, Chulalongkorn, became King.

Though Blofeld strongly criticises Leonowens, he does not dispute that she knew the King fairly well and sometimes acted as his secretary. Nevertheless, later writers such as Warren (2002:47) claim she hardly knew the King at all and that he referred to her in correspondence only once. This view has been debunked by the discovery in 2003 of eight letters from Mongkut to Leonowens in Thailand's National Archive. The letters show that the two were well acquainted and that he did require her to undertake secretarial work from time to time.[79] The discovery of the letters was written about in 'King Mongkut's letters to Anna: when madame teacher plays political negotiator', a 2003 article in the Bangkok *Art and Culture* magazine (in Thai). The English originals of the letters are reprinted in a Thai-language biography of Leonowens, *Palace spy, or, the world of illusion of Anna Leonowens*, by Gailert Nana & Pramin Kreuathong (2004).[80] Morgan shows conclusively that Leonowens's role at the palace became more than just the teacher of the King's children:

> Without having to exaggerate the extent of her influence or the political importance of her role, I can say that Anna was to a small but significant extent privy to matters to state and that the king did occasionally consult her on issues important to Siam. She often disagreed strongly with the king, in terms of his treatment of the women of Nang Harm and also in terms of some of his political decisions. But the important point here is that she was actually in a position to do so. Her job in the Grand Palace had clearly evolved over the years into a lot more than being schoolmistress to the royal children (Morgan 2008:154).

Despite the criticism of Leonowens's work, no-one thought to question seriously the authenticity of Leonowens's portrayal of herself until decades after *The King and I* first appeared on stage and screen, when, in 1976, British scientist WS Bristowe published a biography of her son, *Louis and the King of Siam*. Bristowe revealed that Leonowens had reinvented her background to hide aspects of her earlier life. Among a litany of distortions, obscurities and fabrications by Leonowens, he discovered, on checking official records, that she was not Welsh, but was born in India. Her father was not Captain Thomas Crawford who had been killed by rebels in India in 1841, but Sergeant Thomas Edwards, a cabinetmaker who enlisted in the Bombay Infantry and who died in 1831, three months before she was born. Leonowens, Bristowe continued, also lied about her date of birth, claiming all her adult life that she was born in 1834. Even her gravestone at the Mount Royal Cemetery in Montreal shows her birthdate as 1834.[81] Anna's mother was not Selina Edwards, of an ancient Welsh family, but Mary Anne Glasscock, daughter of a gunner in the Bengal Artillery and a woman named in records only as Anne. Bristowe's *pièce de résistance* is his speculation that Anna's grandmother, Anne, might have been Indian or part-Indian, and that, as he offensively adds, she 'may have had what was commonly called "a touch of the tar-brush" in her veins' (Bristowe 1976:27).

In the new biography, Morgan takes the research into Leonowens's past much further, creating as full a picture of her childhood as is possible and debunking Bristowe's errors. While Bristowe paints a distasteful picture of Leonowens's early homelife as the daughter of a private soldier, living in communal barracks where alcohol abuse and lascivious behaviour were commonplace. Morgan concurs to a certain extent, calling it a 'raucous, putrid and violent environment' (Morgan 2008:32). However, she also says the life wasn't as bad as it might seem from today's viewpoint and there was a positive side, including companionship and a better education that Leonowens could not otherwise have expected:

> Fort children ran around in packs. They played together, watched drills together, and, when suppertime came, ate at their fire or at someone else's. When it was time to sleep, they often lay down with a wrap or a ground cloth in piles like puppies…The privacy we strive for so relentlessly today would have been considered a sign of dementia in the cantonments of the Bombay presidency. In camp life, people lived together in that crowded noisy world with an ease we can no longer understand (Morgan 2008:43).

Morgan agrees with academic and writer Chu-Chueh Cheng (2004:151), who says Leonowens never travelled to England until after she left Siam in 1867, instead receiving her schooling in India and later continuing to study Sanskrit and other languages privately.

Her claim that at 14 she toured the Middle East for three years with the Reverend George Badger and his wife is another event Bristowe accuses her of obscuring. According to Bristowe, 30-year-old Badger was single, and Leonowens went with him alone. However, Susan Fulop Kepner (1996a:9) suggests that Leonowens's trip with Badger was unlikely to have been one that cast Leonowens 'as an Anglo-Indian Lolita'. Kepner claims Leonowens made the trip in order to escape her stepfather, whom Kepner accuses of being sexually abusive, on the basis of Leonowens's lifelong hatred of him and refusal to speak his name. Morgan (2008:52) says she is 'certain' that Leonowens did not travel with Badger at all, but made up the trip after hearing about one the Reverend and his wife had taken. (Contrary to Bristowe's aspersions, Badger was married). Badger was a well known scholar and Leonowens had probably read his books and might even have known him (Morgan 2008:54). Since Bristowe (1976:27) labeled Leonowens's stepfather, Patrick Donohoe, a 'wild Irishman' who was demoted from 2nd Corporal to Private, every other writer has followed the line that he was an abusive, unlikeable man. Morgan (2008:34–39) disagrees, presenting evidence to say he was not a drunk or a wife-beater, but in fact was a steady worker and a good provider, father and husband.

Bristowe also discovered there was no dashing 'Captain Thomas Leonowens'. At 18, Anna had married Mr Thomas Leon Owens, a clerk and bartender. The couple had travelled through Asia and Australia, where Owens took whatever work he could get. The couple lived in Western Australia for four years and, as Morgan (2008:76) shows, Avis and Louis were born there, not, as she later insisted, at St James's Square, London.[82] Leonowens never admitted to having lived in Australia. She said merely that en route from Singapore to England, their ship, *Alibi*, crashed on to rocks and they were rescued and taken to New South Wales, from where they soon sailed back to London. According to Morgan (2008:76–78), the real story is that the Leonowenses were bound for Melbourne when the *Alibi* became stuck on a reef while heading into the port of Fremantle for a supply replenishment. The ship took three months to repair and by that time, the Leonowenses, who had travelled with Anna's uncle, William Glascott, had all decided to stay in Western Australia. Glascott left Western Australia in 1855 to go home to Bombay, and in 1857, the Leonowenses also left Australia and sailed to Singapore.

In 1859, aged 31, Tom died of 'apoplexy'—the term then used for sunstroke—on Prince of Wales Island (Penang) in Malaya, where he had been working at a hotel. He is buried in the Protestants' Cemetery in Penang, the burial ground for European expatriates at the time. Leonowens had claimed her husband's death occurred in more romantic circumstances, that is, after a tiger hunt with his 'fellow officers' in Singapore (then part of Malaya). The headstone on Thomas's grave does reveal that the reinvention of the family's background had already commenced by the time of his burial: it gives his surname as Leonowens.

Writers such as Warren, Bristowe and Alexander B Griswold say Anna Leonowens stretched the truth in order to make money. In his eagerness to discredit Leonowens, Griswold makes unsubstantiated assertions. King Mongkut's choice of Leonowens as full-time teacher to his children was 'unfortunate', Griswold says, adding that she 'was not very successful at teaching and gave up the position after five years' (Griswold 1961:44). On the contrary, Leonowens must have been successful to have lasted that long and she continued teaching and lecturing after she left Thailand.

Warren's criticism, like the majority of others since Bristowe's book, relies on paraphrasing Bristowe's 'unveiling' of Leonowens. Warren adopts Bristowe's stance and takes it further, calling her the 'half-caste' daughter of a woman who 'very likely, was wholly or partly Indian' (Warren 2002:46). Warren accuses Leonowens of 'bald plagiarism', yet he himself has taken material from Bristowe, rewritten it and presented it mostly unsourced.[83] Warren (2002:48) even makes the bizarre suggestion that Leonowens did not write her books herself, but used a ghost-writer. Leonowens continued her writing career long after her Siamese books of the 1870s. In the 1880s, she wrote two other books, *Life and travel in India, being recollections of a journey before the days of railroads* and *Our Asiatic cousins*. Leonowens would have considered herself progressive, liberal and anti-racist, and it is a mistake to judge her writing on the basis of 21st-century ideologies.

Anna Leonowens in mid-life. The picture is among a collection of papers and photographs belonging to Margaret Landon, now held by her Alma Mater, Wheaton College, in Ilinois. Writing on the back of the picture, thought to be by Margaret Landon, says the picture was probably taken between 1870 and 1875. Leonowens looks remarkably young in her early 40s if Landon is correct. Landon thought the picture may have been taken by Napolean Sarony, a famous New York celebrity portrait photographer. Credit: Landon Collection Wheaton College (IL) Special Collections.

Warren also claims Leonowens was forced to make up stories to 'add some spice to what would otherwise have been a rather tepid work' (Warren 1997:87). It is a strange statement, given the uniqueness of her position and the nature of her day-to-day life, which no other European and no Thai man (except the King) had witnessed so fully. Warren takes other opportunities to criticise Leonowens. In his biography of Jim Thompson, another famous expatriate who made a name for himself in Thailand, he says her books 'reveal her to have been ill-tempered, prejudiced, and more than a little ridiculous, even by Victorian standards' (Warren 1998:88).

Leonowens's best work is her lively prose about her life as an English teacher in the Inner Palace. To highlight its value, it is interesting to compare Leonowens's descriptions of the *Nang Harm* with Warren's own experience. He was granted rare permission to walk through the long disused *Nang Harm* while researching his impressive book *The Grand Palace* (Warren 1988).[84] 'Even today, though the women have long vanished, the Inside is forbidden territory to most visitors', he begins. He describes a ghost town, overgrown and in disrepair, although the outlines of 'the pleasure gardens' are still visible and 'a little waterfall still spilled down an artificial hill' (Warren 2002:57). In contrast, Leonowens's descriptions witness the 'city' in its heyday when it teemed with life:

> Here the houses of the royal princesses, the wives, concubines, and relatives of the king, with their numerous slaves and personal attendants, form regular streets and avenues, with small parks, artificial lakes, and groups of fine trees scattered over miniature lawns and beautiful flower gardens (Leonowens 1991:12).

Though Warren criticises Leonowens for being overly dramatic, he cannot resist being so himself when he describes his departure from the old *Nang Harm*, noting that the Thai photographer accompanying him is 'ill at ease' in 'such a place': 'we passed back through the tall gates, which closed theatrically behind us' (Warren 2002:57).

In the 1990s, feminist re-readings of Leonowens's memoirs began to query the attitudes of the anti-Leonowens school (Cheng 2004:141). Susan Fulop Kepner and Susan Morgan are among academics attempting to deconstruct Bristowe's biographical picture and to re-read Leonowens's work in light of its achievements as well as its obvious faults to restore balance to the argument. Morgan (2008:xiv) credits Bristowe as the first to publish her real maiden name, birthplace and birthdate but notes that 'the rest of his short sketch of her life is mostly inaccurate'. While the reading of Leonowens by critics such as Bristowe is exclusively literal and lineal, Morgan argues that, rather than quibble over the historical or biographical accuracy of Leonowens's books, it is more critically productive to look at the value of her work. Morgan (1996:235) points out that although three missionary wives had taught English in the *Nang Harm* 11 years earlier, before being banned for spreading Christian ideas, Leonowens was almost certainly the only Westerner privileged to enter the Siamese harem so constantly over a long period of time.

Detractors, such as Warren, are scathing of anyone who challenges their view that Leonowens was a liar, a fraud and a plagiarist. Kepner, for example, has felt his ire. Kepner is respected as a pioneering translator of Thai books into English, notably the acclaimed novel *Letters from Thailand* (Botan 1982), *A child of the northeast* (Kampoon 1988) and *The lioness in bloom* (Kepner 1996). She has studied Leonowens and Landon extensively. Her research includes meeting Landon's relatives and examining family documents; in Thailand she met Margaret Landon's husband, Kenneth Landon (also an author of books about Thailand).[85] Yet Warren dismisses Kepner's work on Leonowens, making it sound trivial and close to plagiarism itself. Kepner, he says, apparently accepts most of Bristowe's findings, despite her criticism of him, and merely 'adds a few of her own, gleaned from a perusal of Mrs Landon's papers' (Warren 2000:22–3).

Kepner is bemused by Warren's comments: 'I don't know why William Warren was so critical of my painstaking research on Anna—except that he likes to say witty things. I doubt that he sat down and read my article carefully.'[86] While Warren suggests those interested in reading more about Leonowens could consult Kepner's articles, he fails to give any details of them or to include her in his bibliography.

Leonowens's writing was praised by many of her contemporaries, but later critics almost all designate her as a poor writer. FK Exell, who lived and worked in Thailand as a government employee from 1923 to 1936 but did not write about it until the 1960s, says that he found *The English governess* 'interesting' but 'written in very stilted Victorian English and large slices seemed to me fanciful' (Exell 1963:187). He goes on to suggest that Landon's book was 'about 75 per cent fiction', to call the play and film of *The King and I* 'a travesty' and to follow it with 'Anna Leonowen [sic] must have had a very vivid imagination' (1963:187–8), as if Leonowens were responsible for the stage and screen versions. It is likely that Exell's criticism has a taste of 'sour grapes' about it, since he says he turned down missionary Dr Edwin McDaniel's suggestion that he rewrite *The English governess* (1963:187). Dr McDaniel, who spent most of his life in Thailand, subsequently showed both *The English governess* and *The romance of the harem* to Margaret Landon, who used them to inspire her 1943 novel *Anna and the King of Siam*, and who became famous and wealthy as a result. In her Preface to *Anna and the King of Siam*, Landon says Dr McDaniel showed her the books when she visited his house in southern Thailand in the late 1920s, and she remarks that she was entranced by them:

> I took the book and sat down. Outside on the one long street of Nakon Sritamarat in south Siam automobiles honked continuously. There was the jingle of horse-drawn gharries and bicycle bells. An occasional elephant padded by in ponderous majesty. But as I read all of this dropped away (Landon 2000:ix).

Before Leonowens's books were published, Siam was virtually unknown in the West. Because it was never colonised, it was effectively not locatable by Westerners. Taiwan-based academic and writer Chu-Chueh Cheng (2004:139) discusses Leonowens's contribution to putting Siam 'on the imaginary map of western readers'. Cheng credits both Leonowens and King Mongkut with bringing Siam to the notice of Westerners, yet she notes that they did this in diametrically opposed ways. While Leonowens presented Siam as the epitome of the stereotypical *Arabian Nights*-type Oriental monarchy, Mongkut was keen to bring Western technology to Siam and to present it as a 'modern' nation (Cheng 2004:139).

No-one disputes the assertion that Leonowens fabricated and exaggerated some material, yet there are numerous examples in her books of her affection for Siam and its people, particularly towards the women and children she taught. For example, she said she had known many who 'showed a self-sacrificing devotion and a courage not to be excelled by the most saintly of the Christian martyrs' (Leonowens 1991:10). Her dedication in *The romance of the harem* is an indication of her feelings:

> To the noble and devoted women whom I learned to know, to esteem and to love in the city of the Nang Harm, I dedicate the following pages, containing a record of some of the events connected with their lives and sufferings (Leonowens 1991).

The reason for Leonowens's mix of fact and fiction lies partly in her need to make a living. Because she had what would have been seen in the late 19th century as a socially unacceptable background in 'polite society'(her target readers), she was forced to invent, or modify, the details. Others had done so before her, including the great 19th-century explorer and writer Richard Burton, who conveniently edited out aspects of his past that his audience might have found unsavoury.[87] Biographer Dow points out that Henry Morton Stanley also invented a persona more suited to the sensibilities of his audience : 'I wondered why it was so impossible for her [Leonowens's] critics to praise in a woman the very qualities they applaud in male adventurers (particularly Stanley)' (Dow 1991:xiii). Morgan takes the idea of identity reinvention further, saying it is part of American life and when Leonowens went to the US it would have seemed not only desirable but a practical tactic to further her career. Her very fabrications 'were the foundation for her successes', Morgan says (2008:2). She adds: 'After all, do we want to claim that the "real" Cary Grant was actually Archibald Leach all along, or that Bob Dylan inevitably remains Bobby Zimmerman?' (2008:2).

While Thai critics tend to look at the broader issues, Western critics, like Warren in *The truth about Anna...and other stories*, find myriad complaints about minutiae. For example, they repeatedly quibble about the term 'governess', saying Leonowens was merely an 'English teacher', without the apparently more exalted status of 'governess'. This is a comparatively new criticism of Leonowens; earlier writers such as Blofeld do not dispute the term, though he calls her 'the perfidious and mendacious governess' (Blofeld 1987:ix). In addition, an English translation of a letter from King Mongkut's secretary, dictated by the King in 1867, says: 'Mem Leonowens, *the governess* of the royal children, is becoming very naughty indeed' (Seni & Kukrit 1987:220).[88]

Men who wrote about Thailand, such as Crawfurd and Loubère, held important positions in their governments and to a certain extent were able to dictate terms to the Siamese, asserting their imperialist viewpoints. On the other hand, Leonowens was not of consequence in the Western world at the time of her appointment to Siam. In many cases, her critics harbour the very prejudices they accuse her of. Bristowe, for example, maintains that she was never accepted into expatriate society in Bangkok because her 'inexperience in the social graces natural to Victorian ladies was too great a handicap' and her 'pose did not deceive the small population of English people of good family and she was never to enter their social circle' (Bristowe 1976:30). Bristowe does not offer proof of his assertions, only that 'poor Anna' seemed to associate most with the American Protestant missionaries, including 'the formidable Dr Dan Beach Bradley' (1976:31). Like Warren, he seems to forget that Leonowens would have had little time to join the idle pursuits of expatriate wives in Bangkok.

The critical disapproval of Leonowens has led to popular travel guides disparaging Leonowens and repeating misconceptions. The 2006 edition of *Thailand's beaches and islands*, for example, confuses the films with the original memoirs, erroneously stating that Leonowens claimed in *The English governess* to have had an affair with the King (Williams et al 2006:27).[89] Obviously, the writer had not bothered to read or check Leonowens's original—or even, for that matter, any of the films. Though they imply a romantic interest between the two, there is no suggestion of an actual affair. The Eyewitness guide dismisses Leonowens as 'an unreliable source' (Thiro 2004:111), yet directs readers to the writings of short-term visitors such as Joseph Conrad (1986) and W Somerset Maugham (2001). Although, of course, Conrad and Maugham are both literary lions, as descriptions of Thailand go, their texts are highly critical of Bangkok and based on scant knowledge of the country and its people gleaned during short visits, as opposed to Leonowens's more than five years spent living among Thais.

Improbably, *Eyewitness* readers are also directed to Barbara Cartland, whose romance novel, *Sapphires in Siam* (1988) is set in 1898. The novel is not derogatory of Siam, her characters naming it 'the Land of Smiles' (a phrase not in common usage in the 1890s) and a 'strange paradise' (Cartland 1988:157,123), but her romantic picture is hardly useful to tourists. Cartland had visited Thailand four times, travelling to Bangkok, Chiang Mai and Pattaya and, in an introduction to the novel, she writes a mini travelogue: 'Last year I found the newly gilt Palace in Bangkok breathtakingly beautiful, the Oriental Hotel the finest hotel in the East, and Pattaya very exciting' (Cartland 1988). She acknowledges Florence Caddy's 1889 memoirs as a source, but Thailand in the novel is merely an impressive backdrop.

It seems to have become almost forbidden for guidebooks to mention Leonowens's name, except in the most dismissive tones, though critics are, strangely, generally less harsh on *The King and I*. *The magic of Bangkok* criticises Brynner for his 'inaccurate portrayal' of Mongkut (Sheehan 2002:6); *Our world in colour: Bangkok* identifies Rama IV as 'King Mongkut of "The King and I" fame' (Reid 1990:14); Moon Travel's 2000 *Bangkok handbook* reviews the 1946 and 1956 films, blames Brynner, again, for his 'unfavourable portrayal' and refers to Leonowens not by name but as 'a former governess' upon whose 'fictional life' the film was based (Parkes 2000:33, 264). It does, however, include *The English governess* in its reading list. Lonely Planet's latest *Thailand* guide (Williams et al 2007) does not mention Leonowens at all.

Many popular collections of female travellers' tales leave out Leonowens, which is surprising, given the controversy about her.[90] Some of those that do include her, romanticise her story as Hollywood does. In *Wayward women: a guide to women travellers,* Jane Robinson (1990:138–40) retains a cinematic image of the Western teacher in an Eastern harem. Although her book is acclaimed on its cover as 'scholarly', there is no evidence of Robinson having done any research on Leonowens. She even lists the long-corrected date of 1834 as Leonowens's birthdate and makes the outrageous and unsourced claim that King Mongkut 'commanded her services...occasionally (and unsuccessfully) as a concubine' (Robinson 1990:139). So, although Robinson lists three of Leonowens's four books, including her later memoirs of India (Leonowens 1884), she does not appear to have read them. Rather, she seems to have relied on her own fanciful imaginings fired by the romantic spark implied in *The King and I*. Her book would hardly be worth mentioning, except that it is a popular paperback and, as such, perpetuates myths and misconceptions about Leonowens to the general reader.

The snubs continue: a major exhibition of writing, letters and artwork by notable intrepid women travellers at the National Portrait Gallery in New York in 2004, *Off the beaten track: three centuries of women travelers*, left out Leonowens. As a 2004 article by Alan Riding in the *New York Times* remarked, it is odd that Leonowens's 'peripatetic life' was not deemed worthy of inclusion, despite her coming to 'personify the eccentric Victorian female traveler' in the Western imagination (Riding 2004). It would also have been an opportunity to set the record straight about Leonowens's relationship with King Mongkut.

Michael Smithies contributes a chapter about Leonowens to *Adventurous women in South-East Asia* (Smithies 1995). Acknowledging Leonowens as the sole source of much of the material he covers, Smithies nevertheless cannot resist belittling her, noting that the male editor she thanks, Dr JW Palmer, cannot have had much hand in improving her style, since it 'may be typical of young Victorian ladies' (Smithies 1995:100,101). In Smithies's attempt at gendered humour, he perhaps forgets that Leonowens was 39 the year *The English governess* was published, hardly considered young, particularly in Victorian times (Brown 1995:591). Smithies dismisses Leonowens, mostly by repeating unsourced material from Bristowe, yet still uses her story and lengthy quotations from her work to comprise the bulk of his chapter. He is, literally, cashing in on Leonowens's supposedly offensive and embellished story.

Smithies does not appear to rate female writers highly, because his comments about Leonowens are not his only attempt to discredit them by making them seem pathetic or immature. Another example came during a 2001 address to the Siam Society in Bangkok. His comments on the work of missionary Mary Lovina Cort include repetition of the snide remarks of an earlier writer, Norwegian traveller Carl Bock, who described unmarried women as 'evidently disappointed ladies of middle age', followed by Smithies's assessment that 'She was a primary school teacher and this, alas, is clearly reflected in her writing style' (Smithies 2001b:84).[91] Leonowens, too, was a schoolteacher.

On the other hand, Smithies (2001b:82) excuses the writing of de Beauvoir, 'perhaps the first genuine tourist of modern times to visit Siam', because of the nobleman's immaturity. De Beauvoir is 'less than reverent toward King Mongkut behind his back', Smithies says . In fact de Beauvoir is highly derogatory, describing the monarch as 'an old king who does nothing but cough and spit' (Beauvoir 1986:81). Despite his rudeness, de Beauvoir should be excused, Smithies (2001b:82) contends, because he 'clearly loved him [the King] for his eccentricities'. Of de Beauvoir's assertion that it would be advantageous for Siam to be taken over by a Western power, Smithies merely says the 'political musings of a very young man' cannot be taken too seriously (Beauvoir 1986:ix). When de Beauvoir (1986:59) makes factual errors—such as stating that King Mongkut has 875 wives[92]—Smithies excuses him because 'His book has a youthful exuberance which is thoroughly refreshing' (Smithies 2001:82–83).

Despite the fact that the 20-year-old de Beauvoir is revealed to be a liar, a prankster, and a gossip who adopts a position of supercilious condescension towards the court of a nation he regards as beneath him, Smithies uses his work to demonstrate what he sees as proof that Leonowens is unimportant. Smithies finds it strange that though de Beauvoir says he has been allowed entrance to the 'harem', he is not introduced to Leonowens. Yet, de Beauvoir made only two brief visits to the palace during his week-long visit to Bangkok and, as he was not a compatriot of Leonowens, there would have been no reason for him to be introduced to her. In addition, France and Britain were adversaries in Southeast Asia at this time and there were significant class differences between the two—he was a young nobleman and she a working woman nearly twice his age. Besides, de Beauvoir's claim that he was granted access to the harem (Beauvoir 1986:78–80) seems far-fetched, since few other men had been allowed there, and he was a stranger in Siam. Not being a Siamese speaker, he may have been mistaken. He was most likely not in the *Nang Harm* itself but in a reception area where visitors were customarily received, as described by Thai writer and politician Kukrit Pramoj (1998). Though lively, de Beauvoir's description is patently generic and it is possible the young man made up the episode. A clue can be found earlier in the book on his arrival in the streets of Bangkok: 'Ah! well, travellers who spoke of Siam as a dream of the "Arabian Nights" only told the truth…', he says (Beauvoir 1986:21). De Beauvoir is clearly captivated by the thought of the harem:

> Through the chinks of half-open doors sparkled bright eyes, animated with the liveliest curiosity…For a whole hour we stopped in the harem, and saw things that it is almost impossible to describe; living pictures of human forms and jewels, gardens and fishponds, kiosques and dormitories composed of mats, all combine to give this wing of the palace an appearance both material and romantic (1986:80).

To say Leonowens's public retelling of her story contained fabricated information to sensationalise it for financial gain is too simplistic. It is true that she needed to make a living to support herself, Avis and Louis until the children came of age and Avis married, and she knew she had to write a commercially successful account.[93] Looking broadly at Leonowens's life after her time in Siam, however, it is clear that her motives are wider than her critics suggest. This view is supported by the work of Morgan, who has examined the gendered criticism of Leonowens's work offered by male scholars who have disregarded the female perspective (Leonowens 1991; Morgan 1996). In North America, the women's movement and the anti-slavery movement were closely allied. By pointing out the evils of Siam's harems as a system that imprisoned women, Leonowens hoped to promote reconsideration of the state of marriage in the West and the treatment of women everywhere as chattels. In *The English governess*, Leonowens makes sweeping statements, clearly intending to speak out against any society that puts some classes above others, for example when she repeats the words purportedly said to her by the then Prince Chulalongkorn (who became Rama V) on slavery: 'These are not slaves, but nobles; they know how to bear. It is we, the princes who have yet to learn which is the more noble, the oppressor or the oppressed' (Leonowens 1988:284). Leonowens's decades of work in Canada to improve education for women and to promote equality for all are well documented. In 1895, for example, she became president of the Women's Suffrage Association in Halifax (Morgan 2008:202). In 1906 she became president of the board of the Montreal Foundling and Bay Hospital (Morgan 2008:204). As Thongchai Winichakul says (Morgan 2008:back cover), 'Her life and contributions as a writer, a humanist, and a 19th century feminist were far richer beyond being the "I" with the King'.

Leslie Smith Dow's 1991 work, *Anna Leonowens: a life beyond The King and I*, is a mixture of Bristowe's research, some new research carried out by Dow or commissioned by her, unsourced claims and supposition. A typical passage in Dow is her story of when Leonowens and her daughter, Avis, travel to the Catskill Mountains to stay while Leonowens begins writing *The English governess*: 'Anna's dark skin, its natural colour heightened by the tropical sun, and her comical hoop skirts soon had the countryside abuzz with rumours that she was the queen of Syria!' (Dow 1991:65). Dow does not acknowledge a source, simply presenting the information as fact, but it was probably taken from Landon's fictional account of the event (Landon 2000:387).

Dow presents a sympathetic portrayal of Leonowens and says she believes the teacher has been too harshly criticised. Although a third of Dow's biography relates Leonowens's experiences in Siam, the book's main contribution is in its description of Leonowens's achievements after she left Siam, rarely remembered outside of her adopted home of Canada, where she lived for 40 years. She continued accepting paid work, such as lectures about her time in Siam for the then enormous sum of $60 each, and commissions as a magazine journalist, including an assignment in Russia when she was 49 (Dow 1991:79,75). In 1887, she founded the Victoria School of Art and Design, now the Nova Scotia College of Art and Design (NSCAD) University.[94]

As this book was going to press, I was alerted by Anna Leonowens's great-grandson, Louis Leonowens, that another biography was being written.[95] The author is respected US biographer Alfred Habegger, who confirms he has visited Western Australia and uncovered archival material about Thomas Leon Owens, Anna Leonowens's husband. Habegger says he doesn't have a particular 'stance' on Leonowens and wants to stick to documentary evidence. 'Of course, I don't share Bristowe's hostile and debunking attitude, or accept his very sloppy scholarship, but I'm also more critical than Margaret Landon was', he says.[96] A third biography being written is by Canadian archivist Lois K Yorke, who co-authored the entry on Leonowens in the *New Oxford Dictionary of National Biography*.[97] It is to be hoped that Morgan's biography and the two new books to come will make enough impact to change basic misconceptions and errors about Leonowens still promulgated by supposed authorities, such as *Encyclopedia Britannica*. The *Britannica*'s online subscription-based website[98] gets Leonowens's birthdate and birthplace wrong (it says 1834 and Wales) and includes several other errors.

What Thai critics say

Many Thai critics ignore Leonowens; others either comment on her writing seemingly without having read it, or confuse Leonowens with Landon or the films drawn from Landon's work. Manich Jumsai (1991), for example, says the description of King Mongkut 'possessing a fitful, whimsical and tyrannical temperament' as described in Landon's book and in 'the film'—he may be referring to either of the early films, naming only the first, *Anna and the King of Siam*—is untrue (Manich 1991:57). He does not, however, name Leonowens's books and he mistakes the dates of her residence in Siam as 1864 to 1866, showing he is unlikely to have read them (1991:56). Nor does Rong Syamananda appear to have read them, judging from his 11 lines on the subject in *A history of Thailand* (Rong 1990:124). Rong is, however, one of the few critics who separates later material about Leonowens from what she wrote herself.

While repeating Bristowe's revelations about Leonowens's background, Noy Thrupkaew acknowledges her as 'a plucky heroine in her own way' who was forced to 'whitewash' her own background in order to survive (Noy 2003). Though Noy makes some fundamental errors—she says Ayutthaya was the capital when Leonowens wrote about Siam—she also gives an interesting insight into why the official reaction in Thailand to Leonowens was so forbidding. She says a government notice to foreign diplomats regarding the banning of the 1999 film reveals its own racism when commenting on the film's assertion that Leonowens's teaching led to King Chulalongkorn abolishing slavery and other modernisations:

It is suspected that the inclusion of such suggestion is motivated by the jealousy of certain western races that could not tolerate the success of an oriental nation which managed to preserve its independence and [introduce] far reaching reforms. Thus, it must attribute part of such success to Anna Leonowens whom they thought belonged to the superior race but who was in fact an individual with doubtful origin and could even be half Indian (Noy 2003).

Historian Hong Lysa provides a Thai counterpoint to Leonowens's *The romance of the harem* with her article 'Palace women at the margins of social change' (Hong 1999). Hong describes the stories of four palace women from King Chulalongkorn's time as they are detailed in records, both official and unofficial. Hong says the truth of what life was like for women of the Inner Palace was somewhere between the wasted, lazy, repressed lives represented by Leonowens, and the idyllic, fulfilling lives indicated by Kukrit Pramoj in his 1953 novel about court life, *Four reigns* (1998). Both authors, she says, exaggerated the isolation and passivity of the women. In reality, the women 'moved illicitly between wang (palace) and muang (city, town)—the "inside" and the "outside", tradition and modernity, privilege and politics (kanmuang)' (Noy 2003).

In her MA thesis, scholar Pornsawan Tripasai says the problem with Leonowens's writing is that it reduces Thais to stereotypes: the polygamous, barbaric Oriental despot, the construction of a harem as a den of iniquity and the fearsome 'Amazons' who guard it (Pornsawan 2003:11). Pornsawan has since delivered several papers about Leonowens, including 'Anna Leonowens and the imaginative colonisation of Thailand' (2006) and 'Debating Anna: the textual politics of English literature teaching in Thailand' (2004). Pornsawan makes a valid point that Thai people strongly disagree with the way Leonowens portrayed King Mongkut, but unfortunately, herself falls into the trap of using only the work of Leonowens's detractors as her sources, particularly Smithies, Warren and Bristowe. Pornsawan uses Leonowens to illustrate her contention that teaching English is a 'a form of neo-colonialism' (Pornsawan 2006:1). She claims Leonowens's major aim in her narrative is 'to celebrate the authority of the White Master over the native' (Pornsawan 2003:12). This may be the way Leonowens was portrayed in the films, but it was not the way she portrayed herself in her books, although she did think the British culture was the standard that others should aspire to. Far from being the 'White Master', Leonowens was, of course, an employee with a Master of her own—namely, the King of Siam.

In her 1999 PhD thesis, Chalermsri Chantasingh (Chalermsri 1999) concurs with many of Pornsawan's views. Furthermore, in a subsequent paper, Chalermsri (2000) contends Leonowens created herself in her writing as a character American audiences would relate to. Thus, she says, 'The condescending Anna was later revamped and re-created into a charismatic and legendary character by an American writer, Margaret Landon...' (Chalermsri 2000). Chalermsri carefully separates Leonowens's work from the subsequent fictionalisations by Landon, and from the stage and film versions. However, Chalermsri finds even less to like in Leonowens's portrayal of herself than in the way others presented her. Leonowens was, she says in an earlier article, a 'haughty, humorless British governess with a high-handed attitude' whose book *The English governess at the Court of Siam* was 'an unrelated, episodic and repetitive compilation of incidents and stories that she claimed to have experienced personally' (Chalermsri 1998).

An interesting English-language website about the controversy surrounding Leonowens is run by Sriwittayapaknam School in Samut Prakan (Sriwittayapaknam School 1999).[99] The website provides information about Leonowens and has prompted much debate, most of it from Westerners and from Thais living overseas. The site is rather one-sided, however, as it has lifted much of its content from William Warren's scathing article about Leonowens reprinted in the 1997 book *Travelers' tales guides Thailand* (Warren 1997:85–92). The website was formed in the wake of controversy about the 1999 film *Anna and the King*.

Towards a new understanding of Leonowens

Leonowens is the only person with such intimate knowledge of the harem to have written about it so extensively; consequently, her accounts must be valued as significant. In the absence of a larger body of literature, her work should be read for the detail of everyday life in the harem that she provides. Also of interest are her comments on society and her endeavours to apply those comments to life in North America at the time. There are many precedents for this type of social comment, as Chu-Chueh Cheng (2004:124) notes, including Swift in *Gulliver's travels* (1726) and Captain Basil Hall in *Travels in North America* (1829).

Leonowens never claimed to be an historian and she gets her facts wrong often. It must be remembered, however, that Thai history was not meticulously recorded in those days and Leonowens would have had no way of checking whether the stories she heard were true. As Cruysse (2002:68) notes, while the Western concept of history is 'linear and irreversible', the Thai concept is based on a belief in reincarnation and is 'circular', as noted by both van Vliet in the 1640s and Leonowens in the 1870s.[100]

Apart from her need to make a living, Leonowens's objective in telling the tales of the harem women was twofold. Firstly, she vehemently opposed slavery in all its forms and, secondly, she particularly despised the harem as a form of female enslavement. As she says, 'Polygamy—or, properly speaking, concubinage—and slavery are the curses of the country' (Leonowens 1991:10). She felt it was unjust that the women, some only teenagers, were required to spend their lives behind closed gates and were used as political pawns to secure Bangkok's authority over the rest of Siam.

Susan Morgan discusses the judgements of Bowring in the 19th century and Griswold in the 20th, who maintain that slavery in Thailand was not the evil institution of incarceration that existed in the US and British colonies (Leonowens 1991:xxx–xxxi). The key to Leonowens's viewpoint, as Morgan says, is that the degree of slavery does not so much matter—her point is that the women are not free. 'Bowring's account of slavery in Siam is similar to contemporaneous accounts in America describing darkies singing happily on plantations, looked after by their benevolently paternal masters,' Morgan says (Leonowens 1991:xxxi).

Leonowens detested any violation of what she saw as basic human rights to liberty, education and justice, as demonstrated by her extensive charity work later in life in Canada (Dow 1991). Before she went to Canada, she befriended Annie Adams Fields, a celebrated Boston hostess and the wife of literary publisher James T Fields. Leonowens stayed often with them and Annie Fields arranged speaking engagements for her. Fields also introduced Leonowens to writer Harriet Beecher Stowe, whose book *Uncle Tom's cabin* had been discussed in Leonowens's *The romance of the harem*. Stowe was so impressed with Leonowens that she included, in a new introduction to *Uncle Tom's cabin*, Leonowens's tale of the Siamese princess who read Stowe's book and freed her slaves. It is interesting to note that Fields, whose friends included Charles Dickens and who was well respected in the literary community, apparently sought out Leonowens's company, praised her social skills and attested to her talent as a linguist. Leonowens, she said, spoke 'like a lady' and knew 'seven Oriental languages' (Gollin 2002:132). In addition, Fields said Leonowens was a woman of 'modesty and sweetness and special refinement' (Gollin 2002:133). This would appear to negate Bristowe's assessment of Leonowens as unfit for the company of people 'of good family' (Bristowe 1976:30). Bristowe asserts that Leonowens was not successful in her guise as an English gentlewoman:

> The Consul and his two assistants came from good families and she must have been quite unable to sustain her pretences of breeding either in her manner of speech or in her manners for them to have taken no subsequent notice of her (Bristowe 1976:31).

Bristowe was wrong, because, in fact, nobody had thought to question her background for more than 100 years, until Bristowe started digging. Even members of her immediate family did not know the truth.

For much of the 20th century, as has been shown, Leonowens's work was dismissed, particularly by male critics. BJ Terwiel is rare among male historians in acknowledging Leonowens's work as 'not completely worthless' (Terwiel 2005:158). In light of current thinking, much of what Leonowens wrote does today appear racist, far-fetched and pandering to Victorian readers' demands for the 'Orient' promised in *The Arabian nights*. But this does not mean her work is valueless. Travel writer Dame Freya Stark said just that in an introduction to a new edition of *The romance of the harem*, renamed *Siamese harem life*, in 1953. Even then, Stark observed that Leonowens's 'Victorian piety' seemed 'remote' (Leonowens 1953:xiii). However, in Leonowens's time, she adds, this piety was 'the shaft on which her whole machinery depended' and should not now be separated from what Leonowens says about Siam and its people (Leonowens 1953:xiii).

Though it is commonly assumed by critics, including Griswold, that Stark was 'taken in' by Leonowens's tales and believed them all to be true, a reading of Stark's introduction shows that she actually doubted their basis in fact, at least partially (she, after all, also wrote about travel in Eastern lands). As she says, the stories 'read like fiction' (Leonowens 1953:xiii). Stark does, however, credit Leonowens with rather too much ('few people can have wielded a stronger influence in that corner of Asia') and appears to believe that Leonowens's influence was directly responsible for the abolition of prostration and slavery by King Chulalongkorn (Leonowens1953:xiii). In this way, however, Stark is perhaps demonstrating that she is a product of *her* time, when the West was desperate to persuade the East that Western political, social and moral practices were the mark of civilisation, and that they were the only way 'forward' and away from the evils of communism.

Given Stark's specialisation in Middle Eastern travel, it is significant that she was chosen to introduce Leonowens's book because, as this book has shown, Siam has been closely connected in Western minds with *The Arabian nights* for centuries. Lach and Foss (1990:24) note that Galland's translation of *Nights* was so influential in its presentation of an undifferentiated 'Orient' that it became the benchmark for what an 18th-century reader demanded from any book of tales about Asia: 'he expected to be transported to a place of fantasy, a fairyland of stock exotica'. The 19th century was no different, and whole new generations were enchanted with the idea of 'the East' when Burton's translation came out.

The influence of *The Arabian nights* has continued and its images remain central to a great deal of Western writing about Asia. Travellers often see their preconceptions come to life—they 'see' what they want to see, and Leonowens is a perfect example. Both *Romance* and *The English governess* employ many of the stock Eastern characters identified by Lach and Foss (1990:24): 'captive maidens in seraglios, magnificent mandarins and autocratic sultans in settings of fabulous wealth'. This is evident in the illustrations to the 1953 edition of *Siamese harem life* (the edition with Stark's introduction). The richly detailed pointillist illustrations show luscious interiors with fine carpets, intricate ornaments and voluminous drapes, populated by topless concubines draped in jewels. King Mongkut in reality was gaunt and often plainly dressed, and ate sparingly, no doubt influenced by having consumed only one meal a day during his decades as a monk. Yet, in the Stark edition, he is depicted as a rotund, bald persona with a cruel face, dismissively turning away from the slave girl lying before him, while his attendants are pictured with uncharacteristic long beards and moustaches.[101] In contrast, Leonowens's story on 'The Christian village of Tâmsèng, or of Thomas the Saint' is accompanied by a picture of a modest yet clean village in which people are depicted industriously working or cooking; the women are fully clothed with their hair neatly tied back, no jewellery, and one tends her baby (Leonowens 1953:168). The only suggestion of 'Oriental splendour' is a hazy glimpse of a temple in the background. Griswold is correct when he says the illustrations are 'preposterous' and are 'a Victorian fantasy of harem scenes from Turkey to China and have nothing to do with Siam' (Griswold 1961:60). Unfortunately, although these illustrations did not appear in the original edition, the publisher retained Leonowens's acknowledgement to Dr Bradley's daughter, Sarah, for providing photographs for illustrations, misleading the reader into thinking those used in this edition are the originals. In fact, the 1873 edition contained line drawings that were much more realistic than those of the 1953 edition, though there were errors in the captions. The 1953 illustrations are, of course, a reflection of what readers would expect from Leonowens's stories in light of what they already 'knew' of the East. They resemble more closely those used in various editions of *The Arabian nights*[102] than those in the original edition of *The romance of the harem*. Later editions of *The English governess at the Siamese Court*, including the 1980 Folio Society edition and the 1988 Oxford University Press edition, have tended to use the more realistic illustrations from the 1870 edition.

While it is true that the King was an autocratic ruler with great wealth, a glittering palace and a harem of women, some of whom would have been unhappy, Leonowens dwells on the more sensationally awful stories in *The romance of the harem*. Morgan points out that King Mongkut, though he might well have been a more enlightened and better educated leader than many of his contemporaries, was also a product of his era and of his position as an absolute ruler (Leonowens 1991:xxxiv). The King, she says, 'was instructed by both his religion and his culture to view women in terms of their functions rather than their selves' (Leonowens 1991:xxxiv).

Leonowens translated *Nang Harm*, or Royal Women's Quarters, as 'the city...of the Veiled Women', for which Warren justly criticises her for being melodramatic (Warren 2002:56; Leonowens 1991:xxxiv,xxxv). Undoubtedly, Leonowens was speaking figuratively. She would have realised the women in Siam were not, in fact, veiled—after all, she worked and lived among them. She was using a descriptive translation that her readers, being familiar with *The Arabian nights*, would have recognised.

Craig J Reynolds (2006:132) makes the persuasive point that, 'considering the richness of the historical evidence', it is surprising Leonowens's work has not been used to write a history of the inhabitants in the late-19th-century Inner Palace. It is also surprising, given that Leonowens was born in India, that she has not been included in many discussions of the writing of colonials—those who consider themselves to be English, but who are also, as Melanie R Hunter (2002:42) notes, colonial outsiders. Hunter discusses the 'obsession with what it means to be English', which occurs in fiction and travel writing from Robinson Crusoe on (Hunter 2002:43). Leonowens and her desperate desire to be considered English would seem to be an obvious example, and yet, she is not mentioned here, either.

Many crtics have questioned how the working-class Leonowens, with only a basic school education, could have become the highly literate and accomplished writer she was. Some have accused her of pretending to know more languages than she did. Others have invented theories about supposed mentors (such as the Reverend Badger). I have always maintained that from rudimentary beginnings it is possible that Leonowens was intelligent and industrious enough to educate herself by constantly studying, reading and travelling. Morgan concurs, adding that it is likely Leonowens had a photographic memory: her granddaughter, Anna Fyshe, once remarked that Leonowens had an 'extraordinary memory' and that she 'could give a clear synopsis of a book she had read 30 or 40 years earlier' (Morgan 2008:200).

In *The romance of the harem*, Leonowens retells stories as, she says, they were told to her by women there. However, the title of the original work, with its reference to 'romance', suggests a kind of fiction, as Morgan notes (Leonowens 1991:xvi,xvii). The fact that later publications were renamed *Siamese harem life* gave a misleading impression that the book was entirely factual—but this was the fault of the publisher, not of Leonowens (Leonowens 1991:x).[103] Although Leonowens says she wrote down the tales as told to her at the time, the fact that an original diary has never been published probably means one didn't exist. She admits as much herself in *The English governess* when she relates a disagreement between King Mongkut and Sir John Bowring, saying, 'At this distance of time I cannot clearly recall all the effect upon my feelings' (Leonowens 1988:277).

Leonowens did not claim that all the stories in *The romance of the harem* were true. She admitted some of them had been told to her by others and could promise only that 'I tell the tale as it was told to me, and written down by me at the time' (Leonowens 1988:Preface). Nor did she say that all the events happened during her time there, but rather that *most* of the 'stories, incidents, and characters' she wrote about were 'known to me personally to be real' (1988:Preface). She also admits to making up some of the names (1988:Preface). In a population of several thousand, as that of the *Nang Harm*, there are bound to be tales of misery of various types, as there would be in a percentage of any human population anywhere. Leonowens found those stories, collated and repeated them in the most sensational way to create a good narrative. As Spurr contends, it is common for Western writers to be 'a kind of Prospero who transforms the non-Western world into a series of enchanting or disturbing visions' (Spurr 2001:155). Leonowens herself admits she is presenting a condensed story:

> Of the life passed therein, volumes would not give an exact description; but what I am about to relate in the pages that follow will give the general reader, perhaps, some idea of many of the stirring incidents of that life (Leonowens 1991:13).

It may be that the stories interpreted and repeated by Leonowens, written some years after her return from Siam, were incorrectly remembered, were affected by language difficulties, or even referred to an earlier period. To complicate matters, the stories the women told her may not have been true. As Chris Berry notes, there is an oral tradition among Thai women to relate a story to achieve a certain effect, not necessarily as a literal version of real events (Berry 1997:62). Here lies the key to Leonowens's strange combination of hearsay, stories from past times, legends, conjecture, poetic licence and exaggeration of her role. So intent was Leonowens on improving the lot of women that the country itself did not matter so much as the issue she intended to promote. She recognised that an 'exotic' setting in an unfamiliar land would draw in fascinated readers. Having obtained their attention, she then hoped to educate them to despise, as she did, all forms of human bondage, no matter where in the world they occurred. She worked the rest of her life to campaign against slavery and for women's rights, particularly their right to education.

Despite the decades of criticism and the deceptions of Leonowens herself, her legend is very much alive among her descendants. Her great-great-granddaughter, Lucy Bahr, of Guatemala, wrote an article about her father,

Louis T Leonowens (named after his grandfather, Anna's son), in which she reminisced about the family's enjoyment of the films about Leonowens and of the Rodgers and Hammerstein music: 'Of course the movies are romanticised stories based on Anna's experiences. No-one is fooled into actually thinking there was ever a relationship with the King', she writes (Bahr 2001:24). Though many Western critics are so damning of Leonowens, the family is still regarded with respect in Thailand. At the time of writing, Bahr's father, Louis Leonowens, had been the Honorary Consul-General of Thailand in Guatemala for 40 years and her husband, Henry Bahr, had been the Thai Consul in Honduras for 14 years. (Louis Leonowens started his professional life as a journalist but moved to Guatemala when he bought a coffee plantation there in 1954.) The Bahrs and Leonowenses travelled to Thailand in 1997 to attend a conference of honorary consuls-general and Louis Leonowens was introduced to the present monarch, King Bhumibol. Louis recalls that the King was 'curious about any information I might have about Anna and Louis T'.[104] Bahr confirms that Leonowens and the King 'reminisced about their respective grandfathers [Prince Chulalongkorn and Louis Thomas Gunnis Leonowens] who were schoolchildren together' (Bahr 2001:23).

Bahr says her father gave her a diamond ring that was presented by King Mongkut to Leonowens (2001:22), which clearly demonstrates the King's esteem for Leonowens and further challenges the claims of critics that they hardly knew each other. This was not the only present King Mongkut reportedly gave Leonowens; he also presented her with a set of coins that had been a diplomatic gift in 1836 from the US President Andrew Jackson to King Rama III.[105] The 1834-minted set left the Leonowens family when two descendants sold it in London in the late 1950s for a fraction of its true worth. Known as the King of Siam Proof Set, it was sold in 2001 for more than $US4 million and on 1 November 2005 for $US8.5 million.

Kepner believes Leonowens to be 'a much misunderstood and maligned character, very different from the way she has been imagined and reinvented by both Thais and Westerners' and that Leonowens's books about her life in 19th-century Siam were 'a better example than most of Victorian travel adventure writing, replete with invention, as all of them were'.[106] It was, in the end, the novel by Landon and the films it inspired that brought Leonowens to general notice. But, in her own time, she was not the villain she is cast by 20th-century critics. In Lucy Bahr's words:

> She took on the Victorian world when women were supposed to submit and disappear into the woodwork. She loved challenges and adventure. She also fought for causes such as women's rights. Anna is a worthy example for her descendants to follow! I can tell you that all of us are very proud of our

relationship to Anna and feel very proprietary about her and anything related to her (Bahr 2001:22).

The interloper: Margaret Landon

Careful readers will exonerate Mrs. Landon from any share in the blame for giving a false picture of the king. Her stated purpose is not to describe him objectively, but to exhibit him through Anna's eyes without correcting the faults of Anna's vision.—AB Griswold (1961:56)

Margaret Landon's novel *Anna and the King of Siam* sold 790,000 copies in the US and Britain when it was published in 1943 (Wheaton College Archives and Special Collections 2000), so she was a publishing phenomenon for the time, particularly as this was during the Second World War. It is significant, therefore, that there has been no book-length biography of Landon (1903–93). Susan Fulop Kepner planned in the mid-1990s to write a joint biography of Leonowens and Landon, but abandoned the project after publishing several articles and conducting years of research. While Kepner believes Leonowens's character and work to be misunderstood, she can't say the same for Landon's book. Landon, she says, 'took advantage of everyone, grabbed everything, and made the fortune she had always wanted on the backs of Anna, her niece, the family, and everyone involved'.[107] While researching an article, Kepner met Landon's daughter, who, she believes, would have disapproved of Kepner writing a warts-and-all biography of Landon. In the end, Kepner decided it would be too complicated to present Landon and her family in a balanced way: 'To display them in their amazing entirety would be highly problematical,' she told me.[108]

Kepner says Landon identified strongly with Leonowens, so much so that in some ways, she became Leonowens—or Leonowens became Landon in Landon's imagination. Interestingly, as Kepner notes, the screen character of Leonowens was reinvented in Landon's image—tall, fair and beautiful—not in the real image of Leonowens—'dour, dusky, dumpy' (Kepner 1996a:8). Landon was a missionary and, like Leonowens, a teacher, who lived in Thailand for ten years. While Leonowens aims to speak out against slavery and discrimination of women, Landon aims to promote the American/Christian way of life. Both, of course, use Christianity as the tool of what they see as 'civilisation' in an attempt to accomplish their literary aims. Landon's Christianity is at a fundamental level, while Leonowens's is less didactic and, perhaps, is given prominence more because of the expectations of her readers than because of any religious devotion she might have had—after all, it was Landon who was the missionary, not Leonowens. Morgan (1996:239) notes that Leonowens was not a regular churchgoer, though she considered herself a Christian.

Landon's descriptions of Leonowens's teenage life in India concoct a whirl of social engagements, an environment where servants catered to every whim and 'glided about, so quietly that their feet seemed hardly to touch the floor' (Landon 2000:7–8) and where the women were dressed in rich silks, the men in dress uniforms. Though Landon curiously never mentions Leonowens's later book, *Life and travel in India* (1884), as a source, she actually copied whole passages from it. Compare these two passages:

> The sun shone through the mists of early dawn as the young girl looked from her cabin window with mingled curiosity and wonder...In the foreground she saw the stone quays and the great flight of stone steps along the waterfront (Landon 2000:6).

> The sun shone through the mists and haze of the early dawn, and I could see from my cabin window, with a sense of mingled wonder and curiosity, the great stone quays and the long flights of stone steps which led to the beautiful island of Bombay (Leonowens 1884:7).

It is strange that Landon does not mention the book, because in her preface, she describes in detail how she came to own copies of *The romance of the harem* and *The English governess*—after reading them at Dr McDaniel's house in Siam, she found them years later, within weeks of each other at two second-hand book shops in Chicago. *Life and travel in India* did not do nearly as well as Leonowens's earlier books and had been forgotten by the time Landon was writing, so perhaps she thought no-one would notice; indeed, critics have overlooked her plagiarism. Even Kepner omits Landon's use of *Life and travel in India*.

Unlike most of Leonowens's writing, Landon's abounds with sexual imagery that probably prompted the idea of romance between the King and the English teacher in the minds of writers of the later film scripts. Landon describes, for example, 'torches reflected on the rhythmic dip of rows of wet paddles' and dancers on whom 'The soft rain of light sparkled on their bare breasts, their gold ornaments and the gold of their clothes...The music swelled into a rapturous crescendo that seemed a prelude to a choral climax' (Landon 2000:25,51). The seductive imagery, so reminiscent of *The Arabian nights*, makes Landon's tale titillating, suggestive and a more enticing read than Leowowens's. Landon goes further than Leonowens, actually likening the Middle Eastern tales to the surroundings in Bangkok; when Anna and Louis enter the Inside each morning, they step 'into a glittering kingdom out of *The Arabian nights*' (2000:105).

Though Landon habitually dresses up the story to present it as a picture of colonial elegance, she also makes liberal use of Leonowens's material, often using the exact wording. One example is at the beginning, as the ship arrives in Bangkok:

Tables were set on deck and the passengers ate and talked. The reddish-brown water curved between banks of lush green. Monkeys swung from bough to bough. Birds flashed and piped among the thickets (Landon 2000:24).

In the afternoon, when we dined on deck, the land was plainly visible…trees grew on the banks, more and more verdure, monkeys swung from bough to bough, birds flashed and piped among the thickets (Leonowens 1988:2).

Landon's appeal to the audience's own imaginative construction of the East gained her credit in high places. CS Lewis, for example, wrote to Landon on 20 April 1945 after a mutual friend had sent him the copy of *Anna and the King of Siam* that Landon had autographed for him:

It is fascinating—both in the popular sense that one can't stop reading it, and also in the old sense that it exercises a real snake-like *fascination*. Ugh! That palace is like an opium dream of twenty late Gothic cathedrals all tied together in a tangle and then consecrated to devil-worship (Lewis 2004:642).

Despite Landon's admission in the introduction that the book was only 75% true in her estimation, when the book was first released, her readers seemed to believe all the stories were true. Perhaps the most fanciful of Landon's scenes is her report of what happened when Leonowens was granted an audience with King Chulalongkorn 30 years after she left Siam. It is easy to see where the producers of *The King and I* got their idea for Chulalongkorn's melodramatic speech at the end of the film, in which he abolishes slavery (he did, in fact, abolish slavery, but gradually, many years after Leonowens had left Siam). The second-last paragraph in Landon's book reveals most clearly her political agenda. King Chulalongkorn praises Leonowens for teaching him the principles by which he has ruled, and Leonowens reflects on how the King has created 'a free Siam' and how proud she is to have helped instill 'the idea of the worth of a human being' into a king, 'a change based on democratic principles' (Landon 2000:395). As Western writers describing Siam have done since the 16th century, and particularly in the 19th century, Landon is demonstrating her belief that Western culture is superior and that the East will be 'saved' only by adopting it. Dow's account of Leonowens's meeting with Chulalongkorn in 1897 is more realistic than Landon's. She has taken it partly from Leonowens's granddaughter's journal and records that Chulalongkorn asked Leonowens why she had depicted King Mongkut as she had, and that Leonowens had responded that she had told the truth as she saw it (Dow 1991:123).

Morgan (1996:245) says Landon's book situated Leonowens's story in 'the place it still occupies, as the central representation of Siam in the 20th-century ideology of American Orientalism'. Kepner concurs, pointing out that Landon's *Anna and the King of Siam* is a product of her mid-20th-century American viewpoint, while Leonowens's books are perfect examples of late-19th-century travel memoirs. Of both, Kepner rightly says: 'They were, like everyone else, products of an era'.[109] And so, it would seem, is the screen and stage character Leonowens, the glamorous woman whose looks and story bear little resemblance to their real-life source.

The imposter: Hollywood's *The King and I* and other pretenders

Whatever have been the impressions of Western people about the play and the film, they should be definitely looked upon as nothing more than a kind of entertainment cleverly arranged to draw money from those who wish to be amused.—Rong Syamananda (1976:124)

The King and I has been strongly criticised for not being a faithful presentation of the real people, place and events it portrays. Yet there is rarely, if ever, a Hollywood interpretation of a 'true story' that is so. *The sound of music, The bridge on the River Kwai* and, more recently, *Pearl Harbor* and *Titanic* are all examples of films purportedly based on true stories that strayed markedly from real events. Yet it is *The King and I* that has come in for the most damning criticism by historians. Griswold says the stage and screen versions of the story are 'trifles intended more to entertain than to instruct', but that it is 'disconcerting to note that they were advertised as if they were documentaries' (Griswold 1961:56). Yet surely a filmed or staged story, particularly one in which the characters are constantly breaking into song, is understood by the majority of the audience to be only partly true. As Rong indicates in the quotation at the beginning of this section, plays or films, including musicals or light opera, are charming tales that may be based on truth but are usually considerably reconstructed to become suitable as musical entertainment.

The depiction of the possibility of romance between Leonowens and Mongkut is a manifestation of what Gina Marchetti (1993:3) describes as the 'sexual danger of contact between the races' that fascinated 'yellow peril discourses' of the 20th century and fostered scenarios that were really 'a metaphor for the threat posed to Western culture'. *The King and I* is unusual for its time in that such a possibility was presented as something the audience would almost wish for as the film proceeds, but would also be repelled by when the King punishes Tup Tim, a trophy concubine who runs away with her lover. In all the films, except the animated version, the mistreatment of Tup Tim is pivotal to the white woman's realisation that such a romance is impossible because the gulf between them is too vast.

The 1946 film appears more damning of Mongkut's character than the other films, depicting the slave-concubine Tup Tim being burnt at the stake simply because his pride is hurt, whereas in *The King and I* (1956) the King cannot bring himself to whip Tup Tim under Leonowens's glare. Though the punishment of beheading in *Anna and the King* (1999) is shocking, the King is seen to be not responsible for its having been carried out—in fact, Leonowens's interfering is blamed for the court imposing the death sentence, which the King dare not overturn.

Importantly, in the 1946 version, the King and the governess do not dance together as they do in the 1956 and 1999 films. In fact, in the 1946 film there are no romantic feelings between them, although an emotional attachment is constructed. The depiction in other films of Leonowens dancing with the King in Western ballroom fashion (the polka in *The King and I*, a waltz in *Anna and the King*) has been the subject of much criticism in Thailand. The polka scene is one of the best remembered of the film, and was recreated in the 2004 film *Shall we dance?*[110] The titles *The King and I* and *Anna and the King of Siam* or versions of them, have been borrowed and adapted for many books, only some of which are connected with Thailand.[111]

Though the Thai government did not allow the 1999 film *Anna and the King* to be filmed or screened in Thailand, it presents King Mongkut in a more sympathetic manner, even though the actor was about 30 years younger and not Thai. The film's plot is the least realistic of all, though this is not the most problematic aspect. It is, again, the portrayal of King Mongkut falling in love with a Western woman and wishing he were able to act on that love. In his 2006 biography of the present King, which is also banned in Thailand, Paul M Handley maintains that the film was banned 'for niggling and specious reasons' and that it was 'inoffensive' (Handley 2006:420). He is, of course, speaking from a Western point of view; the Thai perspective is obviously quite different.

Interestingly, some of the least damning comments recorded about *The King and I* and the other films reportedly have come from those perhaps most entitled to take offence—King Bhumibol and Queen Sirikit themselves. When the royal couple visited Australia in 1962, the Australian Broadcasting Corporation banned music from *The King and I* from its airwaves for the duration of their stay. However, when Queen Sirikit saw a revival production of the musical on Broadway in 1985, she pronounced, through a spokesperson, that she thought it was 'fun' and added that 'everyone' realised it was not a true depiction of what went on at court (Klein 2003:221). According to William Stevenson in his 2001 biography, the King had seen the film version and had reportedly said it captured 'the spirit' of his great-grandfather, King Mongkut (Stevenson 2001:231). Stevenson says the King later commented on Leonowens: 'Ah well…I suppose she put us on the map' (Stevenson 2001:128).

The Queen and I: Yul Brynner introduced Queen Sirikit to the cast of a revival of The King and I at the Broadway Theatre in New York on 21 March 1985 (the year Brynner died). Credit: AP Photo.

Historian Thongchai Winichakul is among only a few Thais—significantly, overseas-based—who feel able to criticise the government's decision not to allow the 1999 film, *Anna and the King*, to be filmed or screened in Thailand. Thongchai questions the need for films always to depict history accurately and underlines that all history is told as a version anyway, depending on the viewpoint. 'Should the film board ban the film because it makes King Mongkut look too majestic and good looking, thus historically inaccurate?' Thongchai quips (Handley 2006:421). According to Kepner, Landon felt she and Leonowens had presented King Mongkut as 'a living human being…rescuing him from plastic sainthood' but that her opinion 'has never impressed Thais, who have no tradition of portraying their royal heroes with "warts and all"' (Kepner 1996a:16).

At the core of the 1956 film is a post-Second World War message of solidarity from the US to its political allies that even the most 'barbarous' nations, even the most 'Oriental' of Eastern countries, can be encouraged to see their way towards Western enlightenment and, most importantly, veer away from the threatening shadow of communism to what was seen as the inherent good of democracy. Christina Klein says *The King and I* was influenced by Hammerstein's political values; he was an internationalist who later became vice-president of the United World Federalists (Klein 2003:196).

The King and I is of course a belated articulation of the 'white man's burden', the feeling that it is a duty to civilise the heathen, with the added incentive that 'they' would then be less likely to fall for the 'dark side': communism. These changes were brought about principally through bringing modernisation to the East. As if the world existed in two different time zones, the country subjected to this modernisation is pictured as being suddenly 'brought into' the 20th century. There is an assumption that the present exists only for countries who 'catch up' with the West. As Klein (2003:192) says, 'Here, "backward" Siam is transformed through love and friendship, and the premodern is swept away in a spectacular episode of song and dance'.

The King and I almost did not make it to the big screen. A *New York Times* article of 18 August 1953 announced that Columbia was planning a musical film based on Thai harem life that was unconnected with the Rodgers and Hammerstein stage version. The film would be based on Leonowens's 'little-known book' *The romance of the harem*, and would star José Ferrer as King Mongkut, with Deborah Kerr sought to play Leonowens. The film was to be called *The city of veiled women*, and if it had been made in 1954 as planned, it is unlikely *The King and I* would have been produced for the screen in 1956. Interestingly, Kerr did, of course, go on to play Leonowens on screen, but in the Rodgers and Hammerstein version.

The 1999 film *Anna and the King*, starring US actor Jodie Foster as Leonowens and Hong Kong actor Chow Yun-Fat as King Mongkut, reopened the debate about Leonowens, particularly in the popular press. The fact that the film had to be shot in Malaysia was a blow to the producers, who had hoped to be granted access to the real Grand Palace in Bangkok. Unconnected to any other material in the film, the 1999 version starts with Louis questioning his mother's claim to be English; from this start, the film appears to be going somewhere the others did not. It does not, however, continue this thread and Louis's offhand comments would pass by most viewers almost unnoticed. It is as if the screenplay writers, Steve Meerson and Peter Krikes, decided to reveal Leonowens's deceptions about her background, then thought better of it. It is a nod to research since the original films that has uncovered more of Leonowens's true background, including that by Bristowe and his followers. The *Bangkok Post* ran a succession of articles about the film, and Warren used the opportunity, yet again, to regurgitate Bristowe's revelations, repeating as fact Bristowe's assertions that Leonowens had no friends among the expatriate community. Bristowe's findings have become more often identified with Warren's. An article in the *Bangkok Post* claims that Warren has 'done the hardest work in exposing the woman' (Dawson 1999). Warren did write a letter to the Editor, rightly saying it was not his research but Bristowe's that exposed Leonowens—yet in the letter, he does not mention the title of Bristowe's book (Warren 1999).

Other writers debating the 1999 film go even further than Bristowe and Warren. Canadian Tom Regan, the associate editor of *The Christian Science Monitor*'s website, says Leonowens 'made most of it up or lifted it from other sources' (Regan 1999). Regan does not source material he has gleaned from Bristowe, probably via Warren, and as a native of Halifax, he claims that Leonowens was made an 'outcast' in society there and had to move to Montreal (Regan 1999). In reality, her move to Montreal had nothing to do with the truth catching up with her, as Regan claims. She moved there to be with her family—her son-in-law, Tom Fyshe, had become general manager of the Merchant's Bank of Canada (Morgan 2008:202).[112]

The most outlandish claim in the *Bangkok Post* is that Leonowens 'never taught Royal children'.[113] In addition, Leonowens's work is frequently confused with Landon's and with the films. One article says the Thai Film Board claims it is unhappy with the film because it is 'based on inaccuracies in the book *Anna and the King of Siam* written by Anna Leonowens' (Uamdao Noikorn 1998). Another says Leonowens 'is known throughout the world for her popular book, "The King and I"' (Thongbai Thongpao 2001).[114] Handley says Leonowens's book became *The King and I* (Handley 2006:31).

Several documentaries were made about Leonowens in the wake of the 1999 film, including *Anna Leonowens: getting to know you* (ALKI Productions, Canada, and BBC Worldwide, 2000) and *Anna and the King: the real story of Anna Leonowens* (directed by Steven Smith, Van Ness Films & Foxstar Productions, 1999). The documentaries are competent surveys of the controversy surrounding Leonowens's real identity and both interview Leonowens experts such as Lois Yorke and Susan Morgan, plus various other writers and historians. The Fox documentary, while admitting its own film of that year, *Anna and the King*, was historically inaccurate, interviews some of Leonowens's descendants in an attempt to sort out her real story. *Anna Leonowens: getting to know you* also features comments from a Thai courtier, Chitr Jotikasthira. Both documentaries acknowledge the mystery surrounding Leonowens's identity and the revelations of Bristowe, and, although they don't uncover anything new, both ask for a more balanced assessment of Leonowens's work. However, both continue some of the stereotypes that have become part of Western mythology about the East; Jodie Foster is quoted as saying that the thought of working for a 'heathen ruler with a harem of 600 women would have given most proper English women the vapours', exaggerating by hundreds the number of wives Mongkut had (Smith 1999). While the documentaries discuss the controversy surrounding Leonowens's background, they give her credit as one who had an opportunity to document a way of life in Siam rarely seen by those outside the palace. It was a different story in a 1970 BBC documentary on Leonowens, in which Dr Ian Grimble called her 'a mischief maker, a squalid little girl...one of those awful little English governesses, a sex-starved widow'.[115] Oddly, he accuses Leonowens's books of being 'pornographic' and says they are 'rubbish and lifted from other sources' (Leonowens 1991:x–xi).

It is significant that Leonowens is addressed by Thais as 'Sir', because she is 'scientific' and 'not lowly like woman', according to the character of head wife, Lady Thiang, in *The King and I*.[116] Used in all the films, this device highlights Leonowens's assumed superiority to the women of the harem. In effect, it gives her a voice in the male-dominated hierarchy of the palace. Laura Donaldson (1992:37) says it allows Leonowens to be assertive, 'which contravenes the traditional stereotype of women as irrational and submissive'. *The King and I* is, according to Matthew Bernstein and Gaylyn Studlar (1997:40), an example of the colonial woman being used as 'the instrument of the white male vision and granted a gaze more powerful than that not only of non-Western women but also of non-Western men'. The 1946 and 1956 films could also be seen to be highlighting the cause of post-Second World War women intent on maintaining their right to work, to be independent (hence Leonowens's depicted campaign for a house of her own) and, above all, to be taken seriously as the equals of men.

Several books since Landon's have been marketed as 'the sequel to *The King and I*'. As well as Bristowe's book (1976), there have been a novelised biography by RJ Minney, *Fanny and the Regent of Siam* (1962), Stevenson's biography (2001) and my own novel, *The Occidentals* (1999). Of the books inspired directly by Leonowens's screened adventures, the strangest is a companion volume to the film by Cecilia Holland (1999), a disparate collection of myths, facts and hearsay. It is partly a narrative of the film's production, partly a biography of Leonowens that does not differentiate between conjecture, fact, sentimentality and material taken from the script of *The King and I*, Landon's and Leonowens's books. The text is unsourced and contains no bibliography and makes vague statements that should be explained, such as that Louis Leonowens 'married one of Chulalongkorn's sisters' (Holland 1999:94).[117] The glossy, large-format book is presented as non-fiction, yet is accompanied by hundreds of photographs from the film which have little or nothing to do with the text. The 1999 film also spawned another book, called *Anna and the King* (Hand 1999), a novelised treatment. This book did not, however, purport to be the 'true' or 'real' story.

Of all the screen versions, the least connected with its location is the 1999 animated film *The King and I*. Using some of the original Rodgers and Hammerstein songs, the film departs from reality altogether, descending into a retold children's version of *The Arabian nights*, complete with stock characters such as a wicked magician. That it was made at all, on the edge of the 21st century, shows that, despite all the discourse about Orientalism, colonialism, postcolonialism and racial stereotyping, the viewing public in the West has remained virtually unchanged. The reason, according to Winks and Rush (1990:31), is that Asians have always seemed 'unpredictable' to Europeans, so they become 'comic figures in European plays and skits' who eventually transfer to the screen.

Whatever the truth about Leonowens, it is clear none of the films intended to tell a true story about Thailand. That they are set in 19th-century Siam hardly matters. In the case of *The King and I* particularly, Siam is merely an exotic location in which to set a story that earned a phenomenal amount of money for its collaborators. Leonowens might have made a living from her work, but Landon, Rodgers and Hammerstein made a fortune.

Thailand's own film industry has begun to deconstruct Western stereotypes in an attempt to reinvent the way it is depicted in film. The epic *The legend of Suriyothai*, directed by Prince Chatri Chalerm Yukol,[118] is set in 1528, more than 330 years before *The King and I*, yet Thai critics have seen it as an answer to the West's more famous depiction of Thailand and its monarchy. Described by critic Noy Thrupkaew (Noy 2003) as a 'Merchant Thaivory flick that broke all box office records in Thailand', the film tells the heroic story of the real-life Queen Suriyothai. Though the character is 'clumsily drawn', she 'is almost refreshing after the tittering, sobbing Thai ladies of the Anna movies' (Noy 2003). Noy supports the Thais' push to fight misconceptions of their country and monarchy with Thai-made films they hope might help change the West's perceptions and present a more balanced version of their history:

> Although it can't single-handedly set the record straight, the film has lumbered into the war against Hollywood 'colonisation' like Queen Suriyothai's elephant, perhaps helping pave the way for the real substance of the Thai cinema: tales of the ordinary and everyday that provide the best answers of all to a contested history (Noy 2003).

Chapter six

Eroticising Thailand

Bangkok, Oriental setting
And the city don't know what the city is getting
The crème de la crème of the chess world in a
Show with everything but Yul Brynner,
—'One night in Bangkok', from the musical, *Chess* (1994)

The song 'One night in Bangkok' tells the story of an impending chess match to be held 'in an unusual locale for such a cerebral game, Bangkok'. Just why it is 'unusual' is made clear in the song's lyrics—Bangkok, the song suggests, celebrates physical pleasure. It is about seduction ('I can feel an angel sliding up to me/I can feel the devil walking next to me') and sex-for-money ('The bars are temples but the pearls ain't free'). Bangkok is a 'crowded, polluted, stinking town' full of bars, temples and massage parlours, the song says, with the 'warm, sweet' girls 'set up in the Somerset Maugham suite' (of the famous Oriental Hotel). The song insistently talks of temples or religious symbols in the same line as bars and/or sex for hire and the angel/devil lines also combine religion with eroticism. The allusion to *The King and I* establishes that there is a link in the Western imagination between this fictional harem and today's sex industry in Bangkok.The 'harem' has long been used in literature as the focal point of Eastern life, one of the essential differences in the minds of Westerners, between 'us' and 'them'. As Grewal (1996:82) explains, the harem 'became the racial sign for "Eastern" culture'. Juxtaposed with the idea of an eroticised Thailand are Kukrit Pramoj's 1953 novel *Four reigns* (mentioned previously), set among Bangkok courtiers and the *Nang Harm* of the late 19th and early 20th centuries, and the memoirs of an American anthropologist who was ordained as a Thai nun or *maechi*, *Meeting Faith* (Adiele 2005).

As Faith Adiele (2005:96) observes, male writers including celebrated authors such as Pico Iyer, Paul Theroux and Michel Houellebecq, 'never fail to cover Thailand's flesh trade'. (Female writers, too, sometimes use it, of course.) Current writers such as John Burdett (2003, 2005, 2007) and Angela Savage

(2006) are using Thailand's 'skin trade' and 'seedy underbelly' as settings for thrillers with cinematic appeal. In addition, there are several studies of the Thai sex market and a substantial body of discourse focusing on Dennis O'Rourke's controversial 1991 reality film about a Thai prostitute, *The good woman of Bangkok*. O'Rourke is an Australian documentary maker who, middle-aged and divorced, travelled to Bangkok to look for uncomplicated 'love' with a prostitute. There are battalions of books about the Thai sex trade, from salacious novels and guides to memoirs and academic studies, with titles such as *Thailand: land of beautiful women* (Barrett 2004), *Thailand fever* (Pirazzi & Vasant 2004) and *"Hello my big big honey!": love letters to Bangkok bar girls and their revealing interviews* (Walker & Ehrlich 1995). Andrew Hicks's *Thai girl* (2004) is unusual in that it examines the relationship of a *farang* with a Thai who chooses to remain poor in a low-paying job rather than to become a prostitute.

The Somerset Maugham suite at The Mandarin Oriental Bangkok. Maugham first stayed at the hotel in 1923, where he recovered from malaria and wrote parts of The gentleman in the parlour. He returned to the hotel in 1925 and 1960. Credit: Photos courtesy of Mandarin Oriental Hotel Group.

The real romance of the harem

Women constantly fell in love with him. He returned their love, which is not surprising if one considers that his grandfather, King Chulalongkorn, had two hundred wives.—Germaine Krull on Prince Bhanu, late 1940s (Krull & Melchers 1964:29)

Invariably every Asian advertisement serves up a graceful, gracious, smiling, pliable woman, the embodiment of the West's Orientalist desires. Often she is characterized as a flower—the delicate lotus and exotic orchid bending to your will like a green willow or bamboo reed; heady, aromatic jasmine; the slightly titillating cherry blossom you pluck.—Faith Adiele (2005:87)

According to Said (2003:188), one of the most persistent ideas the West maintains about the Orient is its association with 'licentious sex'. The Orient suggests, for Westerners, 'fecundity by sexual promise (and threat), untiring sensuality, unlimited desire, deep generative energies'. In expressing this association, the existence of the harem in the Western imagination has become the quintessential symbol of a feminised East, an imagined location awaiting male penetration, exploration, and discovery.

Of course, most Western images of the harem are not based on experience or observation. Nor are the representations limited to writing by Westerners. In his newspaper-serialised 1931 novel *Ten-ram* (*Dancing*), Thai author Chamnong Wongkhaluang used these fictional representations in one of his character's views of what he imagined was a typical nobleman's household: '…you'll see it's no different from a Turkish harem: their houses are jam packed with women' (Barmé 2002:123). This is a similar view to that expressed by 19th-century Western male travellers, who, like the Thai male onlooker, had no access to such places so could only imagine them. And yet the travellers, as Bernstein and Studlar (1997:49) point out, 'delineate life in the harems with great assurance and apparent exactitude, rather like European Orientalist studio paintings, for example the *Turkish Bath* (1862) which was painted without Ingres ever visiting the Orient'. Not that he would have been any more knowledgeable, had he visited, as he would have been prohibited from entering a harem.

This literary voyeurism is applied not only to descriptions of the harem, but has wider implications for travel writing. An example can be found in W Somerset Maugham's 1930 travel book about Southeast Asia, *The gentleman in the parlour*, which he wrote while staying at the Oriental Hotel in Bangkok. In the book, he admits he has not visited the Grand Palace, but says he does not regret it, because the palace 'thus retained for me the faint air of mystery' (Maugham 2001:128). He proceeds to create his own description of what he *imagines* the palace to be like, complete with 'officials of the court…intent upon secret affairs…and apartments, vaguely scented, dark and cool, in which lie in careless profusion the storied treasures of the East' (2001:128–9). Bizarrely, he then includes a fairy story he has invented about a generic King of Siam and his many daughters, strongly reminiscent of tales from *The Arabian nights* (2001:129–38).

*The view from here: British
writer W Somerset Maugham
never went to the Grand
Palace in Bangkok, but he felt
qualified to describe it from
his hotel room at the Oriental,
in his 1930 travel book, The
gentleman in the parlour. This
picture was taken in 1933.
Credit: AP Photo*

Similarities can be seen in Joseph Conrad's protagonist in the 1917 novella *The shadow-line*, who observes Bangkok from a steamer on the Chao Phraya river. Conrad describes the city as 'Oriental and squalid' (Conrad 1986:168). He sees the Grand Palace only 'in the distance', yet imagines it in detail: 'temples, gorgeous and dilapidated, crumbling under the vertical sunlight, tremendous, overpowering, almost palpable…' (1986:150).

In the same way, the harem is out of bounds and unreachable by Western men, and is, therefore, construed as a concept that can be written about in an imaginary way. CS Lewis found Landon's novel on Leonowens enlightening:

> I never fully realised what a harem meant before: all those moons, and one dreadful sun, like a horrible parody of a nunnery. And yet the real revelation is the beauties of character which apparently existed among these 'forbidden women' (Lewis 2004:642).

Lewis's comparison of the harem with a nunnery is a familiar one; both conjure visions of unreachable, cloistered and covered women living together and worshipping one male (husband/God). Ironically, of course, while the women of the harem are seen as the ultimate female sexual objects, those of the nunnery are asexual, seen, according to Narumon (Pook) Hinshiranan as 'celebate housewives' serving orders of monks (Adiele 2005:34). In Thailand, they are considered misfits, women who have escaped bad marriages, women who cannot find a husband or who are poverty-stricken, old or infirm (Adiele 2005:33)—the antithesis, in fact, of the image of harem women.

Male writers find it incongruous that sex industry workers should have any sort of spiritual life. Adiele refutes this masculine viewpoint in a powerful feminist argument that concerns itself with the subjugation of women in general, in the US as well as in Thailand. In this way, her writing can be compared with that of Leonowens more than 130 years before. Adiele comments on the way Westerners express surprise at what they see as contradictory conditions in Thailand existing conjointly, such as large numbers of both monks and prostitutes: 'Raised on dichotomy, we craft tension-filled narratives that make for a fine holiday: we visit jeweled temples by day and opium dens/sex bars at night' (Adiele 2005:33). She rejects the Western presentation of Thai women as objects of seduction, but notes that it is a habit of males of any race, nation or creed, including Thais, to believe 'the female sexual appetite is uncontrollable (and therefore destructive)' (96–7). As an American woman, she says she feels as vulnerable to abuse by Thai men as Asian women do by Western men: 'Perhaps that is the nature of the world. We lock up our own women and go looking for theirs' (2005:97). Imaginative descriptions of the 'harem' are the literary equivalent to locating the key to them. However, there is a fundamental difference between Adiele's situation and that of a 19th-century harem woman—Adiele is free to leave when and as she wishes.

Adiele first went to Thailand at 16 as a Rotary exchange student to Chiang Rai in 1979. The daughter of a Nigerian father, conceived when he was a student in the US, and a white mother of Scandinavian origins, she says she was Washington State Rotary's 'first black ambassador' to Thailand. No-one even seemed to know where Thailand was, and Adiele agreed to go to Chiang Rai because the white exchange students Rotary had sent there couldn't cope with the food, the language or the climate (Adiele 2005:17). Ironically, Adiele sees herself as akin to 19th-century explorers:

> And once I opened myself to the idea of some unknown country near Vietnam and Cambodia not yet on tourist maps, I too began to see the possibilities. This was virgin territory, literally uncolonized, unconquered, unexplored (Adiele 2005:19).

In her early 20s, the high-achieving but troubled Adiele returns to Thailand on a 'Grand Fieldwork Project' and, for reasons she still cannot determine, decides to become ordained and live as a novice Buddhist nun for several months. She keeps a journal of her spiritual and physical journeys, on which she draws extensively for the book. Her experience goes beyond the touristic, allowing her to make some salient comments on the nature of modern travel, while conceding that she is still a participant in it:

> Ever since my year as savior of Thai-American exchange programs, I had worked hard to distinguish myself as the Ultimate Traveler…We avoided tourist hangouts, instead cultivating Thai friends and practicing our tones and idiomatic expressions. We ate spicy food and sticky rice with our hands, ladled cold water over ourselves before meals and bed, tied sarongs when at home, bargained like mad at the market. We were Authentic! (Adiele 2005:173).

Ultimately, Adiele's time as a *maechi* can be seen as an anthropological experiment, a Westerner's study of Eastern religion and an attempt to define her own identity. Yet, like Leonowens's writing of the *Nang Harm*, it offers a rare description of a world usually inaccessible to outsiders. Despite any criticism that could be levelled at Adiele for profiting from her experience, the fact remains that the narrative is a valuable exposé of this world and an honest depiction of her emotional journey through it. She does not present Thailand as either hell-hole or paradise, but as something in between and with aspects of both.

Apart from that of Leonowens, the only extensive eyewitness account in English about the *Nang Harm* is Malcolm Smith's excellent memoir (Smith 1947). Smith was a doctor in Bangkok and an official court physician during King Chulalongkorn's reign in the early 20th century, 40 years after Leonowens lived there. He 'was associated almost daily' with Queen Saowapa, a daughter of Mongkut who married her half-brother, Chulalongkorn, when she was 16 (1947:8). Smith is familiar with Leonowens's work and, although he concurs with views that she made up some of it, he acknowledges her as a valuable source of information about the harem,:

> Of Mongkut's private life we have only her [Leonowens's] account…But we need not believe all that she said; her books, particularly her second one, show that she was gifted with a vivid imagination which at times took charge of her pen (Smith 1947:42).

He also notes that Leonowens was 'a fanatical opponent of polygamy'. Smith provides a mostly non-judgemental, factual account of court life, much of it from his own observations but he also includes material about previous reigns, particularly that of King Mongkut. He doesn't rely only on Leonowens's work, however, because when he first arrived in Bangkok, there were still people alive who had known Mongkut, among them the Reverend Samuel J Smith, editor of the *Bangkok Calendar*, and Captain Bush, the first Harbour Master there (Smith 1947:40). Smith describes intimate details of King Chulalongkorn's harem, particularly of Queen Saowapa, who was Smith's patient after her husband died and she became the Queen Mother:

> To her personal appearance the Queen paid great attention and spent a long
> time at her toilet every day. Scented water made from freshly cut flowers and
> aromatic herbs was used for washing and bathing. No towel was used, but the
> body was dabbed all over with powder and allowed to dry (Smith 1947:78).

It is not clear exactly how he came by much of this information but it must
have been told to him by someone who knew—presumably, he was not actually
present when the Queen was attended on in her preparations. He gives some
clues as to how he gathered his information, when he talks about the harem's
disbandment after Chulalongkorn's death in 1910 and the empty lives of the
remaining unmarried princesses: 'I did not discover this through inquiry:
information in the East is seldom gained in that way; it came up at odd times
in the course of conversation' (Smith 1947:99). He includes a fascinatingly
detailed account of everyday palace life, including sleeping arrangements of the
King, Queen and harem, which of course, Western audiences find particularly
titillating. We learn that the King's bedroom contained:

> an enormous bed, or to be more correct three beds placed side by side. The
> middle one was higher and larger than the others; no-one could use it except the
> King and his wives, the lower beds were for those in attendance (Smith 1947).

Much of Smith's writing about life inside is more interesting than that
of Leonowens because he does not let his own moral code interfere with his
narrative. Thus, we learn how Chulalongkorn conducted his marital affairs:

> The King could, if he wished, call upon any woman within the Palace walls
> to lie with him. It was the highest honour that any woman could expect, though
> it is on record that not all of them desired it. In actual practice, however, he
> chose his queens and minor wives from a certain class which were set aside for
> him at his coronation…Some of them were his own half-sisters, others were the
> daughters of princes and noblemen, but the absence of rank was no barrier…
> When the King took a liking to any particular girl, he would send one of the
> serving-maids on duty that day—she might be already his wife—to command
> the girl to go to him. That was all (Smith 1947:69–70).

Smith was present frequently at the Queen Mother's bedside in her later life
and became a companion to her as well as her physician. He could speak Thai
and was the only European the Queen Mother saw regularly. His portrait of the
ageing valetudinarian and their friendship constitutes one of the most intriguing
memoirs written by a foreigner about the Thai royal family. He was able to ask
the Queen intimate questions about her family life with King Chulalongkorn.

Kukrit's *Four reigns* is a well known historical novel written in Thai in the
1950s. Kukrit, born in 1911 and a descendent of Rama II, set the book from the
end of the 19th century to 1945, so much of what he writes benefits from his
access to family recollections as primary sources. The book was translated into
English in 1981 but remains little known in the West, yet its literary value as a

fictionalised history of Thai court and *Nang Harm* life, starting during the time of King Chulalongkorn's reign, is considerable. It is the nearest to a comprehensive account of *Nang Harm* life by a Thai. The attention to detail is extraordinary, yet Kukrit said it was the easiest book he ever wrote because, 'it is a novel of a life that my ancestors and myself have lived rather fully' (Kukrit 1998:v). It is not, of course, an eyewitness account of the *Nang Harm*—as a man, Kukrit would not have had access and, anyway, it was disbanded after King Chulalongkorn's death a year before Kukrit was born. It is, rather, reportage of the Inside as told to Kukrit by his female relatives. Leonowens, writing about the reign previous to King Chulalongkorn's, had the benefit of access to the *Nang Harm*, but she lacked the cultural knowledge of Kukrit, and was writing for a Western audience that had certain expectations of a 'harem' story.

In *Four reigns*, Kukrit aims to demystify the 'Inside', to present it as a city within a city, with all the everyday occurrences that could be expected and a range of characters. He aims to show the ordinary Thai what life was like for the upper classes. The women of the Grand Palace are not, for example, depicted as reclining on sumptuous cushions, eating tasty morsels and awaiting their master. Rather, Kukrit presents the *Nang Harm* as a city of individuals, each going about her business. When the protagonist, Phloi, enters the *Nang Harm* as a girl, she is amazed at its size and the different sights within it. As she walks past one building, she sees that 'In one room a couple of girls were embroidering. In another, a woman was having a nap. In the third Phloi had glimpses of some vegetable-peelers and fruit-eaters' (Kukrit 1998:20). When she sees some beautiful white marble steps, she is surprised 'at the absence of loungers' (1998:21).

The depiction of Thailand as somewhere that Western males, both heterosexual and gay, might go to indulge their fantasies of a willing supply of sexual partners, became a popular subject of writing from the 1950s, though actually the sex industry there has been big business since the 1920s. Stephen Conyers-Keynes, who lived in Bangkok before and during the First World War but didn't publish his memoirs until decades later, seems to find polygyny, in particular, rather delightful and even 'old fashioned' in the values it promotes (Conyers-Keynes 1950:87). What he means by that remark becomes clear when he comments later that women in Siam are 'content to remain women, rather than to compete with men for men's jobs' (1950:215). He describes a 'poppet' who sits on his knee as being beautiful but vacant, an 'animated doll' in whom 'West and East could hardly have been closer together, and yet never further apart' (1950:131).

His sentiment is a manifestation of the common vision of the East as existing in the past, particularly before the women's liberation movement. For example, according to Exell, Bangkok was fascinating because you 'left the present behind and entered the past' (Exell 1976:3). This imagined past is a place where men still dominate society and where the epitome of that domination in the imagination is the harem, or at least its possibility. This, in turn, was a metaphor for the West's treatment of Thailand as a whole, for the feminising of a nation, the image of the 'Thai female Other...supine, passively awaiting a visit from the mobile, penetrative West' (Pornsawan 2003:22).

Western writers habitually exaggerate the number of wives of kings from Chulalongkorn back, perhaps in order to increase the shock value of the existence of the harem, perhaps to promote the male fantasy of being able to choose from an unlimited supply of women, and, probably, because they simply don't know the truth (Loos 2006:115). As Loos says, the existence of polygyny was also used by Westerners and Western-educated Siamese to demonstrate Siam's 'backwardness' (2006:117). Loos points out the hypocrisy of Western men in Thailand who, on the one hand, criticise polygyny as morally depraved and yet, on the other hand, in many cases, practise it themselves. 'Western men indulged in concubinage, prostitution, mixed-race marriages, and even polygyny with Southeast Asian women (and men) throughout the colonies and in Siam,' she says (2006:104). Adiele (2005:100) describes an arrangement whereby Western male tourists go through a temporary 'marriage' ceremony with a Thai prostitute which lasts only the duration of their stay. The arrangement mirrors many of the marriages of 19th-century Western males with Thai women, such as British Consul Thomas (later Sir Thomas) Knox, who retired to England, leaving behind his Thai wife of several decades. It is not unique to Western men visiting Thailand, but was a common practice at the time in the British colonies, notably in India and Burma. The attitude is demonstrated in Maugham's description of his friend Masterson's alliance with a local woman in Burma, with whom he lives for five years and has children (Maugham 2001:33–7). When she suggests legal marriage, Masterson rejects the notion and she leaves him, taking the children with her. 'I treated her in every way as my wife,' he tells Maugham; yet, he says he cannot marry her because he wants to retire to England (2001:34–7). 'If I married her I'd have to stay in Burma for the rest of my life,' he adds (2001:37). His treatment of the woman is justified, in his mind, because he claims it was a relationship of convenience for her. She didn't love him, he says: '...they never do, these girls who go and live with white men' (2001:39). Sheridan Prasso (2006:45) examines the colonial disapproval of inter-racial marriage as it appeared in the stories of Maugham and others, which 'repeated the common theme of tragedy befalling the white man who let himself fall for "native" women'.

Loos (2006:117) describes in detail the political role of the *Nang Harm* and of polygyny, but points out that its continuance long after it ceased to be necessary politically shows that it existed also as a demonstration of masculinity and strength. Morgan agrees, acknowledging that the *Nang Harm* was a political tool to help Siam remain united and thus independent—'a kind of social substitute for a national infrastructure or a "Siam mapped"'—but she argues that the system is also responsible for the subjugation of Thai women today (Morgan 1996:233–4). Morgan believes today's extensive sex industry in Thailand, 'complete with child prostitution, poor families selling their daughters, and slave markets where you can buy young girls' can be traced to the 'nineteenth century customs of slavery and the harem' (Leonowens 1991:xxxix).

Reynolds (2006:186-7) concurs with the view that Thai women were traditionally considered lower in status than men, a concept he says is evident in the principles of Thai Buddhism. The subjugation of Thai women by their own culture, including Thai men's well-documented extensive use of the prostitution industry, is partly responsible for the promulgation of a burgeoning sex industry. However, the predatory Western male's propensity for 'exotic' women offering cheap sex that is readily available and not necessarily accompanied by demands from the woman for 'marriage' and/or 'equality', must be largely responsible for the growth of the business. Conjointly, there is an extensive business dealing in boys sought by Western men, many of whom lead a conventional married life at home.

Prostituting Thailand

Scot Barmé's 1920s-based study notes that, by the early 20th century, there was a well-established prostitution industry in the city (Barmé 2002:83–7). According to Warren (2000:219), Maugham in 1922 was given a card in a Bangkok street by a tout advertising the services of an erotic masseuse; Warren also claims that the forerunners of today's girlie bars and go-go clubs appeared then. Bangkok has become renowned internationally as a sex industry centre since the Vietnam War and late 20th-century tourism packages brought an increasing number of Westerners to Thailand. Warren (2000:219–20) blames Bangkok bar girls for breaking up many marriages in the 1960s between foreign university professors and their wives.

One of the earliest English language novels set in Thailand's sex industry is Jack Reynolds's *A woman of Bangkok* (1956),[119] published in the same year as the film *The King and I*. At the time it was published, the novel was critically acclaimed, to the extent that the *Asian Wall Street Journal* named it one of the '10 finest novels written about Asia' (Bishop & Robinson 1998:133). The novel focuses on the adventures of naive 27-year-old English clergyman's son, Reggie Joyce, a salesman who is posted to Bangkok. There he meets Vilai, 'the Number One Dancing Girl of Bangkok'. She is the ultimate seducer, as opposed to the cool blonde former girlfriend in England, Sheila, who rejected Reggie's sexual advances and married his brother instead. It is a literary example of what Marchetti describes as a classic plot of Hollywood screen dramas, which present 'the white woman as the innocent object of lust and token of the fragility of the West's own sense of moral purity'. These dramas also often suggest the white virgin 'may secretly desire her defilement' (Marchetti 1993:10). Instead, in *A woman of Bangkok*, it is Reggie who remains a virgin, while Sheila marries and becomes pregnant to his brother; and it is Reggie, who, desiring 'defilement', pays for it in Thailand. There, Reggie finds he can buy sex, like any commodity, while in prudish England, he admits he never thought of going to a brothel and even doubts such places exist there (Reynolds 1956:46). He employs the familiar religious allusions when referring to his sexual experiences: Thailand is 'a sort of Eden' and he 'a sort of Adam in it' (Reynolds 1956:68). Yet when he sits in a bar in Korat, he sees pictures of nude blonde women on the walls, not Thais. As Bishop and Robinson (1998:134) say, Reynolds subverts readers' expectations by 'rendering the clichéd "good" woman in England as "bad" (that is possessing a sexual subjectivity) in order to posit the clichéd "bad" prostitute in Bangkok as "good"'.

The novel becomes more than a description of the exploits of a Western man's experiences with prostitutes when the focus switches to tell the story from Vilai's point of view. Foreshadowing Dennis O'Rourke's film *The good woman of Bangkok*, Reynolds focuses on the minutiae of Vilai's existence—her beauty regime and her diet, for example. Similarly, O'Rourke focuses on the prostitute Aoi's personal routine and there is a memorable scene in which she becomes angry at being filmed in close-up eating a bowl of noodle soup. She berates O'Rourke, telling him this is not part of his film. In many ways, the picture of Aoi eating is more intimate and personal than any other scene. It establishes Aoi as a normal human being with the same basic needs for and right to sustenance as anyone else. Such scenes draw in the audience, involving them, seemingly, as closely as O'Rourke and Aoi, in what Alison Broinowski (1991:134) calls the 'voyeurism and collusion' of the film.

O'Rourke's film has been the subject of heated debate, some of it collected and edited by Chris Berry, Annette Hamilton and Laleen Jayamanne (1997), who present critical analysis, feature articles, interviews and reviews of the film. Their book is interesting not only for what it says about the film and about O'Rourke and his motives, but also for the broader attitudes it reveals towards Bangkok, Thailand and Asia. In her foreword, academic Ien Ang says the film came at a time of change in Australia, when a country that 'traditionally luxuriated in the imaginary comfort of being a white, Western nation' found itself 'gradually (but irrevocably) marginalised' in relation to Southeast Asia, which it had once seen as the 'inferior Orient' (Berry, Hamilton & Jayamanne 1997:3). Thailand is described as a colonised nation, despite not having been officially colonised. The film, the book's introduction says, 'has forced us to recognise the continuing power of the stereotypes of the White Man and his Desire, the Colonised Woman and her Need' (1997:5). This demonstrates once more that in the Western imagination, Thailand is not differentiated in terms of colonisation from countries such as India and Burma. Jeannie Martin takes the link further, saying the life of the prostitute is a metaphor for a condition where 'racism is a product of colonisation', which she says is why the film was located in Bangkok and not, for example, in Kings Cross in Sydney (Martin 1997:17). Berry describes 'the neocolonial sex trade in Thailand' and says *The good woman of Bangkok* is a variation of the stories that 'represent Australia as a western self constituting itself in relation to an Asian-Pacific other' and as the 'colonial adventurist' (Berry 1997:36). As anthropologist Marcia Langton observes in the book, Thailand has become colonised to a certain extent 'by the fact of the sex tours from Australia, America and Europe' (Langton 1997:168).

In answering his critics in the book's Afterword, O'Rourke says the role of colonialism is not a matter of white versus brown or O'Rourke versus Aoi, but of how the Thai elites have exploited the poor of the north and northeast of Thailand, using 'the most gross forms of economic and cultural colonialism' including 'the business of prostitution' (O'Rourke 1997:216), a view that Thai writer Pira Canning Sudham concurs with.[120]

Bangkok, O'Rourke (1997:216) says, has a 'fantastic, grotesque appeal' to sex tourists. Though O'Rourke's film has value in the documentation of the sex trade as a complicated product of supply and demand, and in showing how women are exploited by it, he has been criticised for its strong element of voyeurism and for becoming a perpetrator of the very exploitation he purports to abhor. At a 1996 seminar at the National Library of Australia in Canberra, entitled 'Documentary Fictions: Bibliography, Truth and Moral Lies', O'Rourke defended his actions by contrasting himself with journalists making current affairs programs about the horrors of the sex trade: 'Any notion of moral superiority on my part was demolished in the one transaction of sex for money/ money for sex,' he said, adding that although he called the film a 'documentary fiction', its truth was in its subjectivity. Meanwhile, the 'crusading film maker or journalist...stands outside the brothel and says, "Isn't this disgusting! We know who are guilty here. Now we will leave."' (O'Rourke 1996).

Many of the articles in *The filmmaker and the prostitute* (Berry, Hamilton & Jayamanne 1997) discuss the film in terms of what it says about Australia's relations with Asia. Thailand as distinct from other Southeast Asian countries is discussed most extensively by the two Thai writers included towards the end of the book.[121] Though the city's name is used in the title of O'Rourke's film, much of the discourse about it is not specifically about Bangkok, but discusses issues such as the moral responsibility of the filmmaker and the implications of the relationship between the Asian prostitute and the white customer. In discussing *The good woman of Bangkok*, Berry speaks specifically of Papua New Guinea, for example, but not of Thailand. Ultimately in this debate, Bangkok becomes, as O'Rourke says in the film, 'the mecca for western men with fantasies of exotic sex and love without pain'. John Powers (1997:103) reiterates that it is Pico Iyer's '"love in a duty-free zone"—sex sparked with the mystery and exoticism of the East, love free from risk, pain or change'. As 'Voice 2', one of a group of Asian women on an ABC radio discussion of the film comments, 'When Australian men see this they are going to see Thai women, Filipino women, Malaysian women as all the same and anyone who is sort of dark, brown, slanty eyed and female' (Martin et al 1997).[122]

Although the earlier novel *A woman of Bangkok* appears to foreshadow the film, O'Rourke says the inspiration for the work and its title was Brecht's *The good woman of Szechuan* (1940) (O'Rourke 1996). While the academic criticism in *The filmmaker and the prostitute* tends to negate Thailand as a separate entity, some of the journalism uses it as a setting in which to contextualise O'Rourke and, obviously, to further titillate readers. Powers (1997:104) says when he met Aoi, the 'star' of the film, he 'looked her over discreetly; she did the same to me'. There is a sense of the camera still being present. Powers becomes a customer himself at O'Rourke's insistence, but is at pains to point out that he doesn't 'sleep with' the prostitute whose time he buys. He is aware of the implications of his voyeuristic position—'I was there to watch...eyeing the naked women and enjoying whatever small taste of corruption enticed me' (1997:108). Powers's story mirrors many others by men who have spent their time in Bangkok lurching from one girlie bar to another as it fulfils its role as a capital of fantasy, debauchery and disease, 'a city shuddering under a murderous plague' (1997:112).

Annette Hamilton (1997) discusses the film in relation to how Thai critics and audiences respond to it. Her comparison of reactions to the authenticity of Aoi between Thais and non-Thai-speaking viewers has broader implications for foreign perceptions of Thailand: while Thais picked up through markers in Aoi's speech that what she was saying was 'untrue', Hamilton (1997:59) says, 'to many Western viewers, it was "the truth", because it was what they expected to hear'. The reviews of the film, too, fall back on stereotypical images of Bangkok. It is a 'sex-for-sale city', says Rick Groen (1997), and, according to MA Deviah (1997), 'the film shows it like it really is; sleazy and seedy, capable of titillating only the most perverse'. Aoi is portrayed by Michael Wilmington (1997) as wandering through the streets among 'the seamy neons of the red-light district, the gaudy tourist hotels, the steamy bustle of the outdoor eateries'.

The descriptions of Thai bar girls by Western writers are examples of what Said describes as the 'exclusively male province' of Orientalism, as found particularly in travel writing and novels, in which 'women are usually the creatures of a male power fantasy. They express unlimited sensuality, they are more or less stupid, and above all they are willing' (Said 2003:207). Many writers since Reynolds have used the eroticised location of Thailand, particularly Bangkok, in fictional tales of the sex industry. They form such a significant percentage of English novels about Thailand today that, despite the sex industry being a relatively small part of the life of the city as a whole (and mostly confined to certain areas), Thailand has become synonymous with sex tourism. Bangkok and other Thai cities such as Pattaya are depicted as 'hotbeds' of illicit sex where any perversion can be bought. Bangkok is seen as a seedy destination that 'real travellers' use only to pass through on their way to 'paradise'—'unspoilt' coastal locations such as that depicted in *The beach*, misty mountains with hilltribes, or pristine resorts in which interaction with Thais except as servants is minimal.

The picture of Thailand as a sex tourism centre has become part of the body of the Western world's information about the East that 'everyone knows'. It is used as a referential prop in popular Western culture. For example, in Mike Mitchell's 1999 film, *Deuce bigalow: male gigolo*, Rob Schneider's character discovers his father met his mother at a Bangkok strip club. His father says she 'could see something beyond the 200 baht' he was paying her and they were married two days later.

Some Thais believe that the way Thailand has been constructed in the Western imagination has led to its depiction as a destination for Westerners to indulge in what they would not dare to do at home. An article in the *Bangkok Post* about a 2006 Thai cultural festival in Paris quoted a Thai spectator as saying, 'The stereotype of Thailand in French media…was now one of only prostitutes and drugs' (Onnucha 2006). Young Thai writer Rattawut Lapcharoensap (Rattawut 2005) documents the belief among tourism industry workers in Thailand in his story 'Farangs': 'Ma says, "Pussy and elephants. That's all these people want"'. Ma continues, telling her son that despite the range of historical and cultural sightseeing available, foreigners really want only 'to ride some hulking gray beast like a bunch of wildmen and to pant over girls and to lie there half-dead getting skin cancer on the beach during the time in between' (2005:2).

Pira Canning Sudham was one of the first Thais to write in English about sex tourism and the women who work within it, in his 1983 short story 'Siamese Drama'. It is the tale of Salee, a rural girl tricked into prostitution in Bangkok, her older friend Nipa, and the various ways they make a living from selling sex, first by setting up Salee as the minor wife of a Thai man and later more profitably as the girlfriend of a German man when he is in Pattaya for a month's holiday. The German promises to come back and marry Salee, but when he does not, she refuses to go back to prostitution and returns to her village. She cannot, however, escape Nipa, who arrives in the village to procure teenaged girls to sell in Krung Thep (Bangkok). Ultimately, Salee murders Nipa and pretends they were set upon by bandits (Pira 1991:29–49).

The women sex workers in 'Siamese Drama', are not painted as victims of male abuse. Indeed, the abusers in the story are the affluent-looking women who trick parents into allowing them to take naive young women to the city. Pira presents Western men as pathetic, unattractive characters who are gullible and easily fleeced of money in return for sexual favours. They are all rich in the character Nipa's eyes and each one is an opportunity for a young, pretty woman to make money. Yet Pira (1991:37) shows that it is the Thais who have paid the highest price for allowing their country to become a centre for sex tourism: the consequence is that it is being 'taken over' by these pathetic Westerners: 'The mighty mark-carrying Germans had colonized the town', he says of Pattaya. Pira (1991:37) depicts Pattaya as a seedy place full of vice, where 'women stalked their prey; men and pimps worked stealthily among drug peddlers and transvestites'. There is salvation, however, in the form of traditional Thai villages in rural areas, and through access to good education that fosters independent thought. However, salvation is only possible if they can free themselves from the 'Masters'—not white visitors, but corrupt Thai officials, politicians, and business people.

There are hundreds of novels, guides and picture books in English about the Thai sex trade, most of them published in Thailand and sold there in English language bookshops. Most collections of short stories about Thailand contain at least one set among the bars and bar girls of red-light districts, Patpong, Soi Nana or Soi Cowboy. James Eckardt's *Bangkok people* (1999), for example, includes a matter-of-fact slice-of-life story, 'A night in the life: the bargirls', set in a Soi

Cowboy bar and told from an observer's point of view (Eckardt 1999:41–49). Eckardt's view does not seem lascivious or even particularly personal—it could be any bar, any night; ultimately the story is about his inability to find out anything from the *mamasan* about what really goes on there. Soi Cowboy is an 'unfulfilled promise and a hint of mystery' (1999:49).

Seedy underbelly: neon lights advertise bars that pander to tourists' stereotypes of Thai women at Bangkok red-light street Soi Cowboy. Credit: Greg Elms/Lonely Planet Images.

Long-time American expatriate Jerry Hopkins (2005:13) says Bangkok does live up to its reputation as 'the wild, wild east' because it is 'one of the great, unruly and untamed cities in the world'. Hopkins employs the language of colonialism in order to somehow explain the Bangkok indulgences of Western expatriates, whom he describes as 'explorers' and 'adventurers'. Even the title of his book, *Bangkok Babylon*, aligns the city yet again with the ancient, phantasmagoric Middle East of *The Arabian nights*. His approach does not seem to include integrating with Thai society. As Hopkins (2005:13) says, he moved to Thailand 'because it had the most interesting expatriate community

I'd encountered anywhere in the world'. In addition, every fantasy, Hopkins says, is both cheap and available. Sex, like drugs, is just another commodity in 'Southeast Asia's prime marketplace': 'It's not surprising that such an environment has appeal for some of what society deems the best and the worst. Missionaries and NGOs come to fix the "problem". Others come to roll around in it' (Hopkins 2005:13).

Lawyer/lecturer-turned-novelist Andrew Hicks's 2004 novel *Thai Girl* is the result of his observations of 'the interaction of Thais and foreign visitors' during his extensive travels in Thailand 'with backpack and notebook' (Hicks 2004a:5).[123] The cover of the 2004 edition depicts the familiar images of a long-haired young woman with a flower in her hair, against a background of deserted beach and palm trees, while the 2006 edition, produced for the wider international market, is even more provocative, featuring a faceless woman posing with her hands behind her head in front of a supine man on a beach. Hicks says the stereotypical image is a ploy to 'induce some of the more thoughtless tourists' to read the book, which he says he hopes will expose the predicament of poor Isaan girls forced to work in the sex industry: 'So many visitors treat Thailand as an adventure playground and the women as a free for all and I hope the book makes them stop and think,' Hicks says on his website (Hicks 2004b).

In *Thai girl*, Hicks says he aimed to write not just 'another trashy Bangkok bar story' or about 'the older hoodlums of the typical sex novel' (Hicks 2004c). The book is, he says, an answer to these types of books, one that is set particularly in Thailand, not in the generic 'paradise' of texts such as *The beach*. He asks his readers a question:

> There are loads of rubbishy novels based around sad old farang grease-balls, mafia types and gangsters celebrating how easy it is to get laid in the sleazy back ends of Bangkok. Do we really need another of this genre and is this what *Thai girl* is all about? (Hicks 2004c)

Of course, the answer is 'no'. Yet *Thai girl* begins in a seedy Bangkok go-go bar of the sort so familiar to consumers of late 20th-century and early 21st-century films and novels. Ben and Emma are young English backpackers who are enticed into a bar and overcharged for drinks (Hicks 2004a:9). By the second page, however, the novel has stepped away from the formula, to examine the way stereotypical views of Thailand have developed. Emma has a rude awakening when she realises her 'preconceptions of Old Siam, of Anna and the King in soft focus, jumbled up with images of temples and mountains, tropical beaches, buffalo carts and rice farmers in conical hats' are incongruous with the reality of Bangkok (2004a:10). Emma can be identified with Behdad's delineation of a tourist as one who does not seek new knowledge by visiting a destination but 'desires to identify the already defined signs of exoticism as exotic' (Behdad

1994:49). Emma also fits Gerster's observation that some travellers are 'more influenced by what they have read about places—especially that place called Asia—than by the places themselves' (Gerster 1995:22). Said, too, acknowledges the importance of literature in the imagination of the traveller, saying that when a book about a location 'acquires a greater authority, and use, even than the actuality it describes', the result is disappointment for the traveller who does not receive what he or she expects (Said 2003:93).

Initially, *Thai girl* appears to have similarities with *The beach*. Hicks seems to perpetuate the stereotype of Western tourists when he bases Ben and Emma in Khao San Road and sends them to go-go bars. Then Ben, 'desperate for a beach', and Emma link up with two others to travel to Koh Samet in the hope that it is the 'the long-promised tropical idyll' of 'amazing Thailand' (Hicks 2004a:26,47). It turns out to be 'a perfect stretch of sand' and, at this point, Hicks parodically invokes *The beach*:

'So this is Thailand at last. The beach!' said Ben in raptures.

'No man, not *the* beach. This one's handy for Bangkok but it's a bit crowded. Almost but not quite paradise,' said Maca.

'Looks like paradise to me,' said Emma, taking in the sweep of the bay, the crystal clear water and the unbroken green of the jungle (Hicks 2004a:26,47).

The irony continues as Ben is described actually reading *The beach* while sitting on 'the beach', hoping to learn from it something about Thailand: 'But it told him nothing' (Hicks 2004a:26,83).

Hicks does not ignore the dichotomies implicit in tourism, such as the potential environmental damage and the impinging on the host country's culture. Though the text is sometimes self-consciously deliberate in its attempt to depict typical young *farang* tourists, it goes some way toward forging a new type of Western fiction. It achieves this by using all the stereotypical staples to show that, although girlie bars, sex shows and cheap prostitutes are indeed available in Thailand, there is much more to find out; Australian character Maca notes, however, employing a typically colonial concept, that the culture is 'difficult to penetrate' (Hicks 2004a:26,83). Hicks has made a valiant attempt at presenting a less stereotyped Western-boy-meets-Thai-girl story, but *Thai girl* also fits what Holland and Huggan (2003:2) identify as a travel story that contributes to 'a new *exotic*', showing that the world remains 'heterogeneous, unfathomable, bewildering'. The novel can be used to examine an assertion made by postcolonial critic Brian Musgrove (1999:33) that travel is about power that is 'supposedly always purchased at the expense of those imagined others who constitute the zone called "elsewhere"'. Ben professes to search for knowledge of Thai culture but he finds himself, guided by the beguiling beach masseuse,

Fon, in yet another traveller's idyll as 'One beach followed another, one lotus eaters' paradise improved upon by the next' (Hicks 2004a:122). When he travels out of his comfort zone with Fon and her sister Jinda to their home village in Isaan, he observes the realities of poverty. Yet Ben is still thinking of his visit purely in terms of his response to it as a traveller and of how it measures up to what he expects, rather than of its realities:

> Though the roads were straight and well-paved, this was the real, rural Thailand that Ben had longed to see. He had left behind the artificial worlds of Bangkok and backpacking and ahead of him lay new and authentic experiences of Thailand (Hicks 2004a:186).

The villagers who meet Ben understandably 'dream of marrying out of rural poverty', but Ben dreams of his air-conditioned hotel room in Bangkok, and continues to see the rural life of his fantasies: 'A life on the land free of urban pressures and surrounded by family and friends strongly appealed to his romantic side' (Hicks 2004a:194).

Ultimately, like many travellers before him, Ben finds the thought of taking Fon back to England impossible. When he returns home alone, the visited country quickly becomes a fantasy once more. As he lands at Heathrow, Thailand seems 'somehow irrelevant, already a distant memory' (Hicks 2004a:294). Similarly, Reggie in *A woman of Bangkok* does not end up with the girl, instead flying home, 'rumbling up into the utter blackness between the invisible earth and the pin-point stars' (Reynolds 1956:347).

There is a sub-genre of books that cash in on the Western male's fascination with the sex industry in Bangkok. They include Dean Barrett's 2001 offering *Thailand: land of beautiful women* (2004), a collection of photographs of women in Thailand, from hilltribe women in their native costumes to historical pictures and artwork, to near-naked go-go dancers. He presents the Thai woman in the familiar role of 'Two in one'—that is, being both innocent child-woman and seductive temptress. The 'two in one' ideal is also examined by Reynolds who describes Vilai's changes to her appearance during the day as she prepares for work that night. Vilai is presented as more 'real' than other prostitutes, however, because she makes up fully only at night, preferring during the day 'to give seduction a miss' (Reynolds 1956:126). Nevertheless, Vilai—or the White Leopard, as she is known professionally—is adept at creating an image that foreign men want: 'Every day, at last, sometimes after hours of labour, she would turn out another work of art' (Reynolds 1956:110–111). Similarly, O'Rourke's film shows Aoi in her dual roles of prostitute and simple country girl.[124]

The mass of popular fiction set in the Bangkok red-light districts and featuring white males making use of Thailand's reputation for providing willing women includes the short story collection *Chairs* (Moore 2000), the 'erotic thriller' *Sleepless in Bangkok* (Quartermaine 2005) and *Skytrain to murder* (Barrett 2003). *Bangkok knights* (Piprell 2001) shows clearly what Pornsawan Tripasai identifies as the three stereotypes of Thai women in Western literature: 'the temptress Eve, the nurturing native, and the *femme fatale*' (Pornsawan 2003:41). The quest for romance is enacted by men as if they are part of the Western tradition of the heroic explorer. The protagonist, Trevor Perry, works as an expatriate in Kuwait yet comes to Thailand to find a wife because, as Pornsawan (2003:44) comments, 'the notoriety of Thailand draws him there. It could furnish him with a desirable product, an amenable native woman'. Books such as these are hard to find outside Thailand, but they are on the shelves of the many English-language bookshops in Bangkok and other tourist destinations and are frequently bought by Westerners on holiday as 'beach reading'.

The typical elements of these books—foreign men becoming involved with Thai women, danger in an exotic location, the perfect beach with white sand and palm trees and so on—are similar to those found in travel writing about Thailand. So the 'beach reading' reinforces what the travel guides have told them before their arrival. Media exposés of children being sold into prostitution, of poor northeastern women being forced to sell sex and so on, combined with the rhetoric of Tourism Authority of Thailand brochures presenting Thai women as smiling, charming and available, serve to increase the perception of Thailand as the holiday destination of choice for sex tourists, according to Morgan (1996:222). She maintains that prostitution has contributed significantly to the tourism industry's expansion in Thailand and that the numbers of American and European men travelling there have increased because they are 'ideologically conditioned by tourist ads themselves to read Thailand as a safe and satisfying outlet for repressed sexual desires' (Morgan 1996:226). The complicity of Thailand in advertising itself as a sex centre is widespread in mainstream publications: for example, the *Bangkok Post* website (www.bangkokpost.net) often carries an advertisement for foreign men wanting to meet Thai women. Pornsawan (2003:55) says Thailand perceives its role of host as 'to make Western visitors feel at home ... In its encounters with the West, neo-Thailand submits itself to the authoritative West and then is transformed into the object of the West's desire'. Such is one of the insidious by-products of colonial hegemony, of either the discursive, cultural, economic or political times—the tendency of the 'colonised' to start looking or behaving in accord with the stereotype. As Salman Rushdie remarks in *The satanic verses* (1988:168), 'They have the power of description, and we succumb to the pictures they construct'.

As demonstrated by works such as O'Rourke's film, there is a thin line between observation, social comment and voyeurism in any work that focuses on the sex trade. In *Patpong Road untold story* (Adul 2005), Thai lawyer Adul Tinaphong, who has an office near the infamous red-light area, has written a broad-ranging book on life and business along Patpong Road. He includes owners, bar and restaurant staff, as well as sex trade workers. Although the book is rather amateurish and is designed and advertised partly to appeal to would-be sex tourists, it cannot be dismissed. Adul has been interested in the street since he was a boy, when he was taken there often, late at night, by his father, Montri Tinaphong. While Montri, who appears in military uniform in a picture in the preface, went about whatever business he had there, the young Adul was watched over by his father's bodyguards (Adul 2005:preface A). It is a strange book, combining biography with titillating information about bars, prostitutes and sex shows, plus interesting legal information. The book is not scholarly—by choice, Adul says, so everyone can understand it—but it is interesting in that most of the information is based on Adul's observations, his interviews with workers and customers and anecdotes they told him. The result is a hotch-potch of stories linked by Adul's opinionated commentary; it conveys perfectly the steamy, seedy, confusing atmosphere of Patpong Road. While all the stereotypes are there—the women forced into prostitution to support their families, the prostitutes who constantly cheat gullible *farangs*—Adul also does his best to debunk them. For example, he tells several tales of successful marriages between *farangs* and bar girls:

> I once introduced a bar girls [sic] to a foreign friend of mine who first came to Patpong Road. Several years later, they fell in love with each other and married. Another seven to eight years passed by, I met this couple again with their three children…Now this guy is the President of a corporation in Europe and his Thai wife is the vice-president in the same corporation. She fluently speaks three languages (Adul 2005:176).

Irish musician and activist Bob Geldof is among international celebrities who have written about Patpong. *Worst journeys* (Fraser 1993) includes a sharply observed excerpt about the Bangkok sex industry from Geldof's autobiography (Geldof 1986). Geldof uses the lure of voyeurism to point out some distasteful realities that he believes sex tourists ought to be aware of. The night starts pleasantly, if disconcertingly, when Geldof enters a bar in Patpong for a drink and finds bar girls dancing to one of his songs (Geldof 1993:144). To Geldof, they are 'beautiful creatures, blank-eyed and indifferent' (1993:145). As Geldof's own voyeurism becomes more demanding, the scene to him is like a movie and he wants to see 'all these things I'd read about in *these places*' (1993:145, italics added).

While Geldof starts the piece with a specific description of Bangkok, the city becomes generic, vaguely anywhere in Southeast Asia, as he aligns it with the 1978 film *The deer hunter* (Geldof 1993:144,145).[125] Geldof's awful final scene depicting skeletal drug-dependent prostitutes simulating sexual acts, the antithesis of an erotic sex show, brings him to his senses. He leaves, knowing he has orchestrated the performance to a certain extent, seemingly to satisfy a morbid curiosity. Yet the experience does not appear to teach him anything: 'I think we'd have found those Deerhunter scenes if we'd wanted. Who needs it?' (1993:146). In other words, what you do not choose to see does not exist, except as something fictional, such as a film. It seems an extraordinary comment from Geldof, who is renowned for his humanitarianism. It is, however, a brutally honest depiction of the tourist's path: consume, retain only what you choose, leave the rest behind, and after the holiday, go home to the 'real' world.

Pico Iyer's chapter about Thailand in *Video night in Kathmandu* centres on Bangkok and his reaction to the sex industry (Iyer 2001:307–36). Everything is available, he finds, in 'big bad Bangkok' (2001:310). He meets a 21-year-old Canadian who has lived in Bangkok three months and who has a Thai prostitute 'girlfriend'. He tells him the best introduction to Bangkok is 'a pilgrimage to the heart of the Patpong Road' which has 'nothing in mind but the bodily pleasures of foreigners' (2001:312–3). Like Geldof, Iyer (2001:313) imagines himself in a film about Saigon during the Vietnam War. Iyer, 15 years on, criticises his early writing about Bangkok for its lack of breadth; he can be forgiven, he says (Iyer 2003), because, as a male in his 20s, his 'reflection seldom left the bars'. He was on his first trip to Southeast Asia, spoke no Thai and 'could not begin to know anything more than the hotel workers, tuk-tuk drivers and bar girls who clustered round me'. He is intimating, therefore, that Thailand is partly responsible for his two-dimensional view of the country because that is the way he says it presented itself.

Since the 1970s, most guidebooks have contained some reference to the sex industry and/or its euphemistic stand-ins (go-go bars, massage parlours, coffee shops). The 1970s *AOA Bangkok Guidebook* praises the nightlife, which it says offers 'an exciting variety of opportunities for entertainment, enjoyment—yes, even adventure' (*AOA Bangkok Guidebook* c1975:12).[126] It is coy about what is on offer at massage parlours but manages to convey its message anyway: 'What really goes on in those places? Only you and your masseuse will ever know' (*AOA Bangkok Guidebook* c1975:114). While it acknowledges concerns about how workers are procured for the sex industry, it repeats the familiar line that the workers are paid well and reiterates the urban myth of the successful bar girl who drives to work in a BMW limousine (c1975:114).[127]

Poole's 1970 guide *Bangkok!* devotes one of its five chapters to nightlife, also adopting a tongue-in-cheek attitude and noting, for example, that negotiations after bar closing times 'involve more than a dance' (Poole 1970:42–6). While proclaiming that 'The night life itself no longer involves opium dens and child brothels', he later has a warning about bar girls: 'They range from demure, child-like creatures to spectacular ladies of the night. Behind make-up and décolleté it is hard at first sight to tell the difference' (1970:46).

Three decades later, the prim *National Geographic Traveler Thailand* does not elaborate on the sex industry, though it acknowledges its existence, remarking that 'few doubt that many men come to Thailand for the purpose of having sex with Thai women' (Macdonald & Parkes 2001:340). Meanwhile, Parkes's other guide, Moon Travel's *Bangkok handbook*, expects a large number of its readers to be interested in sex tourism, as there is a comprehensive guide to the scene (Parkes 2000:175–80). The nightlife in Bangkok, the guide (Parkes 2000:175) says, is 'perhaps the most notorious in the world' and adds that 'the range of sexual services is simply amazing'. It claims the sex industry 'all begins' at Bangkok Airport, where, its says ludicrously, 'male visitors are sometimes propositioned by transvestites who boldly drag their unsuspecting prey into terminal bathrooms'!

Parkes's chapter on entertainment bundles the sex industry with cultural performances, nightclubs and bars outside the sex industry and shopping, making sex just another tourism commodity. Like many other guide writers, Parkes also, however, feels the need to give what Bishop and Robinson (1998:86) call 'a bit of potted sociology'. He discusses proposals to legalise prostitution in order to decrease the spread of AIDS and asserts that the sex industry was not a result of American soldiers on rest and recreation from Vietnam but is part of Thai culture. The Patpong shopping market, he says, is 'obnoxious', but go-go bars welcome everyone, 'even families', to have a look inside (Parkes 2000:176).[128] However, in a section about live sex shows he warns tourists that 'Very few visitors enjoy these shows' (2000:177). So, presumably, he is saying it is the Thais themselves who perpetuate the industry—yet these shows are performed in areas such as Patpong for an audience made up almost exclusively of tourists, who are not necessarily all Western.

The most recent guidebooks are a mixture of those that steadfastly avoid all mention of the sex industry, such as *Globetrotter Travel Guide Thailand* (Hoskin 2006) and those that treat it as a necessary evil or just another tourism possibility. In *Lonely Planet Bangkok encounter* (Williams 2007), China Williams also attributes the sex industry to Thais themselves. Most prostitutes cater to Thais rather than to foreigners and the industry was well established by the time American GIs got to Bangkok—they merely took advantage of what was already there, she says; like Parkes, she does not source her information

(Williams 2007:167). *The Rough guide to Bangkok* says that while 'the gaudy neon fleshpots of Patpong give a misleading impression of an activity that is deeply rooted in Thai culture—the overwhelming majority of Thailand's prostitutes of both sexes...work with Thai men, not farangs' (Gray & Ridout 2007:124). *Rough guide* also links polygamy with the Thai sex trade and treats the *farang* sex industry as a separate entity that grew from R&R trips for US GIs during the 1960s. Many recent guides also look at the gay sex industry scene, which *Rough guide* says 'bears a dispiriting resemblance to the straight sex trade' (Gray & Ridout 2007:200). *Bangkok inside out* has a chapter on the red-light street Patpong, but says it includes the area 'with great hesitation'—not because of a moral stance, but because it's simply not very interesting, being 'hardly the "Must See" attraction of guidebook hype, and is in any case covered ad nauseam by nearly every piece of literature on the city' (Ziv & Sharett 2005:107). It ridicules tourists to the area, particularly the busloads of 'fat retired European women' who visit with the idea that 'they think they are about to see or do something very, very naughty' (2005:107).

Lonely Planet Thailand in 2007 takes a more tongue-in-cheek approach to describing the Bangkok sex industry than its previous editions. Bangkok is indeed 'happy-hooker land', it says (Williams et al 2007b:171). It lists the most 'palatable' website guide to Bangkok's 'sexy underbelly', while propagating a stereotype of bar girls who have become attached to their customers:

> For a fly-on-the-wall perspective, stop in at the nearby Internet cafes to see groups of bar girls writing love-letter emails to their new sugar daddies; the well-worn piece of paper in front of them is something of a 'master' copy (Williams et al 2007b:171).

Some of these love letters are the subject of the aforementioned *"Hello my big big honey!"* (Walker & Ehrlich 1995) which examines the bar scene in Bangkok and gives an insight into much of the interaction between Thais and foreigners and into the way the boundaries between romance, love and sex for hire intersect (1995:12). As with much of the literature about the bar scene, *"Hello my big big honey!"* can be read on one level as a study of this interaction; on another, of course, it can be read as a literary peep-show. Walker and Ehrlich write separate introductions, both of which warn Western men of the consequences of being seduced by Thai bar girls. The girls 'touch aspects of the Madame Butterfly syndrome', Ehrlich remarks somewhat absurdly, and 'A tropical girl speaking some kind of a beautiful, ancient bamboo language can quite easily hypnotize an innocent Western man abroad for the first time' (1995:12). Walker is more straightforward, saying it's easy to see how a Westerner could fall in love with a bar girl: 'They can be gentle, fun-loving, uncomplicated, slim and sultry. But they can also be cunning, ruthless and manipulative' (1995:6). Thai academic Yos

Santasombat, however, blames the men's inability to see beyond the dictates of Western culture for their naivety and their usually misguided attempts to 'rescue her from this hell hole and give her a chance to recover her own dignity, in a Western concept' (Walker & Ehrlich 1995:17).

While *"Hello my big big honey!"* does not debate the social implications of the sex trade, there are several books that do, including *Patpong sisters* (Odzer 1997) and *Night market* (Bishop & Robinson 1998). In attempting to correct the stereotype of the sexually available (for a price) Thai woman, Robert and Nanthapa Cooper point out that, if estimates are correct and between 1% and 5% of Thai women are prostitutes, at least 95% are not (Cooper & Cooper 2005:134). Other works, such as the Thai-Western relationship guide *Good medicine for Thailand fever* (Pirazzi & Vasant 2004:110) say the percentage of prostitutes is lower.[129] However, most visitors, the Coopers add, receive the wrong impression of Thai women because prostitutes 'naturally gravitate around the male visitor's world—where the money is' (Cooper & Cooper 2005:134). If readers of novels over the last 50 years from *A woman of Bangkok* to *Bangkok 8* are influenced to believe they present a true picture of Thailand, it is easy to see why the capital is viewed as a city full of sex for sale and not much else, apart from the vices that go with it. As John Urry notes, 'The male look through a kind of "porno-tropics" is endlessly voyeuristic' (Urry 2002:151).

In virtually every piece of writing about Thailand's sex industry, whether 'literary' or not, lasciviousness and voyeurism combine to titillate the reader. One of the most compelling examples is Michel Houellebecq's controversial novel *Platform* (2002). This disturbing, uncompromising story about Westerners who sell and buy sex-tour package holidays, parodies and exploits much of the gratuitous and pornographic material about the sex industry. The novel centres on the story of Ministry of Culture civil servant Michel, who uses part of his inheritance from his murdered father to join a package tour to Thailand and take advantage of its sex industry. On his return, he links up with travel agent Valerie, whom he met on the tour, and helps her and her boss to set up a more profitable enterprise, catering to sex tourists. *Platform* is part of what Gerster describes as the 'revisionary impulse' in writing that satirises male fantasies of Asia (Gerster 1995:358).[130] Michel believes tourism is essentially a self-centered act, whether it be sex tourism or the pursuit of 'historical' sites such as the Death Railway at Kanchanaburi. It amounts to the same result: a penetration by the tourist, whether of prostitutes, land or culture. The tourist observes from a safe distance: Michel views the jungle from his hotel room vantage point, from which he contemplates the dangers that might lurk therein (Houellebecq 2002:66–7). Later in the book, Houellebecq's characters face the ugliness of real danger, as opposed to the manufactured tourist industry kind, when a bomb blast in a

Krabi girlie bar frequented by Westerners kills Michel's girlfriend (2002:331–3). The scene is eerily, yet unwittingly, similar to the Sari Club bombings in Bali in 2002, the year *Platform* was released in English. Instead of being full of happy tourists accompanied by Thai women, the bar is now full of the dead, the injured, and 'the genuine screams of the damned' (2002:332). Much of the language Houellebecq uses, too, is like that of the reporting of the 2004 tsunami. In the book, the terrorist bombing is used by the international media to provide a platform from which to lecture about the ills of sex tourism. One article is accompanied by a photograph 'taken from the German advertising campaign', an example of the 'paradise lost' approach (2002:340). Another article, headlined 'The return of slavery', uses the event to rail against the humiliation suffered by women forced to work as prostitutes (2002:341). Although it professes to care about these women, it mentions only the deaths of the tourists: 'what do the deaths of a few of the well-healed matter', it says, forgetting that beside the tourists were the Thai prostitutes (2002:341).

The hypocrisy of would-be moral do-gooders is exposed throughout *Platform*. Earlier in the book, a member of a sightseeing tourist group, Josiane, screams in righteous indignation: 'It's sexual slavery!…There's no other way to describe it' (Houellebecq 2002:72). Yet Josiane, too, is guilty of using Thailand for her own gratification, viewing and surveying its sights, even deliberately smashing a plate at a restaurant during her outburst and walking out without offering to pay for it. Houellebecq's point is that all tourism, no matter what form, is the same. Josiane refuses to go to a Thai dinner and show because 'It's all a bit touristy'—yet, as Michel thinks to himself, 'What did she mean by that? Everything is touristy' (2002:48).

Houellebecq presents Thailand as a sexual smorgasbord for European tourists. As another member of Michel's group, Robert, says, 'In Thailand… everyone can have what they desire, and everyone can have something good' (Houllebecq 2002:74). Verbal protests such as Josiane's are about as useful a deterrent as the rails against sex tourism in Michel's 'strange publication' called *The white book*, which is, in fact, a travel guide for sex tourists including paedophiles (2002:78–9). Houellebecq intersperses comments about the sex industry with passages about the history of Thailand, much as a travel guide does, so that the sex industry becomes just another sight for tourists to tick off: the bridge over the River Kwai at Kanchanaburi, temple ruins at Ayutthaya, a sex show at Pattaya or Patpong.

Dangerous Thailand

Hand in hand with 'lascivious sensuality', the idea that the land of the 'Other' is 'characterised by inherent violence' is an important theme in Western constructions of Asia, according to Kabbani (1994:5–6). Thailand is commonly portrayed in literature and on film as a potentially dangerous location where inexplicable things can happen. However, it is this very sense of romanticised 'danger', the sense of 'what if…' that attracts many visitors to Thailand. As Adiele asserts:

> LET'S BE HONEST! Danger was partly what drew me to Thailand. I watched myself pass through the countryside, traversing towns owned by bandit kings, climbing up to drug lords' lairs, jumping off trains in the middle of the night, and felt powerful (Adiele 2005:96).

Her sentiments are echoed in the novel *Thai die* by Australian comedian Greg Fleet. The novel is purportedly the true story of events that occurred when Fleet was travelling in Thailand in 1989. He chose Thailand for a holiday because it fitted his criteria: 'it had to be somewhere cheap and it had to be somewhere exotic' (Fleet 2002:9). The ensuing tale of himself as gullible tourist who is kidnapped by gangsters, escapes and joins Burmese rebels in the jungle is, to a large extent, a parody of the travel memoir, complete with photographs, even if some or most of what he says really did occur. The book's existence is testament to the common belief that there is real danger in travelling in Thailand. It also accounts for the interest in books written by *farangs* who have been imprisoned in Thailand, such as *Forget you had a daughter* (Gregory & Tierney 2003) and *The damage done* (Fellows 1997). The back cover of Fellows's book entices readers with its description of life in the legendary 'Bangkok Hilton', which has become locational shorthand for the horrors of incarceration in a foreign jail: 'A place where sewer rats and cockroaches are the only nutritious food, where autocratic prison guards giggle as they deliver pulverising blows and where the worst punishment by far is the *khun deo*—solitary confinement, Thai style'.

The nightmare of ending up in jail in Thailand is reinforced on screen, notably in the Australian 1989 mini-series directed by Ken Cameron, *Bangkok Hilton*, in which Thailand conveniently provides the 'hell hole' in which a young, pretty white woman is locked up for a crime she did not commit. [131] A later example is the US film *Brokedown palace* directed in by Jonathan Kaplan in 1999, about two young women who are tricked by a drug dealer and imprisoned in Thailand.

Bridget Jones: the edge of reason[132] plays on every traveller's nightmare of being set up as a drug 'mule' and thrown into a prison among the 'natives': 'Am in stinking Third-World cell with eight Thai prostitutes and a potty in the corner', Bridget says (Fielding 2004:303). This storyline has echoes of the familiar 'white slavery' scenario, the 'captivity narrative' described by Marchetti (1993:46) that instills the fear that the innocent white traveller could be captured and held in a foreign culture against her will. Stories of Westerners imprisoned in Thailand all promote the belief that justice will not be served outside the West, and then only if it is based on Western ideals, that life in Asia is 'cheap', that the punishment meted out will far outweigh the crime for which it is designed.

In David Foster's *Plumbum* (1983), an Australian rock band is hired to play a season in Bangkok, but the venue turns out to be a brothel catering to Japanese. The fear of white slavery surfaces several times and band member Pete recalls a friend who was enslaved in Manila for six months (Foster 1983:177). This comment shows how, in Westerners' minds, Bangkok is interchangeable with any other city in Asia. Band member Sharon wonders why 'they can't put more of those pistol-packing teenage cops that infest all Third World cities on to some form of traffic control' (1983:176).

The captivity narrative is carried further in Carey Furze's novel *Held* (2003), in which not only is the protagonist, Kelly, kidnapped and imprisoned during a holiday in Thailand, but she is subjected to sexual abuse along with a group of other women. The novel, the cover says, is 'based on a true story' about four *farang* tourists 'who are abducted into sex slave prostitution in Asia' and 'based on an experience she [the author] encountered, while travelling through Thailand in 1989'. The 'Author's Note' at the back of *Held* vaguely describes the 1980s as a dangerous time in Thailand when travellers 'started disappearing without a trace' (Furze 2003:281–2). Worryingly, Furze does not source her information and does not give statistics of how many people disappeared; nor does she explain how she was involved.

One of the better stories about foreigners facing danger in Bangkok is a children's book written in the 1960s by Swedish author László Hámori and translated to English in 1966, entitled, rather unimaginatively, *Adventure in Bangkok*. It is the story of a 14-year-old boy, Jan, who joins his parents in Bangkok, where his father works as an airline adviser. Jan meets an engineer drilling artesian wells for the World Health Organisation and befriends an impoverished Thai boy, Snit. When the engineer disappears, a mystery ensues, including a search through Bangkok and a train journey to Chiang Mai. The novel can be read simply as a children's story or in a more complex way as a comment on the provision of Western aid to Asia and the consequences of corruption. It also contains an interesting portrayal of Bangkok—not as a tourist destination but as a place of work and business—and, in Snit, a memorable Thai character.

Hámori presents both the Thai and *farang* point of view. In a northern village, the headman says of the foreigners:

> 'Certainly, we have seen other *farangs* here before,' the headman explained to Snit and the driver, 'but none of them has ever had such strange light eyes. Never could I have imagined that there were people this peculiar' (Hámori 1966:155).

Thailand's reputation as a risky location is perpetuated by travel writers. As Paul Theroux (1977:239) says, while Calcutta 'smells of death' and 'Bombay of money', Bangkok 'smells of sex' as well as of death and money. The media cash in on this reputation of Thailand as a dodgy destination, too. A 2007 press release by Australia's Channel 9 promoting a story on its current affairs show *Sunday*, worded an investigation into a budget Thai airline crash in this way:

> Hundreds of thousands of Australians will fly to Thailand this summer; large numbers of them buying cheap tickets to holiday destinations beyond Bangkok, using budget airlines based in Asia. But the question they should be asking is: is it safe? (Nine Network 2007).

Thailand's reduction to a series of malevolent stereotypes as a centre for organised crime, particularly related to illicit drugs, as a city of chaotic traffic, swirling pollution, tropical heat, cheap sex for sale and immense population give it the perfect atmosphere in which to imaginatively portray the proverbial 'hell hole'. Paul Theroux subscribes to all these stereotypes, lending to them the authority of non-fiction and his reputation as a critically acclaimed travel writer. Bangkok, he says, is responsible for its own reputation because of its success after the Vietnam War in 'advertising itself as a place where even the most diffident foreigner can get laid' (Theroux 1977:239). He sums up this view of the city succinctly: it has, he says, 'an aspect of violation' that is seen everywhere, in the streets, on the *klongs* and even in the temples, of which he makes the absurd claim that they have been repaired by foreign tourists, not Thais (1977:239).

In recent years, Thailand has increasingly been used by writers as a suitably seedy backdrop for mainstream fiction set in the crime world, a trend noted in *Traveller's literary companion: South-East Asia* (Hudak 1994:77). The trend has continued with John Burdett's thrillers *Bangkok 8* (2003) and its sequels, *Bangkok tattoo* (2005) and *Bangkok haunts* (2007), Angela Savage's *Behind the night bazaar* (2006) and Nick McDonell's *The third brother* (2005). This increase may be due to what Said describes as 'the appearance of success' (Said 2003:93). If experience confirms what has been read, the reader will believe the author, will buy more books by that author and believe them, thereby encouraging other authors to write about the topic. For example, if a traveller read *A woman of Bangkok* and then travelled to Thailand and spent most of his time in a red-light district, he would believe Reynolds's narrative to be a realistic depiction. However, if he had spent his time visiting temples, shopping and having non-erotic massages, he might decry Reynolds's book as unrepresentative.

Savage's and Burdett's works are well written detective novels that concern violent crime in the drug and sex trades. Burdett is unusual in that he writes from the perspective of a Thai police officer, Sonchai Jitpleecheep, who has a white father he doesn't know and a Thai mother who is a brothel madam. The book shows Bangkok as a dangerous, drug-riddled city whose life revolves around its brothels and girlie bars. Interestingly, the author feels the need to explain himself in an 'Author's note', saying that in his many trips to Thailand he has never come across corruption in the Thai police force and that, 'Most visitors to the kingdom enjoy wonderful vacations without coming across any evidence of sleaze at all'. He then says there have been many reports of police corruption 'for more than a decade', but retreats somewhat and asks forgiveness of any Thai police officer who reads the book. The sex industry in Thailand is smaller than that of many other Asian countries, he says, but is better known 'because Thais are less coy about it' (Burdett 2003). While this may be true within the industry itself, Thais are, in fact, sensitive about the sex industry, which is still officially illegal, and Thai authorities have been quoted in the popular press as denying the existence of brothels altogether. Burdett excuses his depiction of Thailand by saying novelists are 'opportunists' and that 'This is an entertainment within a very Western genre, nothing more. No offence is intended' (Burdett 2003). In other words, it is set in Bangkok but it is really about what Westerners imagine and expect Bangkok to be.

Burdett does attempt to dispel some of the West's assumptions about Thailand, though in so doing he ultimately conjures others, such as in the following comment by sex industry worker Kat, delivered while conducting target-practice for her dart show: '*Farangs* don't understand us Thais. They think if a girl sells her body, then she has no dignity, no limits. Actually, the opposite is often the truth' (Burdett 2003:120). Similarly, in *A woman of Bangkok*, Vilai is outraged when a client asks to sleep with her 'for love' and not money: 'Only the lowest girls slept with men for nothing—for love, as the foreigners said—but she was a very high girl, she had a price, and if a man liked her he would show his respect by paying that price' (Reynolds 1956:121).

Travel writer Robert D Kaplan remarks in *The ends of the earth* (Kaplan 1996:374) that male tourists 'too timid to venture into such places in the West' have no qualms about visiting sex shows and brothels in Thailand. It is because, he claims, sex is simply a commodity there, 'separated from all moral prohibitions and, therefore, from its normal danger and mystery'. Kaplan goes on to justify prostitution because, he says, it helps women break the poverty cycle (1996:385). The message to Western readers is that it is acceptable to buy sex in Thailand because Thai women want to sell themselves and their culture condones it, further underlining the chasm between West and East. More than 50 years earlier, Olle Strandberg (1953) feminised Thailand as a whole. While the countryside, he says, is 'a naked and sunburned lap', Bangkok is a 'jewel in the lotus flower' which is 'shooting forth out of slime and mud', and he, the tourist, is 'like a young bride, enveloped in but her veil' who wakes to realise 'that Bangkok awaits me' (Strandberg 1953:83.85).

Thai men are virtually negated in this landscape, appearing merely as peripheral characters. *Thai girl*, for example, has no significant Thai male characters, despite Fon's mention of a Thai boyfriend. They are reduced to minor roles, subjects that the reader will find comical or distasteful, such as the group Ben stumbles upon roasting a rat for dinner. Hicks cleverly picks up on a Western male perception that, by paying Thai prostitutes, they are actually doing something good for them. His character Jack, an English expatriate living in Thailand, puts it succinctly: 'The girls that go with the farang can usually look after themselves but it's the ones getting screwed by Thai men for a few baht that I worry about' (Hicks 2004a:164). In *The good woman of Bangkok*, also, Thai men are depicted as 'emasculated, crippled, pimps: they are corrupt menservants in a vast seraglio' (Martin et al 1997:18).

Burdett does include a strong Thai male protagonist in the *Bangkok 8* series, in which Sonchai's white half helps him to see the foolishness of *farangs* rather than to identify with them. Sonchai is adept at seeming to be what Westerners imagine he would be. He scoffs at what he perceives as Western superiority cloaked in political correctness, the 'Sympathetic American Abroad' who can assert the superiority of his culture and the inferiority of the Thai culture 'subliminally', without saying anything that sounds ostensibly critical (Burdett 2003:93–4). Burdett allows Sonchai to muse about the Thai sex industry and he describes how bar girls concoct a 'fantasy in the Western mind, a world which is mysteriously difficult to let go of'. In the process, they create their own fantasies of escaping poverty and 'the indignity of their trade' by 'finding a *farang* who could support them for life' (2003:88). Burdett writes with a keen sense of irony and parody, which is evident to an even greater extent in the *Bangkok 8* sequels, *Bangkok tattoo* and *Bangkok haunts*.

Despite his use of stereotypes, Burdett, unlike many other Western writers using Bangkok as a setting, does make the city integral to the story. It is not merely a backdrop, but is virtually a character in its own right, even if a rather two-dimensional character, as Burdett admits. In reviewing *Bangkok 8*, Pico

Iyer (2003) says it has 'more verve and urbanity than most', but criticises it for perpetuating the view of Bangkok as a centre for cheap sex and drugs and little else. However, at least Burdett tries to include a Thai point of view and complex Thai characters who may be villains or heroes, or a mixture of both. He makes some poignant observations, particularly in *Bangkok tattoo*, on the effect of Western culture on Thailand. An example is his explanation of why a Thai delicacy, fried grasshoppers, has almost disappeared from Bangkok hawkers' food stalls. Encroaching Western sensibilities have made Thais feel embarrassed about their taste for grasshoppers, he says. Ironically, however, one of the few places fried grasshoppers can now be purchased is at Nana Plaza, a notorious enclave of bars for Western sex tourists, because 'avant-garde *farang* cottoned on to this culinary exoticus with the enthusiasm of the pretentious' (Burdett 2005:33). Ultimately, however, as Burdett admits and Iyer reiterates, this is Bangkok served up typically the way foreigners like and expect it to be—mysterious, besmirched, seductive: 'This is a Bangkok that only a *farang*, or foreigner, could love, and it felt oddly familiar even 50 years ago, when Jack Reynolds gave us his nakedly titled *Woman of Bangkok*' (Iyer 2003).

Angela Savage goes beyond Bangkok to Chiang Mai, only to set her novel in the northern city's own 'seedy underbelly'.[133] Like Burdett, she writes with a sharp sense of humour; her content, like much of Burdett's, is rather bleak. Savage's style, however, is closer to the classic murder mystery with the bonus of exoticism, in the tradition of an Agatha Christie for the 21st century. The book's plot concerns a child prostitution racket that protagonist Jayne Keeney helps smash and a corrupt police official who gets his comeuppance—it is, as Frances Atkinson in *The Age* put it, 'Crime with a conscience' (Atkinson 2006). Although *Behind the night bazaar* is set in the red-light bar district of Chiang Mai, it is not a voyeuristic view, nor is the sex industry presented in the usual dichotomous way as simultaneously thrilling and repelling. Instead, it is wholly ugly and exploitative, an illicit industry run by ruthless men for the purpose of generating wealth.

In *The third brother*, McDonell locates his protagonist firmly in that stereotypical Bangkok territory that Iyer so strongly criticises. The scenes in Bangkok all take place in the city's well known seedy zones: Khao San Road, sex clubs with names such as 'Triple Happiness', among drug sellers and crooked cops. *The third brother*'s opening scenes, like those of *The beach*, concern a young American, Mike, recently arrived on Khao San Road. Mike concludes that Khao San could be anywhere in Southeast Asia, where the restaurants are 'all different…but they are all the same, like everything else on Khao San Road', where 'every backpacker in Southeast Asia starts and ends' (McDonell 2005:15).

Mike claims Khao San Road as a westernised and Western territory; the fact that it is part of Thailand and run by Thais is of little consequence.

Three New Zealand women tell Mike they like Thailand because it is cheap and because 'foreigners come up and talk to them' (McDonell 2005:17). In this way, the visitors construct Thailand as an extension of the West in the context of their social lives at home, a depiction also shown in *The beach*. Considering themselves 'travellers', they are, nevertheless, visiting the Thailand of their expectations and going home with little more knowledge than when they arrived, except, for example, where to buy the cheapest food, T-shirts and, for some, drugs, in areas frequented by Westerners. As well as their *Lonely Planet* guides, they carry the imprint of empire, the belief that they are Great White Explorers discovering new territories. The freelance journalists Mike meets have résumés, he says, that sound 'right out of Kipling' (McDonell 2005:51). Acclaimed on the book's cover by Hunter S Thompson as a literary voice of youth ('the real thing'), McDonell, who was 21 when *The third brother* was published, seems to reflect the mentality of the travellers of his generation. As his character 'imagines the horrors of prison in Thailand', the possibility of 'danger' is never far away (McDonell 2005:102).

Chapter seven

Other Thailands

Siam being a country of plentiful food and easy-going Buddhist village communities, no man in his right mind would even think of heavy physical labour in such conditions! Is this what we can look forward to? We thank our knowledgeable informant for his encouraging little discourse, and settle down to sleep.—Ian Denys Peek, prisoner of war in transit to the Burma-Thailand Railway (Peek 2003)

Although a significant proportion of Western literature about Thailand in recent years has located it as an eroticised zone, there has also been a variety of other responses that should be examined, particularly in the writing of Second World War prisoners of war, of independent female travellers, and in literary fiction by both Westerners and Thais.

The memoirs of prisoners of war working on the Burma–Thailand (or 'Death') Railway are exclusively by and about men. The body of work about prisoner-of-war life in Thailand continues in retrospect, with new books published every year.

Although Western representations of Thailand have been dominated by men, there is a small but significant body of work by women that deserves critical assessment. Some of these writers have lived in the country as expatriates, many accompanying men, the notable exceptions including Anna Leonowens, Faith Adiele, and Karen Connelly.

While today's solo travel stories about Thailand by males invariably contain some description of the sex industry, even if it is only watching bored topless dancers at Patpong, independent female travellers are more concerned with traversing the landscape successfully, avoiding danger and forging a greater sense of self-identity. While many foreign men today go to Thailand to find someone else, many women go to find themselves.

Gendering Thailand

Historically, women often have travelled 'East' to obtain a kind of freedom they could not find at home. For Leonowens, the impulse was financial, for Adiele, spiritual, for Connelly, cultural. This association of 'the East and liberty' is incongruous with the dominant representation of the East as a virtual prison for women. Barbara Hodgson (2005:1) says many Western women have followed the lead of female trailblazers, such as Lady Mary Wortley Montagu in early 18th-century Turkey, in pursuit of liberty from the constraints of what was considered a proper life for a lady at home. Hodgson (2005:2) remarks on the incongruity of Western women's experiences in the East alongside the fantasy/horror stories of women of the harem who are portrayed as imprisoned and veiled. Though Hodgson concentrates on women travelling to what was the eastern Ottoman Empire, her comments have relevance to the Western women in this study who travel to Thailand. Many are seeking some sort of escape, a greater freedom than home offers, in Thailand, whose very name means 'Land of the free'. In this respect, men and women are alike in what they seek in Thailand.

Behdad (1994:110) remarks that Orientalism is traditionally a 'patriarchal system' in which 'the female traveller is the excluded Other who is included only as the token exception in a field defined as masculine'. That does not mean women are above colonialist attitudes themselves; the existence of classically Orientalist attitudes in women's travel writing has become a subject of scholarly discourse. Ruth Jenkins (2004:15) describes the typical 19th-century independent female traveller to the East as eccentric and middle-aged. Thailand, however, was not part of the usual itinerary for most of the Victorian women travelers Jenkins writes about. Leonowens is an exception, but she was not strictly a 'traveller'. There appear to be no extant published accounts of Siam by foreign women before the 19th century. Accounts in the 19th and early 20th centuries are principally by female missionaries accompanying husbands and obliged to adhere to 'company' policy.

In his 1995 introduction to Marthe Bassenne's 1912 book *In Laos and Siam*, Tips observes that women's writing concerns itself more with personal, emotional and domestic detail than men's writing does (Bassenne 1995:vii). Women writing about Thailand. however, at least seem to reach the same conclusions as men: that Western culture is indisputably superior to that of the East, and that Western religion and the morality and values it teaches are the true path and the only way 'forward'. Lillian Johnson Curtis demonstrates this belief when she describes the Chiang Mai house of the missionary, McGilvary, which is in 'the Indian bungalow style' with an English garden:

It is difficult to estimate the power of a Christian home in a heathen land. This one has ever stood for all that makes a Christian home the ideal home of the wide world. Its tidy look, its fragrant flowers and vines, its gardens and fruit trees, have all preached more eloquently than words that the Christian religion is meant for life as well as death (Curtis 1998:305)

Acknowledging that 19th-century women's travel writing has been inadequately discussed, Monica Anderson in *Women and the politics of travel, 1870–1914* says the 'connections between women's travel and complicit agency' need to be more thoroughly examined (Anderson 2006:19). Most books about women travellers, including *The blessings of a good thick skirt* (Russell 1986), *Spinsters abroad* (Birkett 1989) and *Wayward women* (Robinson 1990), do not discuss women travellers in Thailand and this demonstrates the need for discourse in this area, which it is hoped this book will initiate.

Bassenne travelled to Southeast Asia in the early 20th century with her husband, a doctor, and kept a detailed journal. She exhibits a disdain typical of her time for races other than her own. The Siamese, she says, are ugly, lazy and animal-like. Though she complains bitterly about not being allowed to sleep in a cabin on the upper bridge because that part of the ship is barred to women, she does not identify with the Siamese women similarly barred. They can be happy in the one metre-high steerage bridge because, unlike her, they 'have the dislocated legs of the yellow women who are accustomed after centuries of atavism to living on all fours'. So Siamese women, she is asserting, do not warrant equal treatment because they are closer to animals than humans. While in the sleeping area with the Siamese women, Bassenne further segregates herself by setting up her bivouac bed and hanging the blankets round it like curtains 'to isolate ourselves from our neighbors, the Siamese travelers' (Bassenne 1995:126). However, in what can be seen as a metaphor for tourism, she cannot avoid contact altogether, because their feet brush past her when they board or depart the boat (1995:127).

Bassenne is more critical of Siamese women than she is of Siamese men. In describing a Siamese prince, princess and their son, she is particularly scathing of the woman, who, she says, 'Much more than her husband…retained the Oriental aspect' so that she appears physically 'hideous', and her 'manners were surely those of her race' (Bassenne 1995:129). As Jenkins (2004:17) says, women travellers in Bassenne's time felt compelled to maintain 'a rigorous code of propriety'. That meant prescribed behaviour, dress, and separation from the 'natives'. Of all the hardships suffered during her expedition, the most awful for Bassenne is when she is forced in dirty, torn travel clothes, to meet the well-dressed Siamese Governor of Uttradit. Of course, anyone would be embarrassed in such a situation, but for Bassenne, the event takes on a more serious nature than it should because she is forced to break with propriety. Standing beside the Governor, whom Bassenne says is 'all glittering like a Louis XV nobleman who has forgotten his wig', she is mortified: 'my vagabond-like get-up ashamed me' (Bassenne 1995:116–7). According to Monica Anderson (2006:209), a belief in the importance of being well dressed is in accord with the view at the time that the traveller represented 'the Empire' and that 'socially correct dress was seen as a measure of one's social respectability'.

Never caught dressed as a vagabond was Florence Caddy, who travelled in the 1880s aboard a luxury yacht as geographer and naturalist and wrote *To Siam and Malaya in the Duke of Sutherland's yacht "Sans Peur"* (1889). As Grewal (1996:83-4) comments, many women travellers experienced and described only the upper classes of women during their travels: the apparently idle women of the seraglio were presented as the norm, and the majority of the female population was thereby unrepresented, including the vast number of peasants. This wasn't the travellers' fault—they had little opportunity to ineract with ordinary women. Nevertheless, it gave them an unrealistic view of Siam. Caddy seems, like many others, to think of Bangkok as not quite real. It is, as she describes it, 'a city made to live in watercolours, not warranted otherwise to last' (Caddy 1992:227).

Women travelling alone in the 19th and early 20th centuries were seen as oddities for, as Dea Birkett (1989:xi) says, allowing themselves 'to roam with the freedom of men in lands so very different and distant from their own'. Solo female travellers today, while no longer regarded with suspicion, continue to seek that freedom, to search for an experience 'without the filter of someone else's viewpoint', as described by Faith Conlon and others (Conlon, Emerick & Henry de Tessan 2001:x). A story by Faith Adiele in the Conlon collection was written soon after her experience as a Buddhist nun. In 'Passing Through Bandit Country', Adiele is travelling through the south of Thailand looking for *maechi* to interview, but has heard the area is dangerous because of bandits who rob and murder travellers. While the story is ostensibly about 'dangerous Thailand', it is more about Adiele becoming self-reliant. Its climax occurs when a Thai businessman, a would-be protector, exclaims, 'you don't need any help' (Adiele 2001:71).

Thailand is still seen by Westerners as a potentially difficult destination, making the very act of travelling there alone appear somewhat risky. When that person is a woman, the risk is seen as greater; in Adiele's case, the man who offers to help her is unreliable and, ultimately, she has to rely on herself. Adiele again travels beyond the normal tourist zone, which makes her story an interesting counter to the many stories of travellers in Thailand being attended to by legions of Thai servants and guides.

Like Adiele, Karen Connelly was a Rotary exchange student to Northern Thailand. Also like Adiele, her year in Thailand was a life-changing experience: 'Thailand remains a crucial geographical point in my landscape. Whenever I go there now, I feel as though I have returned to the centre of the world', Connelly (2001:preface) explains. She laments the loss of certain cultural practices and artefacts 'in their natural and unselfconscious form' that have been swamped by mass tourism and Westernisation. Despite that, she says the country has much to offer; visitors who complain that 'Western tourists have ruined it' are missing 'a fascinating history, several languages, a great distance of fields, rivers, mountains, seas—not to mention nearly sixty million human beings...'

Connelly's description of everyday life in the Thai village of Den Chai, Phrae Province, in 1986 gives a greater insight into life in Thailand beyond tourism than most other books written by foreigners. It is not about the sex or drug trades, expatriate life, tourism or the idealistic escape to paradise. It is rather the cultural journey of a self-described 'privileged' Westerner as she lives in rural Thailand, learns the language and goes to school. Rather than the usual traveller's tale of fleeting engagement and commercial exchange, Connelly's is one of participation, self-discovery and sometimes isolation. She learns quickly that the hyperbole of travel brochures has little in common with this actuality: 'this is Thailand, the land of smiles, the Venice of the Orient, the pearl of Asia. The travel-agency phrases run off my tongue as mosquitoes settle on my thighs, arms, neck' (Connelly 2001:4).

Connelly is the only *farang* in town. She hates the 'staring eyes, the claps and whistles' that set her apart: 'I lied! I have no tolerance at all for living in a different culture. I have no facility for languages and I am viciously narrow-minded', she says, quoting from journals kept at the time (Connelly 2001:14). Although Connelly learns to love Thailand, she is never completely comfortable: 'The solution is not in being *like* a Thai, but in being a Thai completely, which is impossible. I will never wash sheets by hand without gritting my teeth. I will never wear a uniform without secretly laughing at it' (2001:76).

In contrast to Adiele and Connelly who lived among Thais, many expatriates experience Thailand vicariously, from the safety of secure apartment buildings or gated housing estates, air-conditioned cars with drivers, social functions mostly consisting of people just like them. William J Lederer and Eugene Burdick explain this phenomenon at the end of *The ugly American* (1958) which is set in Sarkhan, a fictional Southeast Asian country. In 'A factual epilogue', they describe the 'ingrown social life' of Americans abroad, noting that Thais in Bangkok dub an American social gathering there a 'SIGG'—that is, 'Social Incest in the Golden Ghetto' (Lederer & Burdick 1958:277).

In the 20th century, the term 'expatriate wife' became synonymous with rich, idle women who incessantly complain about their host country, particularly about the quality of their domestic staff. The community of supposedly bored expatriate wives features in Emmanuelle Arsan's erotic autobiographical novel, *Emmanuelle* (1967), which later became a popular film.[134] It uses the setting of Bangkok to form a titillating parody of the Eastern harem among Western women. In the first scene in Bangkok, the 'half-naked' expatriate women bathe together at the Royal Bangkok Sports Club; the eponymous heroine observes that they live in 'idleness and luxury' and that they exist only 'to seduce or be seduced' (Arsan 1971:34,35). For the expatriate wives, Bangkok is a suitably sensual setting where sexual experimentation is permitted, the reward for being 'in this place' (1971:33). The Thais in the novel are almost invisible, being referred to only vaguely as, for example, 'the chauffeur', 'the houseboy' who walks so silently that Emmanuelle is afraid of him, 'the old cook with red teeth', and 'the little servant girl' who is 'straight out of one of Gauguin's dreams, with her flowery black hair, her ochre body, and her scarlet sarong' (1971:52). In this way, *Emmanuelle* depicts mid-20th century Bangkok as what Pratt calls a 'contact zone' (Pratt 1992:6) in which the Europeans are positioning themselves as colonials—although in Thailand, they are not, of course, colonial masters but masters in their own small circle only.

The Bangkok of *Emmanuelle* is a backdrop, a generic tropical spectacle. As Jean comments when he crosses a bridge and sees naked children playing in the water below: 'Isn't that the Orient you see in films?' (Arsan 1971:95). For Emmanuelle, Bangkok becomes surrealistic, her imagined 'setting' for a 'kind of ballet': '"Setting" was the right word, in its theatrical sense, with its evocations of false perspectives, platforms, cardboard walls, unstable assemblages and scaffoldings' (1971:184). In a clever irony, the atmosphere of unreality is broken for a moment when Emmanuelle realises the terrifying giant Genghis Khan before her is actually one of many discarded promotional billboards for films (1971:187). Her night-time walk with her lover also takes her to a mysterious phallus shrine. The setting is clearly the Lingam Shrine on Wireless Road in Central Bangkok, hardly the jungle Emmanuelle imagines.[135]

The fame—or infamy—of *Emmanuelle* as a result of the film and a string of inferior sequels has given it recognition far beyond its original status as an erotic novel. Pico Iyer (1988:319-20) comments that everywhere he goes he sees the caricature of the balding, middle-aged white man with the Thai 'doe-eyed Lolita', who are the oddest of bedfellows and that Thailand has been thus 'reduced into nothing but the land of Thai sticks and the setting for *Emmanuelle*'. Despite its reputation, however, *Emmanuelle* is expressly *not* about that stereotypical male sex tourist whose partnering with Thai prostitutes Iyer (1988:320) likens to John Cadet's story 'Occidental Adam and Oriental Eve'.

Of works of non-fiction, probably the most lauded expatriate wife's story is *Mai pen rai means never mind* (Hollinger 1977). Carol Hollinger lived in Thailand when her husband was stationed there with the US Foreign Service. *Mai pen rai* is still widely recommended to newcomers to Thailand as a useful handbook.[136] Hollinger (1997:93) says her employment enabled her to gain a better understanding of Thais as distinct from other Asian races, so that she was 'no longer confined to meeting a few bland Orientals at official functions'. Her account of life as a foreigner in Thailand takes her from culture shock through a valiant attempt to understand Thai culture, to celebrate the differences from her own culture and to describe this journey with neither condescension nor through rose-tinted glasses. She admits she had a lot to learn when she first arrived in Thailand:

> I had had giddy intentions of living in an underdeveloped country and sharing with the natives, whom I regarded with great affection from afar, our civilization. I even studied in graduate school the technique of accomplishing this…Foreign Service officers lectured to me on methods of adjusting to strange cultures and I listened as though their word was gospel (Hollinger 1997:95).

Hollinger (1997:95) also admits that the more she learns about Thailand, the less she feels she knows, and she criticises so-called Southeast Asia experts and academics in the West of concocting statistics and 'hocus pocus', singling out Cornell University as one of the few to publish good 'objective writing'. Also in for a caning are 'American matrons' who play bridge all day with other American matrons, but feel they can discuss Thais and Thailand with authority: 'After all, they were there weren't they?'

Hollinger learns about her host country because she wants to. She is open-minded but not blind to Thailand's faults, chief among them rampant corruption. She is rare for her time—she wrote the book during the Vietnam War—in that her experience in Thailand made her question what she thought she knew:

> At first I thought smugly that I was bringing democratic freedom of speech to a group that knew only oligarchy and dictatorship, but as the classroom discussions deepened I found with enforced humility (I was clobbered) that somehow I had become the learner and my students were on the pedagogic end (Hollinger 1977:86).

Meanwhile, female tourists have been viewing Thailand from within the safe confines of the package tour since the 1960s. They are transported, itineraries in hand, in air-conditioned buses to sights, cultural shows and 'adventures' that carefully follow Tourism Authority of Thailand's 'Amazing Thailand' and 'Land of smiles' advertising spiels. Yet, the best of their memoirs reveal that, despite the nature of their travel, some tourists do see beyond the travel gloss. Australian Edith Emery (1969:9), travelling in the 1960s, was enchanted—'the countless sparkling temples more like Hollywood film sets than places of worship'—but not fooled. She says her time in Bangkok was 'a little spell in fairyland', yet she suspects she has been shown 'only the shell...that reflects perhaps the dream-image the visitor wants to see and hides the seedier side which must be there'. Emery's observations demonstrate the hackneyed 'land of contrasts' theme, which insists that Thailand is either an unreal fairyland sparkling with jewels, or a centre of turpitude, when, in reality, it has elements of both. For the tourist and traveller alike, however, the mundane belongs at 'home'. To Emery (1969:9), Thailand is 'a complete contrast to Australia's sensibleness and monotony'.

Another Thailand story in *A woman alone*, by Michelle Kehm, uses the familiar tale of the search for the perfect beach. Kehm doesn't want to go to south coast beaches such as Koh Samui, because they are 'pretty cosmetic and meat markety' (Kehm 2001:185). Instead, she seeks 'a paradise in the rough' and chooses Koh Chang, ironically ending up staying in a hotel full of *farang* tourists that is run by a European (2001:185). It is important to Kehm, however, that she imagines the location as more 'authentic' than Koh Samui and its environs, that she feels 'adventurous. Raw. Real' (2001:187). Consequently, she spends most of the time in her room suffering from sand flea bites—'Oh the price I pay for paradise', she says wryly (2001:191).

Canadian medico Louise de Courval's book of short stories, *Papaya salad (make it spicy, please!)* (2001), is free of the typical tourist's drive to find adventure, to be first, to 'discover' the landscape. De Courval is more interested in learning about the culture, though not in an invasive way. She is a gentle, considerate traveller willing to learn the language and to get to know Thais. She does not kid herself, however, that she is becoming one of them and she is not averse to joining a tour group of foreigners.

De Courval's story about her trip to Koh Samet is an interesting counterpoint to most other tourist tales of the search for the perfect beach. For a start, she says she does not usually like 'lying half-naked on a sandy beach waiting to be grilled by the tropical sun', but she has decided that, after all, she needs a relaxing beach holiday (Courval 2001:19). Eschewing Phuket as too dangerous at that time of year (ironically, for the book was published only three years before the 2004 tsunami), she chooses Koh Samet, which she is told is 'the love island' (2001:20). For the reader, the phrase might have connotations of what that might mean to a Western tourist in terms of sex for sale, but guilelessly, de Courval does not even consider that suggestion. Instead, she explains that the island is 'where young Thai couples go for a romantic weekend' (2001:20).

She finds the beach that has been recommended to her by a Thai friend and, indeed, it appears to be perfect; accessible only by foot, developed only enough to be comfortable, it is 'the exact place where I had dreamed of spending a few days' (Courval 2001:21). Masseuses ply the beach looking for customers, as they do in *Thai girl*, and de Courval becomes a daily customer, chatting to them about their families and their lives. She leaves the island with 'friendly memories' and a feeling of 'well being' (2001:25). While for the protagonist in *Thai girl*, his friendship with the masseuse becomes the focus of his stay and he will always wonder what might have been, de Courval's beach holiday is merely one of many pleasant experiences in Thailand. The endpoint, however, is the same as that of travellers everywhere: both leave the island with their memories, to return home and resume their normal lives.

A recent notable book about Thailand is the collection of stories and poetry by the Bangkok Women's Writers Group called *Bangkok blondes* (2007). It is rather different to other material written by foreigners in that it deals not with culture shock, comparisons with home or the search for a postcard-perfect beach; rather, it deals with everyday life in the capital. After all, expatriates don't spend every day feeling homesick and remarking to themselves and others on the exotic nature of their experience. Mostly, day-to-day life goes on as normal, wherever you live. You still have to go to the supermarket, go to work, take children to school, pay the bills and shop for clothes. The many contributors to *Bangkok Blondes*—members of a group that has been meeting fortnightly since 2000—have written with enthusiasm and often autobiographically about life in Bangkok. They haven't restricted themselves to the expatriate experience and many of their subjects are universal. There are love stories, driving stories, tales of work and play, as well as humorous stories about coming to terms with Thai culture. For example, 'Extra', by Anna Bennetts, is about the hilarious experience of appearing as an extra in a TV commercial:

> I survey my fellow stars for a day. Backpackers seem the norm; as a Bangkok resident I'm the odd one out. Apparently Guy Pearce was here shooting a French film recently and the production team had been so desperate for extras they'd scoured Khao San road at the last minute. I wonder if they'd done that to amass the motley crew I see here today. I wish I'd been on the Guy Pearce shoot instead of this mysterious commercial rumoured to be about mobile phones (Bennetts 2007:58).

The women also make some apt observations of fellow expatriates, such as this one in 'Hovering in between', by Myra Betron, in which she describes how many foreigners come to Thailand to find an 'alternative lifestyle':

Fleeing from broken marriages, hectic careers or all-around ennui, expats here find the Otherness that Thailand offers to be a perfect escape from their Western realities. This escape may be in a soft-natured Thai woman, an island beach paradise or the hushed corridors of a meditation camp. Despite the Otherness of Thailand, one can still easily access the conveniences of Western life, usually at a fraction of the cost. After all, were else can one get Internet access for pennies while sitting on an idyllic beach? (Betron 2007:79).

As it turns out, Betron's experience of Thailand doesn't turn out as she expected, when she finds it difficult to obtain the volunteer work she thought she would so easily walk into. She soon finds the cosmopolitan, Westernised nature of Bangkok overtakes the 'mystique of Thai culture' and, as she says, 'like many others, I escaped to Cambodia and Laos for a more "authentic" Southeast Asian experience' (Betron 2007:83).

A whimsical book about Thailand written by a British woman travelling alone, is Clare de Vries's *Of cats and kings* (2002). It is about her search through Burma and Thailand for the perfect cat to take back to England, interspersed with sightseeing. Bangkok at first view is polluted and full of freeways, 'more Houston than a city of Eastern mystique', as de Vries says (Vries 2002:195). Her search for the cat becomes a metaphor for any tourist's search for perfection and reveals many of her own Eurocentric assumptions about Thailand. Everywhere she goes, Thais try to overcharge her for boat, *tuk tuk* and taxi rides (2002:208–11). Many visitors have this experience: tourist areas throughout the world are frequented by opportunists, after all. But her account of Thailand does not seem to be balanced—she is constantly finding fault. The Thailand of Connelly's experience is far away; de Vries's sightseeing choice is the impressive house of expatriate Westerner Jim Thompson (2002:212).

Later, she does decide to veer off the usual tourist track, travelling to 'the small frontier town' of Tak, where her dingy hotel is 'full of sinister men slamming doors' (Vries 2002:236). De Vries meets a German woman working in a border camp who, she says, looks like a 19th-century missionary. De Vries is surprised that the German eats in the traditional northern Thai way with her hands, while the Karen hilltribe girls in the camp eat with a fork: 'Oh how the East loves the West and the West loves the East,' she comments (2002:241). Moving on to the tourist town of Phuket, de Vries is surprised to find 'no sign of Thailand' among the designer fakes, and the 'hideous conglomerate' of Western chain stores where everything is 'grossly overpriced' (2002:249). There is an idea that the 'real' Thailand must exhibit something unspoilt, untouched by Westernisation. Thais working in the tourism industry or catering to tourists are not part of the Thailand of the Western imagination.

Ultimately, de Vries's book highlights only the differences between her own culture and that of Thailand and the shortcomings of the latter. This, of course, is the nature of a great deal of travel literature—in the end, it celebrates not the journey and the discovery of somewhere new, but the security that home offers, the superiority of the home culture over the visited one. De Vries (2002:254) admonishes Thai women in a schoolmarmish way: 'I wish they wouldn't give men the impression that it's fine to hanker after submissive women', she thinks while watching a classical dancing troupe at the luxury spa resort, Chiva Som, at Hua Hin.

Australian writer Tamara Sheward adopts an even more superior tone in her travel book *bad karma* (2003). Searching for 'the ideal, exotic, bizarre and Birkenstock-free destination', she decides to go to Southeast Asia, which an acquaintance, Wazza, who is living in Cambodia, has recommended (Sheward 2003:6). While not devoid of 'package-tour geeks', the region is 'less affected than, say, Nepal or Tooting', Wazza assures her. Though Thailand hosts 'hordes of Westerners' who travel there for the drugs,

> …Wazza touted it as a good launching pad for the rest of the trip and promised there were still some places which retained a folksy innocence. 'And the whole bloody place is as cheap as chips,' he said. 'It's a fuckin' paradise.' Lonely Planet couldn't have put it better (Sheward 2003:6).

The book is a tawdry collection of Sheward's culturally insensitive travel experiences. Proudly announcing on its back cover that it is a 'not entirely politically correct traveller's tale', it starts with Sheward figuring her friend El will make a useful travelling companion in Thailand because she has lived in Japan and so 'would be able to make at least some sense of our surrounds' (Sheward 2003:8–9). It is the equivalent of saying someone who has lived in France will be able to better understand England. Every stereotype is in the book, including 'nasty' Khao San Road, a swindling rickshaw driver, and 'weird squiggly things' that Sheward (2003:11–7) 'guesses' are Thai writing. Sheward has already made up her mind what she will see outside Bangkok and describes the countryside as she imagines it might be, even though she cannot see it out of the night-running train:

> Outside, Thailand was clacking by, a dark wonderland of eight-syllable villages and chattering people and rogue elephants. And in less than ten hours, we'd be a part of it. No backpackers, no stench, no Donut King. Just uncharted territory (2003:20).

Armed Thailand

> He too was a prisoner, like the five hundred other wretches herded by the Japanese
> into the camp on the River Kwai, like the sixty thousand English, Australians,
> Dutch and Americans assembled in several groups in one of the most uncivilised
> corners of the earth, the jungle of Burma and Siam.— Pierre Boulle (2002:3)

Naturally, the elements necessary for survival and the desire for freedom
are the driving forces in the body of writing, almost exclusively male, about
the experience of military bondage in Thailand during the Second World War.
Among them were young men from provincial backgrounds who, like renowned
Australian surgeon Edward 'Weary' Dunlop in his *War diaries* had 'yearned for
the high romantic ground of adventure in strange lands' (Dunlop 1986:1). For
the prisoners of war, paradisal Thailand becomes a hell on earth, as evidenced
by the Western-generated names associated with it—the Death Railway and
Hellfire Pass. There has been little critical discourse about the prisoner-of-war
(POW) experience in Thailand as a debased form of travel, though *Hotel Asia*
(Gerster 1995) and *On the war-path* (Gerster & Pierce 2004) include extracts
from Ray Parkin's brilliant 1963 POW memoir *Into the smother*.[137]

*Bridge on the River Kwai: tourists ride a train crossing the famous (reconstructed)
bridge, actually on the Khwae Yai River, Kanchanaburi. Credit: Andrew Bain/Lonely
Planet images.*

Thailand as a location has been peripheral to most material written about the
railway in books and films such as *The bridge on the River Kwai*. In the minds

of Westerners on the Allied side, the area is still part of 'The War', suspended in time, even though generations of people have lived and worked in Kanchanaburi since the 1940s. The Death Railway has, in effect, become in the imagination of Australians and other nationalities who endured the POW horror, a part of 'our' history, as have Gallipoli, Kokoda and Tobruk. It is easy to forget that while up to 16,000 Allied prisoners of war died, some 92,000 Asians died working on the railway (Parkin 1999:369). As Prue Torney-Parlicki notes in *Somewhere in Asia*, there was outrage in the press after the war at the imprisonment of white men forced to become slaves, who, they said, were not treated as white men should be but rather as 'white coolies' (Torney-Parlicki 2000:72–3).

In Boulle's 1952 novel *The bridge on the River Kwai*, the location is a device with which to tell a war story. The Siamese exist only as marginal characters, nameless and faceless. Siam is used because it was the historical location, though the novel is only loosely based on a true story and the film departs even further from reality than the book. Yet the Kanchanaburi province of Thailand, with its famous (reconstructed) bridge and Hellfire Pass area, has become one of the country's biggest tourist drawcards, despite—or perhaps because of—the book's description and the film's depiction of 'the jungle of Burma and Siam' as being 'one of the most uncivilized corners of the earth' that white people were 'herded' into by their Japanese captors (Boulle 2002:3). There are reconstructed POW huts to view, cemeteries, museums and memorials to visit, some funded by the Australian Government. Tourists can ride the train across the re-built 'Bridge on the River Kwai' and can walk along part of the railway at Hellfire Pass. As a Thai tourism guide says, Kanchanaburi is 'a real Complete [sic] land of touring' where tourists can 'stay in a jungle resort deep in the wilderness' (Guide to Kanchanaburi 1992). Significantly, the fame of the bridge is based not on fact, but on Boulle's largely fictional book and the film it inspired. The guide refers to Western films such as '*The bridge Over* [sic] *the River Kwai*' and locations where scenes from *The deer hunter* were filmed: 'We're HISTORIC', a large headline in the guide proclaims.

Many tourists to Kanchanaburi today are Australians interested in visiting the war cemetery, memorial and museum that bears the name of one of their country's heroes, senior medical officer Sir Edward 'Weary' Dunlop. *The war diaries of Weary Dunlop* (1990, first published 1986) was a bestseller in Australia. Dunlop's memoirs are mostly, as he says, the edited 'diaries of a working doctor' (Dunlop 1990:436), revealing the most extraordinary tale of courage and survival against great odds. Yet, from time to time, he records also his observations of the scenery, the 'almost untouched jungle' (1990:368) and the Siamese people:

This was our first real sight of the Siamese, whose dress is more European than in Malaya—most seem to be wearing trousers rather than sarongs and hats of a European type…We pulled out through the paddy fields in the late evening and Billy remarked that he felt a little more cheerful now we were in Thailand. I am not so sure! (Dunlop 1990:172–3).

War writing becomes a type of anti-tourism and could be expected to consist of mostly negative interpretations of the countryside, such as at Hellfire Pass, where the heat, humidity, dense jungle and mosquitoes—in addition to the brutality of the guards—made life miserable to the point of being unbearable. The familiar image of a menacing jungle is depicted on the cover of the original 1963 edition of Ray Parkin's *Into the smother*. Often used in Western literature to symbolise the horrors of an uncivilised East, it becomes here symbolic of the harsh conditions to which the prisoners were subjected. Throughout the novel *The bridge on the River Kwai*, too, Thailand is cast as a primitive landscape the Japanese use to their advantage against the prisoners. The Siamese jungle is frequently branded uncivilised, with Boulle (2002:51) describing 'the wild nature of the jungle-clad mountains inhabited by lawless tribes of hunters'. While the West is 'the civilized world', Siam is 'this God-forsaken place' and 'a strip of virgin jungle' (Boulle 2002:61,71,106). Similarly, in *Into the smother*, Parkin calls the Thai jungle 'uncivilization' (Parkin 1999:572). For Rohan D Rivett (1946:258) the jungle 'remains primitive, savage, untrammeled and unconquerable'.[138]

The author on a walk through the jungle near Hellfire Pass, Kanchanaburi, in 1992. I have been there more recently, but that first experience was rather eerie as there were no other visitors. These days, the popularity of battleground and war memorial tourism has seen the number of tourists to such sites rise sharply. Credit: Ian James.

Because POWs lived in a defined area and were not at liberty to interact with Thais, other than to carry out a small amount of trading, their writing about their observations of the country is mainly about its landscape, rather than its people. Parkin, whose ability to transcend the POW nightmare is remarkable, equates the landscape to the Garden of Eden in *The sword and the blossom* and comments on its fecundity (Parkin 1999:685,710). His descriptions of the jungle flora are extraordinarily detailed, accompanied by many sketches. Some of his observations are incredibly lush and even sensual:

> The jungle continues to flourish. The wild banana is flowering and the stiff red spearpoint shows crimson against the young green of its fanlike leaves... The rocks, besides tenacious vines, also support rock orchids—neat, pale green and sienna things with little hoods and cups like sensuous lower lips (Parkin 1999:123).

His most intimate communications with nature occur when he is sent to do a task on his own in the jungle. There, away from the Japanese guards and the regulation of camp life, Parkin feels a deep peace: 'I feel a contentment which makes me burst out singing and whistling...I have ants and lizards for company and, occasionally, a small lizard cocks me a friendly glance' (Parkin 1999:197). Parkin is somehow able to rise above the terrible conditions of POW life and appreciate the surroundings of Thailand as it would appear otherwise, untainted by the horrors of war:

> Here, it is Saturday night in Thailand. A green, wet jungle and the million plants and creatures I have not yet begun to know and the noises of un-civilization. No cinema. No plays...I am sitting here on this Satuday night with my bag of rice, to take my place amongst it all for a while—maybe I will surprise a secret! (Parkin 1999:202–3).

From time to time, the POWs do have the chance to observe Thai villagers, when they perhaps allow inherited biases to inform their idyllic views of the 'natives'. To Parkin (1999:710), two young Thai mothers with their children are 'very placid, surrounded by a fecund, strongly growing nature bearing fruit all around them' that 'preached fertility'. This is the 'nurturing native' of the Western imagination described by Pornsawan and Pratt (Pornsawan 2003:43). Parkin (1999:698) observes a 'young, almost childlike' wife whose breasts 'invite, almost demand, the whole world to nurture'. Weary Dunlop (1992:173) also comments on the Thai women, who, he says, 'are dark and buxom, with raven black hair, good teeth and a rather pleasant smile'.

Ernest Gordon's description of the Thais contradicts Parkin's picture of fecundity, underlining the fact that everyone reacts to travel experiences differently, including POWs, and particularly if they are not being told what to expect by a guidebook. Of the Thai villagers, Gordon (1963:86) says, 'Their existence was frugal and they had little to spare'. He blames their religion for their lack of mercy towards the prisoners, particularly Buddhist monks who 'were on their way to salvation by non-attachment' (Gordon 1963:121–2). Significantly, he then describes a village in which the POWs are treated differently, where villagers give them money, food and medicine. 'Later we learned that this village had been converted to Christianity by missionaries', he says (1963:122)—an unlikely scenario.

While Parkin's and Gordon's books were written about two decades after the war, Ian Denys Peek's memoirs were not published until 2003. This is typical of much war writing, often because the returned soldier feels too close to the terrible events to write straight away and, in some cases, does not even think of writing until many years later, when it is normal to review the events of one's life. Weary Dunlop says he shrank from publishing his diaries for more than 40 years because 'it seemed they might add further suffering to those bereaved, and add to controversy and hatred' (Dunlop 1990:xxi).

Peek (2003:xi) insists that, even though it is half a century since the war, the way he describes events is exactly how they occurred: 'They were not forgotten and dredged up after fifty years; they have been part of my life since they happened', he says. In many ways, Peek's account of his time in Thailand can be seen as part travelogue, though the circumstances were, of course, far from the carefree jaunt usually associated with travel.

Like Parkin, Peek describes the Thais as having an abundance of food and as being kind, happy and easy-going. As Peek's title, *One fourteenth of an elephant*, suggests, the book is partly about the elephant, a stalwart of Western travel writing about Thailand. In this case, elephants are more than an accessory to a description of the exotic nature of the country, but are workers themselves on the same project as the POWs; each elephant was able to do the work of fourteen men, hence the title. He anthropomorphises the elephants, imagining what they are saying to themselves about the situation, and his descriptions of their majesty are similar to those found in the work of other travellers, particularly 19th-century accounts (Peek 2003:115–6). He is grateful to the animals, he says, 'in some faintly mystic way' (2003:123). Yet for Peek, the elephants are not so much the sign of exotica, but of the familiar: 'this was the sound made by the elephants at London's great Regent's Park Zoo as they patiently carried small children in howdahs on their backs at tuppence a ride' (2003:107). Peek's description of Bangkok on his liberation could come from the pages of any travel memoirs, except that this typical 'arrival' scene is at the end of the book, not at the beginning:

Everywhere are brilliant colours, flowers, fruit and vegetables piled in the canoes, and the cheerful sounds of people shouting and calling to each other. In the background is the pulsing pom-pom-pom of hundreds of boat engines—the air vibrates with sound (2003:449).

He has with him in the camp a book about Phaulkon, *Siamese white* (Collis 1936), and, interestingly, says it is useful as a kind of guidebook, in detailing a route from near his camp to Siam's central plains (Peek 2003:355). With the exception of his descriptions of the Japanese, he uses less of the stereotypical language that today is regarded as racist—perhaps because he was brought up in Asia (in Shanghai and Singapore) and is fluent in Malay. However, as already noted, Peek did not write his book until 50 years after the events he describes. Nevertheless, the trappings of colonialist ideology are apparent in some of his observations. The British and French colonial rulers in Asia were 'not perfect by any means, but at least tolerant and respecting of the dignity of others', he notes (2003:453). The idea of the 'white man's burden' is in evidence, too, when Peek expresses his disappointment that the Allies could not 'save' Siam: 'It is curious and interesting that we, as representatives of white colonial powers who failed to defend them from invasion, are so popular…while the Japs, who are an Asiatic nation, are hated and despised with great intensity' (2003:453).

In further demonstrating how Orientalist biases are revealed in war writing, Rohan Rivett's *Behind bamboo* is noteworthy for his 'Chapter from the Arabian nights'. Beginning the chapter in Bangkok just after the POWs are liberated, Rivett starts with a quotation from *Sinbad*, in which, after carrying a heavy burden, Sinbad looks into the house of a rich man to behold many slaves, luxurious appointments and a lush garden. In the space of a few days, Thailand for Rivett has changed from prison camp to the pleasurable surroundings of the Oriental Hotel from which to view, like a play unfolding before him, the 'ever-changing river scene' (Rivett 1957:319).

Civilian expatriates living in Bangkok during the Second World War were also incarcerated there, although their conditions were nowhere near as difficult as those of the Allied soldiers in the jungle. One such civilian prisoner was Gerald Sparrow, who includes this time in his 1955 memoirs *Land of the moon flower*. In contrast to the deep anguish and suffering revealed in Death Railway memoirs, Sparrow's read more like a travel adventure as he describes the prisoners' search for alcohol and female companionship (Sparrow 1955:96). When they are released, Bangkok is once more the city of pleasures that it was before the war—and, as Sparrow (1955:105) notes, it is a 'haven' for Allied soldiers who, he claims, come to find mistresses 'after the long and terrible Burma campaign'.

After the POWs of the Second World War, the next major group of Western soldiers to arrive in Thailand was from 1961 to 1973 during the Vietnam War. They were either posted there as support troops for the US or visiting for rest and recreation from the war zone in neighbouring Vietnam. Thailand certainly lived up to Rivett's earlier pronouncement of it as 'the land of milk and honey' (Rivett 1957:257), though in a context that was different to Rivett's meaning. While the writing of Second World War POWs is reminiscent of 19th-century accounts of a close interaction with the terrain and the difficulties it presents, the accounts of Western soldiers during the Vietnam War are forerunners to casual, carnal, late 20th-century and early 21st-century interactions with Thailand—importantly, the soldiers in Thailand during the Vietnam War were not prisoners there, but associated the country primarily with pleasure.

The influx of soldiers to Thailand during the Vietnam War was the catalyst for its transition to a widely acknowledged sex industry centre for Westerners. Indeed, many accounts from the 1960s and early 1970s describe Thailand only in terms of this reputation. From here originated the concept by Westerners that they could buy Thailand. A passage in Hicks's novel, *Thai girl*, demonstrates the belief that Thailand is 'for sale':

> '[T]he GIs were randy so the Thais sold them their women, maybe the soul of the Thai people too…the nicest people money can buy.'
>
> 'Sold for a serving of KFC,' said Stewart (Hicks 2004a:261).

Peter Loria's novel, *Soldiers in Siam*, written in poetry, letters and narrative, reveals how military personnel posted to or visiting Thailand regarded it as 'a locale equipped to satisfy the fantasy of any soldier'—a heaven, as opposed to the hell they experienced in Vietnam (Loria 2002:2). When social misfit Joe Petersen is posted to Thailand, he goes with the idea that it represents 'everything about the East that was quaint, calm and mysterious' (2002:2). He hasn't read much about Thailand, but pictures in guidebooks have told him all he thinks he needs to know:

> There were temples, small dark-skinned people, water buffalo, rice fields, traffic congestion in Bangkok and beautiful women dancers in bright costumes assuming languid poses (Loria 2002:2).

His preconceptions about Thai women are underlined when the plane lands at Bangkok and the female passengers are asked to leave so an American medical officer can talk to the men about how to protect themselves from venereal disease in Bangkok (Loria 2002:3). Sure enough, Joe finds that the bars are 'not what they are back in The World. Here they have bordello accommodations' (2002:48). For the army deserter, Hughie, Thailand is reduced to a set of stereotypes, as he writes in a letter: 'Matt, I must say the place was more beautiful than it sounded in Pidgin English. "Oh you go Pataya [sic], have wave, have palm tree, have boat, have sand, have pretty girl'" (2002:60).

The Thais themselves capitalised on the soldiers' preconceptions of Thailand in a clamour for profit from large numbers of tourists. As William Warren (2000:223) notes in 'Bangkok in the Sixties', rest and recreation leave entailed 'two-week visits during which, for a remarkably low price, they got an airconditoned hotel room, a girl of their choice, and a selection of cultural and shopping tours'. Susan Morgan (1996:226) says the cultural and political history of Europe and the US are a continuing influence on the way prostitution in Thailand has developed.

Arguably the most important novel set in Thailand during the Vietnam War era is Lily Tuck's *Siam: or the woman who shot a man* (1999).[139] It is one of the rare books written by a foreigner that successfully interweaves history, contemporary (1960s) current affairs, contemplation of international politics, culture shock and atmospheric suspense plus a heightened sensibility of Bangkok as a location. The novel tells of young Americans Claire and her husband, James, a government contractor, who fly on their wedding day to Bangkok, where he is posted. Like other visitors, most of what Claire knows about the country comes from American popular culture—a guidebook that tells her Bangkok is the 'Venice of the East', the stage production of *The King and I* and Anna Leonowens's 'book' (she does not specify which one) (Tuck 1999:108).[140] Tuck lived in Thailand in the 1960s and knew silk company owner Jim Thompson. His unsolved disappearance intrigued her, as it does her character Claire, who spends many hours reading Thai history and newspaper articles about Thompson and trying to work out what happened to him. Visiting his house, Claire contemplates the contents of his desk and the guest book open 'to a page on which there was a pen-and-ink drawing of a man with a bird perched on his shoulder' (Tuck 1999:60). Claire also ponders the fate of King Ananda, who died of a gunshot wound in 1946, which may or may not have been suicide. Though the novel is, in some ways, autobiographical—like Claire, Tuck was a young newly-wed in Thailand whose husband's work consumed most of his time—Tuck claims she and her husband had no idea of the political implications of the US involvement in the Vietnam War at the time, nor did they think about them.[141]

Tuck's novel contains substantial, yet subtle, political comment on the US's involvement in Southeast Asia. Claire's is a philosophical journey beyond the battlefield to its implications. Through imagined scenes, newspaper reports and discussions with other Americans about the war, Tuck portrays the encroachment of the West upon the East in 1960s Thailand. Paraphrasing Jim Thompson's views, Claire shocks a fellow expatriate wife when she declares: 'We Americans have the Thais hogtied…The American presence in Thailand has eliminated any hope that the Thais can reach any kind of agreement with their neighbours… Vietnam, even North Vietnam' (Tuck 1999:176).

Jim Thompson's house: a book lies open on Thompson's desk, as visited by Claire in Lily Tuck's novel Siam or the woman who shot a man. *The house, located in Bangkok near Siam Square, is a tourist attraction with guided tours to view Thompson's extensive Southeast Asian art collection. Credit: Mick Elmore/Lonely Planet images.*

On another level, *Siam* can be read as a travelogue, an interesting observation of sightseeing and expatriate life in 1960s Bangkok, at the start of the city's modern tourism boom. While Claire makes a valiant effort to learn Thai, which she finds a struggle, and to come to terms with her new life, the city is so alien to her, she cannot possibly fit in. Having experienced culture shock herself, Tuck conveys perfectly the sense of displacement that Claire feels, without reverting to assumptions of superiority or adopting a patronising tone.[142] While Claire is disturbed by their visits to remote villages, James relishes the chance to 'discover out-of-the-way places' because, 'In a couple of years…all these villages will be full of backpackers, hippies, tourists' (Tuck 1999:35). The nature of Thailand as an emerging tourist destination and the implications of Westernisation are examined:

Then Claire let her mind wander further back to the early days, the days right after the war, when little was known about Siam except that it was always hot and the people were gentle and smiled a lot, and except for in Bangkok, the roads were mud and the country was made up of rice paddies and impenetrable bamboo jungle unexplored still by foreigners. And she liked to think how during this time Jim Thompson and his important and wealthy friends were busy making plans—plans for the democratic reform of Thailand (Tuck 1999:164).

Narrating Thailand

Is it too much to hope that someone might go past the "lavish hotels and low-life bars" (in the typically overheated words of a back-cover blurb) which leave the visitor "sucked into the jagged netherworld of Bangkok"?—Pico Iyer (2003)

It is a critical truth that many books set in Thailand and written by Westerners use it merely as a location of convenience. They could be set anywhere non-Western to accommodate stereotypes of an 'exotic' location far removed from the ordinariness of the readers' day-to-day lives. As Greg Fleet (2002:7) asks rhetorically, 'Why do we travel? Is it to go somewhere great, or is it to get away from somewhere mundane?'.

US actor Leonardo DiCaprio receiving a Buddhist amulet from Prakoo Wichitsangapairoche, the abbot of Samkond Temple, Phuket Province, in 1999. DiCaprio was in Thailand for filming of The beach. DiCaprio played the lead character, naive young traveller Richard. Credit: AP Photo/Handout.

Alex Garland's *The beach* is full of stereotypes: Bangkok is seedy, vice-ridden, the antithesis of paradise, while the unspoilt island that a group of foreign travellers 'discover', creating their own little world, is ultimately destroyed by Thai drug-dealers. There are no Thai characters of any significance in either the book (1997) or the 2000 film Danny Boyle directed—though, to be fair, this is probably a realistic portrayal of the experiences of many tourists, who meet the locals only as hospitality and tourism workers. The story begins in Khao San Road, famous for its backpacker hotels and drug culture, which Garland (1997:5) says is 'a halfway house between East and West'. In some ways, the opening of *The beach* is similar to that of *The English governess*. Both books, and the films they inspired, incorporate classic travellers' arrival scenes. Every Leonowens screen interpretation begins, like *The beach*, with the arrival, depicting the strangeness of the new surroundings, the very un-Englishness (or un-American-ness) of it all and the traveller's brave decision to continue regardless. As Pratt (1992:79-80) says, the arrival scene in travel writing is a site 'for framing relations of contact and setting the terms of its representation'.

Paradise unplugged: locals on the beach at Maya Bay, Krabi province, 550km southwest of Bangkok, in late 1999 after the film The beach was shot there. Environmentalists claimed that changes made by 20th Century Fox to make Maya Bay look more like 'paradise' permanently damaged it. Credit: AP Photo/Sakchai Lalit, File.

Films reinforce and extend stereotypes generated in literature, and *The beach* is a prime example. Thai residents of the area where *The beach* was filmed protested against it being used as a location, but the Government allowed the production to go ahead, while prohibiting that of *Anna and the King*. And yet, in many ways, *The beach* is a markedly less authentic story about Thailand than any of the books or films about Leonowens. While *Anna and the King* (1999) shows Thais in charge of their own country and winning against a threatened foreign takeover, for example, *The beach* depicts a group of travellers making their own kingdom in a paradise where Thais are peripheral to the main action and anonymous. Ironically, the real beach at Koh Phi Phi chosen as the shooting location in the area depicted in the book was not good enough for its screen portrayal; the film company (Fox again) insisted, despite protests on environmental grounds from nearby residents, that the beach required 'landscaping and the replanting of coconut trees to make it fit with the producers' idea of a tropical paradise' (*Bangkok Post* 1998).[143]

Many novels about Thailand are based on true stories. A good example is *God's fool* (Slouka 2003), a novelised biography of the original 'Siamese twins' Chang and Eng, 'discovered' swimming in the Chao Phraya river by British merchant Robert Hunter in 1829 then exhibited in circus freak shows in the US and Europe.[144] Slouka, writing from Chang's point of view, captures not only the sadness of their exploitation, but the presentation of them as some kind of monster: 'And yet, through it all, we had remained exactly who we were, familiar to ourselves. It was the West that made us freaks' (2003:111). The story has similarities to Mary Shelley's *Frankenstein* (1818) in its examination of the way people react to others who resemble them, but who make them uncomfortable because they are different. 'We were the monster in the looking glass, the rustle in the wilderness of realities,' Chang says (Slouka 2003:112).

Another novel based on the theme of truth is *Golden pavilions* (2004), Melbourne designer Robert Brunton's autobiographical story of constructing the Australian display at the 1966 United Nations-sponsored trade fare in Bangkok. The novel is not the usual travel story in which Thailand is placed on show to meet the expectations of the visitor. Instead, Australia becomes the exhibition, a small piece of Thailand becomes Australian, reminiscent of Australia's claim to imaginary ownership of particular overseas destinations (Kanchanaburi and Gallipoli after the Second World War, Bali after the bombings and Phuket after the tsunami, for example). The protagonist, William,[145] is determined the pavilion will give visitors the opportunity to escape the 'crushing humidity and heat of Bangkok' (Brunton 2004:87). Instead of the usual tourism hyperbole selling Thailand to Australia (paradise, sand, sun, sex, shopping), William must try to sell Australia *in* Thailand (ironically using many of the same drawcards).

For William, Thailand is not that paradise of tourism literature, but is, rather, 'The grubby, uncared for airport terminal, the carping nasal sounds of the language, the heavy, sweet smell of the spiced cigarettes, the general feeling of chaotic disorder of the place...' (Brunton 2004:87). The pavilion is an air-conditioned oasis, though it can't escape the odour of nearby effluent. Moreover, the Australian pavilion is not seen by Thais as a little part of Australia, but as a triumph for Thailand, the Thai press ironically calling it The Golden Pagoda and Thai Heaven (2004:404).

Brunton tells part of the story from the point of view of Sumbart, a poor country man who comes to Bangkok and works as a driver for the pavilion builders, while his estranged wife finds work in the sex industry frequented by foreigners. Brunton presents Sumbart as a rounded character, not a token Thai extra, and many readers will identify with him more strongly than they do with any of the book's other characters. Brunton (2004:191) uses the seediness of the Patpong bar scene to add atmosphere, juxtaposed with the luxury of the Oriental hotel, with its 'kitsch, artificial oriental garden'.

Rather than being either glamorously raunchy or disgustingly debauched, the bars the expatriates frequent in *Golden pavilions* are run-down and not particularly enticing. Brunton's portrayal of the 'old Asia hand', Clive, is cringe-makingly accurate of my experience of a certain type of expatriate, seemingly left over from earlier times, who existed in large numbers in the 1990s when I lived in Thailand. Clive tells the brothers not to worry about carrying their bags to the car: 'Leave 'em mate, you are in Asia now, they do the carrying, we do the drinking and stuff' (Brunton 2004:168). These expatriates relate to their experience not so much as living in a foreign country, but as taking a step up, in their view, from the way they lived in the home country. They are delighted when manual work they once had to do for themselves, such as carrying bags, cleaning and driving, is now done by someone else—and for a fraction of the price it would cost at home.

Australian writer Lynette Chataway says her novel, *Noble Sindhu horses* (2005), was inspired by her time living in Thailand with her family, working for Australian Volunteers International. Chataway refutes the tourism industry's unrealistic presentation of Thailand when protagonist Ava discovers that Chiang Mai is not what she expected:

> It is so hot over here and not as green as it should be. It's not like a jungle at all and you can't see the mountains for all of the smoke. I think they burn the fields after they pick the rice. The guidebook I read on the plane coming over gave the impression that Chiang Mai was a kind of Shangri-La in a misty valley, but really it is a very hot, dusty and noisy place (Chataway 2005:53).

Yet, despite Ava's attempt to dispense with guide-book images of Thailand, when she returns to Australia, she becomes part once more of the phantasmagorical presentation of 'the East'. As her husband, Francis, imagines her in 'diaphanous garments, earrings, a genie vest and harem pants', she tells a story of their time in Chiang Mai, 'like Sheherazade, the spell-binding narrator of *The Arabian nights*' (Chataway 2005:93). The experience of living in Thailand has become, after their return to Australia, a set of anecdotes that metamorphose into fairy stories served up for the consumption of those at home, 'story after story like the Brothers Grimm' (2005:96). Yet she and Francis have to be selective, for reality beyond guide-book-type euphemisms would not be socially acceptable, and Francis knows 'that if the talk were to turn to poverty, for instance, or the toll AIDS is taking on rural Thailand, all eyes would glaze over' (2005:96).

Like *Golden pavilions*, *Noble Sindhu horses* has a strong Thai character, Nikkon. He learns English at school in Chiang Mai, but the teacher is not very good at English, the teaching materials are poor and 'When Nikkon finishes primary school he is amazed at how little he has learned' (2005:21). English lessons from books provided by the Dutch government and from reciting the fairytale *The Emperor's new clothes* parrot-style do nothing to equip Nikkon for life beyond school.

Reflecting Thailand

US academic Benedict Anderson remarked 30 years ago that scholarly writing in English about Thailand was a strange case, in that there was so little of it (Anderson 1978). Of the few books that did exist about Thai political life, all the major studies had been written two decades previously (1978:193). This was largely the result of Siam not being officially colonised, he says, so there was not a large number of Western scholars in Thailand who studied the language and culture; nor were there the meticulous records kept in Western archives that colonised countries had (1978:195). No doubt because of this lack of knowledge, Westerners have been easily led into a false sense of what Thai culture is about, particularly the notion of 'Old Siam':

> [I]n talk and texts, 'Old Siam' manifests itself as a typical blend of comfort and exoticism. Steam-powered river transport, modern tropical medicine, a stable currency, and easy communications with the Western world combine with colourful ceremonies, picturesque sights and sounds, piquant cooking, cheap antiques, plentiful servants, and a 'relaxed' attitude on sexual matters. Needless to say, this 'Old Siam' does not date further back than about 1900 (Anderson 1978:227).

In reality, traditional Thai culture such as art, architecture, music, dance and drama declined when King Chulalongkorn ascended the throne, he maintains (Anderson 1978:228–9). However, since the second half of the 20th century, some arts have been resurrected and, despite criticism of the interest in 'Old Siam', the demands of tourists to see traditional arts must have contributed to this resurgence. This is evidenced in a book published in English about Thai dance, *The Khon and Lakon dance dramas* (Dhanit 1963). More recent examples of impressive books in English about Thai arts are *Thai textiles* (Conway 1992), *A century of Thai graphic design* (Anake 2000) and *Architecture of Thailand* (Nithi & Mertens 2006).

Anderson and Ruchira Mendiones edited one of the first Thai short-story collections in English translation, *In the mirror,* when the literature of Siam was little known outside Thailand (Anderson & Mendiones 1985:9). The title story by Kon Krailat is set in the Bangkok sex industry of the 1970s and tells of an intelligent young man from the country who qualifies as a teacher then heads to Bangkok, where he is paid to perform live sex shows. In his introduction to the book, Anderson examines the story as a reaction to the advent of 'temporary wives' for American soldiers, noting that it was jet travel, chain hotels and the cheap package holiday that 'turned Bangkok from an exotic byway for the adventurous into a standard port-of-call for mass international tourism' (Kon 1985:68). Kon chooses to make his protagonist a male, 'in a mordant juxtaposition' of the many sad stories about female sex industry workers (Anderson & Mendiones 1985:69) and sets the story in a bar with exclusively Thai customers. He is making a political point, Anderson says, by reminding readers that 'such specialized sexual entertainments are no longer only responses to the foreign tourist tide, but have become embedded in metropolitan Thai society' (1985:69).

In 'Michigan test', by Wanit Jarungkit-anan, the protagonist reluctantly arrives to sit an English test to help attain an American visa, but finding it too hard, berates the other candidates for 'applying to become a slave of American imperialism' (Wanit 1985:152). The story concerns the Thai perception of the US and its implications. It is also a criticism of the social values of Thailand's new urban middle class and its greed for the materialism of Westernisation (Anderson & Mendiones 1985:53). While in Western literature, Thailand often becomes a fantasy location, in 'Michigan test', as Anderson says, the US assumes that role for the Thais and the protagonist wonders 'whether or not it was really like what I saw so often in the movies' (Anderson & Mendiones 1985:53). By the end of the story, the US has become even more unrealistic, as have those who seek visas to study there: 'You're dreamers, the whole lot of you! Seeing a lot of movies has made you want to go abroad', the protagonist says to the other Thais in the examination room (Wanit 1985:152).

Over the last 25 years, a counterbalance to the Western quest for the exotic has emerged from among Thai writers. Though Thailand has a well established literary tradition, particularly in poetry, it is only since the 1980s that a significant amount of literature by Thais has become accessible to English speakers. This includes historical material, such as *The Chiang Mai chronicle* (Wyatt & Aroonrut, 1998) and *The Royal chronicles of Ayutthaya* (Wyatt 2000), as well as Thai writing about early interactions with foreigners, such as *The diary of Kosa Pan* (Cruysse & Smithies 2002). There are also modern novels, such as *The teachers of Mad Dog Swamp* (Khammaan 1982), set in Isaan and translated to English in 1982. This entertaining book, about rural teachers, was a bestseller in Thailand and was made into a popular film. As its translator, Gehan Wijeyewardene, says, such translations help to correct the 'selective, perhaps distorted' view that exists in foreigners' writing and provide instead a view 'closer to the reality of the society as perceived by those who live in it' (Khammaan 1982:xliii).

An increasing number of Thais, led by Pira Sudham and SP Somtow, are writing in English. Pira's *Shadowed country* (2004) and Somtow's *Jasmine nights* (1994) are semi-autobiographical novels that examine the influences of Westernisation and modernisation and the reactions of their Thai characters to these phenomena. In *Jasmine nights*, which is about growing up in 1960s Bangkok, the protagonist, Sornsunthorn, called Little Frog by his family but who calls himself Justin, befriends the boy next door, Virgil, a black American. Somtow cleverly juxtaposes the usual stereotypes of white foreigners about Thais, with Justin's preconceptions about African-Americans: 'They are exotic creatures, reeking of ancient times, barbaric splendour, jungle savagery', Justin thinks (Somtow 2002:29). In their games, Virgil becomes 'the ferocious cannibal king' who speaks 'the mellifluous poetry common to barbarian races' (2002:31). Whereas in books set in Thailand by Westerners, the Thai characters are mostly servants or in a service industry used by foreigners, Justin's wealthy father owns the estate on which Virgil lives and is his landlord. Although they are so different, the two boys form a strong bond and Justin learns a valuable lesson concerning race, culture and identity: 'It occurs to me that perhaps we are not so unalike after all. He too is of two worlds', he thinks to himself (2002:39). The boys' preconceptions about each other are revealed when they visit a 'witch doctor'. When Virgil berates Justin for believing in magic potions, saying 'You people too damn superstitious [sic]', Justin takes umbrage, citing canonical Western literature:

'What do you mean, "you people?" What about you people with your cannibals and your voodoo? You sit around worshipping King Kong, for God's sake! You strangle your wives, too,' I add learnedly, for I have recently read an annotated edition of *Othello* that was lying around the ruined house (2002:46–7).

Somtow presents the West, particularly England, as a metaphor for growing up, in what becomes something of a parody of the West's self-designated proprietorial role over the East. When Sornsunthorn/Justin has to leave Thailand for boarding school in England, his father equates it with leaving paradise, with joining 'the real world'. Thailand becomes a paradise lost, soon to be located by American soldiers and then 'discovered' by the mass-market tourist:

> [I]n this tiny Eden, there is no hint of the change that will sweep the world. We're not really of this earth, and that's the truth of it; but it can't last... Sornsunthorn, you see, the thing about all paradises is that we *must* leave them (Somtow 2002:377).

For Justin, England also is a paradise lost, for it is not the England of his dreams, not the romantic England of history that he has come to expect from the classical literature he has read. So, England is not paradise and Thailand will soon no longer be paradise. However, in the last chapter, poignantly titled 'I Have a Dream', Somtow makes the point that paradise is not a physical location but a state of being, no matter how fleeting. Justin has a dream that he and his friends—Virgil, South African Piet, family servant Piak and white American Wilbur

> ...would sit in our little treehouse, sheltered against the chaos of societies we did not make, just being together. Not masters and servants, and not members of different races and cultures, but just ourselves, together (Somtow 2002:383).

In *Shadowed country*, Pira's themes are an apt illustration of Said's contention that separating people into categories exposes 'the way in which understanding is complicit with the power to produce such things as the "Orient" and the "West"' (Said 2003:349).[146] Class distinction runs through the story of country boy Prem who wins a scholarship to study in England in the 1970s. Pira's usual themes of the injustices and imbalance of Thai society are there, but the story has wider applications as a study of class, cultural and racial discrimination in England and between 'Orient' and 'Occident'.

In a scene that mocks Westerners' views of Asians as 'all the same', homesick Prem goes to the red-light district of Soho, not to visit the sex shops but to eat at a Chinese restaurant 'where its particular smell and the Oriental faces of the customers and waiters brought home closer' (Pira 2004:153–4). In a send-up of Western tourists' tales of erroneously spelt menus and Asians' pronunciation gaffes, Prem orders fried rice and says he takes particular care 'not to say "fly lice"' (2004:154). The story becomes tragic when a group of thugs attack him in the street later that night, and it seems even more insulting that they call him 'Chink' (2004:154). The presence of the 'seemingly universal Chinese' that was a comfort at the restaurant earlier, now becomes a taunt, a mark of the chasm between East and West. Prem's poverty contrasts with the wealth of his highly connected and Westernised benefactor/flatmate Dhani, who lives in a state of cultural cringe in a home tastefully decorated with Thai objets d'art and adopts the persona of an English gentleman. Dhani, also referred to as Dani and Danny, depending on the context, has rejected Thai culture as backward and irrelevant to his life. When he has to return to Bangkok to live in his parents' house, a bizarre and vulgar copy of England's Buckingham Palace, he has to think again about his blasé attitude to the riches that have been heaped upon him over the years. Meanwhile, Prem returns to Isaan in his quest to educate the people back in Napo village.[147] The biggest twist in the story comes when impoverished Prem inherits a fortune and must learn how to use it.

Pira does not offer solutions to the problems he addresses—and that, perhaps, is his point: that each person must decide for himself how to live an authentic life. As Australian academic JR Bernard says in a foreword to *Shadowed country*, 'Part of what is at issue is the encroachment of the tempting artefacts and expectations of the West upon the age-old and conservative patterns of the indigenous East' (Pira 2004:9). *Shadowed country* offers the Western reader a picture of Thailand that is more fully rounded than any that foreign writers can offer, and some of the images it presents are surprising, even shocking, Bernard says:

> At very least they are likely to cause an uncomfortable enlarging of the images of Thailand typically held in the Western mind, adding less romantic pictures to place beside those of exotic resorts like Phuket, and of golden Buddhas in scented temples. The heartlessness, and above all the greed, are the same unattractive coins as circulate in my country and no doubt in yours (Pira 2004:14).

Among other Thais who write in English is politician and businessman Pongpol Adireksarn. He is interesting because he uses the pseudonym Paul Adirex, a European-sounding rearrangement of his name, in an attempt to attract more English-speaking readers, although his books are not readily available outside Thailand. His historical novel *Rattanakosin* (Adirex 2004) begins in 1767 and has several *farang* characters who are soldiers in the Thai army, although by that year, when Ayutthaya was sacked by the Burmese, there were only a few Westerners left in the country and the storyline seems unlikely. Nevertheless, Adirex tells an exciting adventure story set between the 18th century and the present. It appears to be the first novel in English about how Bangkok came to be the capital of Thailand.

While many of the best known Thai writers in English are men, Susan Fulop Kepner (1996b) has edited and translated a wide-ranging anthology of Thai fiction about women, most of it, but not all, also written by women. The book includes a useful overview in its introduction and biographical sketches of each author. Kepner concedes that most of the works included focus on negative subjects, because most of the best 20th-century Thai writing is by authors who are dissatisfied with Thai society. There is, however, a balancing mix of positive, popular and romantic fiction. As she says, '...if Thailand is not really the land of smiles, as it has sometimes been called, nor is it the land of sorrows' (Kepner 1996b:xi).

In an extract from Botan's novel, *That woman's name is Boonrawd*, a Thai woman goes to live with an American expatriate engineer. Boonrawd's brother is embarrassed that people might think she is a 'rented wife', and convinced that 'he'll go home to America someday. They all do' (Botan 1996:145). Yet, Boonrawd's mother is horrified that her daughter has made no financial arrangement with the man, other than for household management expenses. By living with a *farang*, Boonrawd cannot be considered by her family as having a 'normal' romantic partnership, no matter what the reality. Kepner identifies an interesting and ironic problem with the novel, given that English-speaking readers will be looking for the story to provide a more authentic look at Thai-farang marriage: non-Thai readers, she says, may find the character of Robert, the *farang* engineer, unbelievable (Botan 1996:163).

Recently, several collections of short stories by Thai authors writing in English have been published, including *Sightseeing* (Rattawut 2005) and *Fragile days* (Tew 2003). Like the stories in *In the mirror* (Anderson & Mendiones 1985), the stories in both of these collections are set in a changing Thailand reacting to encroaching Westernisation, and some include *farang* characters, notably the young tourist Lizzie in 'Farangs' (Rattawut 2005:1–22). The presence of foreigners in Thailand is remarked upon in many of the stories in both books, often in a less than favourable light.

In Rattawut's title story, 'Sightseeing', a mother and son become tourists in their own country and visit a tiny island on the Andaman Sea off the coast from Trang (Rattawut 2005:69–94).[148] They go because they want to see if it really does have fine sand, turquoise water and countless fish, as Ma's boss has told her. Rattawut turns the rhetoric of tourism, meant for foreigners, upon itself:

> Her boss had called it paradise, and though I remember Ma telling me as a child that Thailand was only a paradise for fools and farangs, for criminals and foreigners, she's willing to give it a chance now. If paradise is really out there, so close to home, she might as well go and see for herself (Rattawut 2005:70).

Tew Bunnag's 'Epilogue: an ode to the city' (Tew 2003:131–6) is startlingly vivid as a foil to the countless descriptions of Bangkok in tourist brochures, travel guides and travel writing by Westerners. The picture he paints is far from a Venice of the East or a centre of sensual delights; it is, at times, ugly, tragic and unredeemable. Yet Tew comes closer to describing Bangkok adequately than many other writers, employing the familiar images of travel industry promotion to make his point:

> Those postcard-pretty moments that smile out of the pages of tourist brochures—the gilded temple stupas, the riverside scenes of children waving, a corner of Chinatown in twilight, a colourful marketplace stall overflowing with tropical fruit—merely emphasise the honky-tonk mess of the rest of the place, which is not exactly picturesque (Tew 2003:131).

In 'Jeed Finds Her Brother', Tew turns the viewfinder the opposite way from that to which English readers are accustomed. Thai country woman Jeed observes Western tourists travelling on the Skytrain in Bangkok:

> There were a few scruffy *farangs* as in Sukothai—the ones with the rucksacks wearing Thai fisherman's trousers and peasant tops who went to visit the old ruins and the temples. It always disappointed her to see *farangs* like this. She thought that with their wealth they should always be dressed well, even the young ones (Tew 2003:48).

With the rise of new Thai literature in English, perhaps readers can come closer to Iyer's plea (Iyer 2003) to move beyond the 'tawdry clichés' towards a new understanding of the complexity that is any country, Western or Eastern, including Thailand. Said's description of how that understanding might be achieved could guide this new direction:

> It is more rewarding—and more difficult—to think concretely and sympathetically, contrapuntally, about others than only about 'us'. But this also means not trying to rule others, not trying to classify them or put them in hierarchies, above all, not constantly reiterating how 'our' culture or country is number one (or *not* number one, for that matter) (Said 1994:408).

Conclusion

[I]t remains a curious—but telling—irony that the one country in Asia that boasts of never having been conquered is colonized in the imagination night after night after night.—Pico Iyer (2003)

As I wrote my PhD thesis and then this book, a number of momentous events occurred that put Thailand in the world news media's spotlight: the December 2004 tsunami; the coup d'état in September 2006; and the restoration of democracy in January 2008 after elections that reinstated the People Power Party of deposed leader Thaksin Shinawatra. Though the natural disaster and the political upheaval are not, in themselves, alike, the media's coverage of them reveals much about the way Thailand is portrayed in the West in the early 21st century.

Asia is presented in the media as 'a constellation of "hot spots"', Gerster (1995:237) writes, and 'bad news from Asia is good news', because it makes us 'feel better about (our)selves'. There is certainly an element of cultural superiority in the reportage of the coup of 19 September 2006, a nanny-like observation of 'them' as opposed to 'us'. The ousting of Prime Minister Thaksin 'should be a lesson for all those Third World leaders who use their new private jets to attend important international meetings and mingle with the rich and powerful', preaches Bruce Palling (2006) on a British news website.

There was concern, at the time of both the tsunami and the coup, that the tourism industry would be adversely affected, and, certainly, when I visited Phuket in March 2005, the beaches were bare, the bars almost empty, the souvenir shops desperately needing customers.Today, most, but not all of the tsunami-affected areas have been rebuilt and the tourists are back. In mass-market weekend newspapers, stories about Phuket read as if the tsunami had never happened. In the *Sunday Herald Sun* newspaper's *Sunday Magazine*, for example, Carlie Oates admits she thinks of Phuket as 'a little slice of cliché heaven' with 'idyllic scenery and exceptional service from the loveliest of people' and, instead of a headline, the story has a statement: 'Phuket: If poolside foot scrubs, cocktails and canoeing through secluded lagoons sound like paradise, this island may just be your heaven on earth' (Oates 2007:50).

It is difficult to gauge how much the 2006 coup affected tourism, if at all, although there are many anecdotes of travellers changing their plans to visit Thailand just after it. In July 2008, the coup and its aftermath were still being named as contributing to the Australian Government's warning to exercise a 'high degree of caution' when travelling in Thailand.[149] The coup actually became *part* of tourism as tanks and soldiers lined the streets of Bangkok. The *New York Times* published an article with the headline 'Thailand Tourists: "Coup? What Coup?"'(Considine & Purnell 2006). It was accompanied by a picture of a white female tourist flanked by two Thai soldiers with guns. She is smiling and holding up the front page of Bangkok's *Nation* newspaper with the headline 'COUP!' The article quotes tourists in pubs and shopping centres in Bangkok treating it as something of a joke, another picturesque traveller's tale to take home: 'In fact, when tanks rolled into Bangkok, Thais presented soldiers with flowers and candy, and many troops gladly posed for photographs with foreigners. In Phuket, unperturbed beachgoers sipped "coup cocktails" at beachside bars' (Considine & Purnell 2006).

Travellers' tales: a military coup becomes just another photo opportunity for tourists in Bangkok, including this one pictured with Thai soldiers on 23 September 2006, which appeared in a New York Times article entitled 'Thailand tourists: Coup? What Coup?' Credit: AP Photo/Apichart Weerawong.

Business as usual: a group of Thai dancers dressed in a go-go-bar-style take-off of military gear, performs in front of a line of tanks parked outside the Royal Plaza in Bangkok on 25 September 2006. The women handed out pink roses to soldiers. Credit: AP Photo/Apichart Weerawong.

Thailand obviously wants to promote the idea that all is well for tourists. As such, coverage of the coup is an excellent example of the complicity and reciprocity involved in the tourism process. This complicity was revealed by a picture in *The First Post* on 26 September 2006, which shows a group of young Thai dancers dressed like bar girls, dancing for coup soldiers to show the coup is not threatening to tourists, that it is business as usual for tourism in Thailand. The *Bangkok Post* underlined this view in an article on 4 October 2006 which quoted the Kasikorn Research Centre as saying the photographs of tourists with soldiers and tanks would help foreigners 'realise that Thailand's political situation has returned to normal'. Meanwhile, a Tourism Authority of Thailand newsletter, also dated 4 October 2006, cited the coup as just one more tourism attraction of Thailand:

> Sawasdee ka! There's lots of news this month from Thailand, with the successful and peaceful introduction of a new government; the recent opening of Suvarnabhumi International Airport in Bangkok and the upcoming Surin Elephant Round-up, Phuket Vegetarian Festival and Royal Flora Ratchapruek in Chiang Mai. As always—there is something to keep everyone happy!

One frequent visitor who had 'fallen in love with the country's shrinking unspoiled areas' said he wished the coup had affected tourism so that fewer travellers would go there (Considine & Purnell 2006). This is reminiscent of Alisa Tang's sanguine claims about the tsunami having the 'positive' effect of 'washing away rampant development' (Tang 2005). Both quotations demonstrate the (neo)colonialist nostalgia that permeates Western writing about Thailand, stamping an assumption of ownership by the 'West' upon the 'East' so that, as Said maintains,"'our'" East, "our" Orient becomes "ours" to possess and direct' (2003:pxiv). Prasso (2006:130) cites an example of this attitude from a *Washington Post* editorial of 26 December 2003, about Thai-US co-operation on counter-terrorism strategies. Referring to then Prime Minister Thaksin, the editorial is headlined 'Our Man in Bangkok'. As Prasso (2006:130-1) points out, 'The editorial editors at *The Washington Post* would never think to refer to Silvio Berlusconi [of Italy]—who in many ways is Thaksin's political and businessman equivalent—as "our man in Rome"'.

The continuing promotion of the East as mysterious and exotic has its origins in early travel writing such as that by Polo and Mandeville. Like Mandeville, many travel writers use the work of others as inspiration and, in some cases, simply copy them. In the case of Thailand, early accounts of Ayutthaya by Westerners set the tone for future travellers' accounts and led to the coining of enduring phrases such as 'the Venice of the East'. However, the real sense of ownership of the East was propagated as a consequence of the later 'scientific' categorisation of races. By the mid-18th century this had resulted in Europeans believing themselves to be racially superior. As Said maintains, in constructing 'Asia' in the cultural imagination, Europeans associated it with 'theses of Oriental backwardness, degeneracy, and inequality with the West' (Prasso 2006:206). Today, despite a chorus of postcolonial damnation, the ideologies of imperialism still assert themselves in Western cultural forms, particularly in writing.

This book has examined the origins of various assumptions about Thais and Thailand that exist in almost everything written about it by Westerners, incorporating what Said describes as a 'free-floating mythology of the Orient' (Said 2003:53) and what JV D'Cruz and William Steele (2003:37) term 'The superiority-of-being-us'. The mythology becomes part of the body of knowledge that 'everyone knows', that is accepted as fact by the majority of people in the West, even though it is actually the result of a mixture of assumption, prejudice and expectation.

Most literature about Thailand presents it as a location that promises eroticism, the possibility of danger and, most importantly, adventure, even for the package tourist. For the independent traveller, there is the feeling of travelling into the unknown and of bravely undertaking a mysterious journey. Evidence of this can be found in the introduction to one of my own travel stories:

'You're going to Tak? A woman alone? Hmmm…adventurous.'

The words of my Thai friend in Bangkok did not exactly inspire confidence before I set off to the northern province on the Myanmar (Burmese) border.

After all, if a Thai was wary of the place, how would I fare? (James 2001:14).

Travel writing perpetuates this body of knowledge by creating an expectation of what a location is 'like'. This is particularly true of guidebooks, which tell you what you will see. Houellebecq (2002:82) parodies this process in *Platform*, when he describes the city of Surat Thani, which, he says, guidebooks judge as being 'of no interest whatever'. He then comments wryly: 'Nevertheless, people live there'. Sure enough, *Lonely Planet Thailand* says Surat Thani has 'little of historical interest' and there is nothing to do there, but that a nearby village makes an interesting day trip 'if you find yourself stuck in Surat for a night' (Cummings et al 2005:547,551). The latest *Lonely Planet Thailand* has toned down the condemnation, though it maintains that Surat Thani is 'a point you zip through on the way to somewhere better' (Williams et al 2007:578).

Synonymous with expectation is the notion of exploration, that the tourist is somehow able to travel back in time to 'discover' territories. Western wanderers consider themselves discoverers as much today as they did in the 19th century—more so, in fact, because travel 'adventures' are available to a much higher percentage of Western populations than ever. The accessibility and methods of travel and the trappings of tourism might have changed, but the expectations are the same.

Those expectations are given credence in travel guides and newspaper travel sections, which promise the traveller a paradise of unspoilt beaches, virgin jungle, and smiling locals, combined with the thrill of exploration. Even more so than in the past, travel guides have adopted the rhetoric of Orientalism in order to promote themselves and their destinations. Guidebooks and travel articles frequently cite the fact that Thailand has never been politically colonised by the West as evidence of the 'authenticity' of Thailand's ancient culture. Travellers then complain that the destination is not as 'authentic' as they had expected, as in this description of the Grand Palace from Exell's memoirs:

> There was nothing wrong with the Audience Hall, of course, except that it was not my idea of the East. I would have preferred a setting which was essentially Siamese. But perhaps I was biased. I had come to the East to see the East and not Italian buildings or State Capitols (Exell 1963:77).

Thailand in travel literature becomes a dream world, and if the confronted reality seems different, the traveller feels cheated. Lonely Planet author Joe Cummings tells Jerry Hopkins in *Bangkok Babylon* that he despises the advent of mass tourism on Koh Samui, which there is no doubt, of course, he helped create: 'It's total tedium and it's no longer Thailand. It's sort of Thai, you can make an argument either way, but as far as what I get out of it, I don't feel like I'm really in Thailand' (Hopkins 2005:189). Criticism because of failed expectations has a long history. In the late 19th century, H Warrington Smyth (1994:9) asks, 'But where was the Bangkok I had read of?' Instead of the gilded temples of a 'Venice of the East', there is only the mud and industrial ugliness of 'an eastern Rotterdam', he complains.

Western assumptions and expectations about the country are exploited by Thailand itself. The Tourism Authority of Thailand's 'Amazing Thailand' campaign, launched in 1997, has ensured that iconic images of bejewelled dancing girls, glittering temples, lumbering elephants and coconut palm-fringed beaches are synonymous with tourists' expectations. The use of Western information by Thailand in constructions of itself is not new, of course. A large proportion of written representations of Thailand before the 18th century were by Europeans, and Thai scholars have used foreigners' accounts for much of their information about Ayutthaya.

Many writers agree that Thailand was subjected to what Osterhammel (1997:20) terms 'quasi-colonialism'. Benedict Anderson (1978:210), for example, says Siam was 'plainly semi-colonial'. Travel literature about it in the 19th-century reflected colonial aspirations and acquisitions elsewhere, such as in Egypt, India and Burma. In addition, 19th-century writers discuss Siam as if it were about to be—or at least ought to be—colonised. Its people are branded inferior to the white man and, in turn, to races in colonised countries such as India. Key racist concepts that historically had been used by Europeans to subjugate others are employed equally in reference to Thais. There are numerous descriptions along the lines of Smyth's, in which he says the Siamese can show 'earnestness' and 'endeavour', but that they exhibit 'a thoroughly Oriental luxuriance of idleness, frivolity, intrigue and dishonesty' (Smyth 1994:18). As Said (1994:181) says in describing Kipling's Orientalised India, any survey of late-19th-century Western culture 'reveals an immense reservoir of popular wisdom of this sort'. Bishop and Robinson say travel brochures have taken colonial descriptions and used them to explain how tourists should deal with the locals. They quote an extraordinarily insulting and almost unbelievable British brochure (probably dating from the late 1960s), that says Thais should be treated as 'Peter Pans. Eternal children who have never grown up…The lights are on but nobody's at home' (Bishop & Robinson 1998:89). Thankfully, travel brochures have moved on in the last 40 years and such blatantly racist material is no longer acceptable.

For long-term visitors, expatriate life turns out usually to be no more than a platform from which to view a foreign culture and results in much the same views and conclusions as the tourist or traveller has—in some cases, it results in an even narrower perception as frustration and dissatisfaction with life away from 'home' increase.

The habit of the expatriate European communities to separate themselves from society at large arose partly from the desire to maintain one's supposed racial superiority and not to 'go native'. (It is, of course, also about being near like-minded people who speak the same first language.) Most expatriates, with the exception of the missionaries who almost all made a valiant attempt to become fluent and literate in Thai, seemed satisfied that they could not or would not learn to speak Thai and that they refused to adopt local dress more suited to the climate or to socialise with any Siamese other than those of the upper class. For some, this was evidence in their minds that they had not succumbed to the lascivious pleasures of the flesh or the unruly life of the 'native' so readily accessible in exotic locales; others simply couldn't see the point. Grewal cites Harriet Martineau's advice in *Eastern life: present and past* (1848), in which the Englishwoman traveller, in particular, is advised to dress, eat and drink during her travels as she would in England, or as close to it as possible, because if she adopts 'native' dress it might signify 'her rejection of English ways'(Grewal 1996:93).

In essence, 19th-century and early-20th-century visitors believed they must bring the social mores of the home country to the foreign locale, setting up colonial-style houses and decrying the lack of good servants, holiday resorts and the like, even in countries such as Siam that were not officially part of any empire. It was the fostering and continuance of 'civilisation' that was important. The culture of the host country was deemed to be an interesting diversion at best, and, at worst, was used by writers to point out the savagery of non-Western people and to justify the need to introduce Western ideals and practices. Even long-term residents who claim to abhor discrimination retain their sense of superiority in some way. Many of the writers studied reveal that the longer they spend in Thailand, the less open-minded they are towards its culture. Some become scathing, while others profess to understand Thai ways, but succeed only in further showing their Eurocentricity.

Writing by 19th-century visitors shows clearly that the basis upon which missionary work is justified is that of the 'white man's burden', the duty to teach non-white people what Christian Westerners believe is the true religion, morally correct social values and Western education and languages (principally English). So-called civilisation and Christianity are inseparable and are the desired result of missionary labours. It was the missionary's duty to save the souls of the heathens and thereby to civilise them. They were to be drawn away from the dangers of 'savagery'—from abject nakedness, worshipping heathen idols, unbridled bodily urges and unsavoury habits. In their writing, the jungle becomes the geographical embodiment of this savagery, always lurking at the edges, ready to claim its own back—and the white man, too, if he is not vigilant. Nor are the 'savages' allowed to pick and choose what aspects of Westernisation they want to adopt, for some, such as film, it is maintained, could be subversive. Meanwhile, 'native' religious views are considered equally dangerous.

There is a central belief common to most 19th-century Western writing—and to a fair proportion of later writing, too—that modernisation is for Thailand's greater good, that all Western ways mean taking the country 'forward' and that there is an ongoing need to lead the Thais step by step towards becoming 'developed'. The authority comes not from the experiences of the sovereign state itself, but, in the minds of Western teachers and advisers, from the lessons of Western civilisation. The attitudes continue today, albeit in a less obvious manner. It is a pity more writers did not heed the wise words of Carol Hollinger:

> Because a nation is underdeveloped does not mean that it is populated by underdeveloped citizens...There is no such person as a simple man. The pathos and absurdity of human life is as complex in a tribal village as it is on Fifth Avenue. The man who lives in a thatched house on stilts has wisdom and ignorance, love and death, mirth and tears, anger and peace, youth and age in his life as we do. There is no East, no West...there are people and no one of these people is a statistic to himself (Hollinger 1997:98).

While Westerners' images of Thailand, particularly before the advent of mass tourism in the 1970s, might have once been influenced by Leonowens's books, they were filtered, adapted and added to via novel, screen and stage to change the view to an almost wholly fictional one—comparatively few people today have read Leonowens's original works. The films featuring Leonowens, particularly *The King and I*, plus the books by Landon and Leonowens, can be viewed as part of the body of work by certain Westerners, including travel writers and filmmakers, who, according to Said (1994:xix), 'deliver the non-European world either for analysis and judgement or for satisfying the exotic tastes of European and North American audiences'. By not allowing Leonowens to stand as a product of her time, however, the value within what she actually wrote has been ignored. It is time Leonowens took her place among other 19th-century travel writers as a significant chronicler of her life and times in Siam—and as the only outsider, Western or Thai, to have been able to intimately observe and write about the *Nang Harm* over a number of years.

A large amount of literature promotes Thailand to the West as a centre of sensuality, of sex for sale and of romanticised danger. This includes travel writing, tourism brochures, novels, guides and memoirs. In particular, there is a body of popular writing, most of it by white male expatriates, set in the sex tourism industry and portraying Bangkok and other tourist areas of Thailand as places that exist by and of the sex industry and the vices associated with it. Perceptions of the ideal Thai woman are crucial in this depiction of Thailand as a sex tourism centre. The stereotype of the Asian woman, 'eyes almond-shaped and usually downcast' persists, as Warren (2000:131,135) says, despite the existence of images to the contrary in Western literature, such as Vilai 'the White Leopard' in *A woman of Bangkok*.

The images of subservient and seductive women portrayed in literature today about Thailand have their origins in entrenched Western stereotypes about Eastern women, particularly those of 'the Inside'. The very term 'harem', a word of Turkish origin which has been used in English since the mid-17th century, conjures visions of voluptuous, idle, jewel-covered women, of sumptuous cushions and plates of sweet treats, and of the wealthy, omnipotent master who controls the women's lives.

Thai women are portrayed as always available, young, smiling, but ultimately all alike. This is illustrated perfectly in David Foster's novel, when Felix says he customarily has sex with a woman only once, so in Bangkok, after the first prostitute, he cannot go to another because 'They're *all* the same!' (Foster 1983:191). This belief persists well beyond the images of the sex industry. An example is a 2005 magazine advertisement for a Thai-style food kit sold in Australian supermarkets. 'Go a bit Thai', Pillsbury's advertisement for Wraps of the World says. It is accompanied by a picture of a typical family—mother, father and three children—whose faces have all been replaced by that of the same young Thai woman, smiling and wearing a gold headpiece, with 'A Taste for Adventure' written below the picture.

A dominant image of Thailand in many Westerners' eyes is that of an adventure holiday destination, with pristine scenery and the lurking possibility of danger. As Robert Sam Anson says, it is easy in Bangkok to be 'seduced. lured. And then, even without realizing it, you are captured' (Anson 1997:6). Overwhelmingly in male writing about Thailand, the image is of a seductive, feminised land open to and awaiting penetration by the white man. In return, the white man pays for the privilege, his patronage supposedly benefiting the entire country and helping it to develop further along Western lines while keeping its special identity from times past, thereby becoming an even more comfortable destination for the Western tourist. Iyer portrays perfectly this desire for both the exotic and the familiar:

> Bangkok was the heart of the Orient, of course. But it was also every Westerner's synthetic, five-star version of what the Orient should be: all the exoticism of the East served up amidst all the conveniences of the West (Iyer 2001:333).

The word 'exotic' has become synonymous with what Thailand is seen to offer the traveller—idyllic beaches, cheap sex, shopping and drugs, sultry weather and tropical adventure. However, not all literature about Thailand is of clichéd exotica. Women sojourners such as Connelly, Adiele and Hollinger participate in the culture rather than merely observing it from safe touristic sidelines. Instead of trying to pass themselves off as culturally aware and politically correct, all admit their failures and prejudices. All make not only a physical journey, but a psychological journey of discovery. While many men go to Thailand to seek sexual encounters (in classic Orientalist fashion), many more women than men go to search for a higher self-identity. Yet in the end, most travellers' stories have the same outcome: the traveller returns home to resume his or her 'real' life, sifting through memories of the holiday or overseas posting and retaining only those that have significance for them. Many travel memoirs ultimately celebrate the superiority of the home culture over the visited one, using traditionally male colonial attitudes to validate themselves with their audience. This was particularly true in the 19th century, when, even though women's travel writing often concentrated on the domestic detail of daily life, the conclusions reached were the same as those of the men—that Western culture and religion are superior and should be instilled in the East in order to civilise it. Of course, attitudes today have changed markedly but some of the old trappings of empire remain, even if unwittingly. There is nothing wrong with travelling to find an unspoiled beach or a relaxing tropical resort *per se*—the trouble lies in the endless repetition of such images to the exclusion of other balancing reflections.

Liberty and escape were the desperate desires of POWs in wartime Thailand and as such, the landscape plays a big part in their writing. Thailand for them becomes the antithesis of paradise, a hell on earth, and its tormenting jungles a hindrance to escape. It is remarkable that, despite the psychological and physical agony of their position, some POWs, notably Ray Parkin, were able to appreciate the beauty and even sensuality of their surrounds. In this way, Parkin's narrative is at times reminiscent of peacetime travel writing about Thailand.

In contrast to the memoirs of Second World War veterans, Vietnam soldiers' accounts are the precursors of late-20th-century textual presentations of Thailand as a location of beach-tour packages and cheap sex. From here the idea was promoted among Westerners that Thailand was and is 'for sale' (at a cut rate). It becomes not a real destination, but a place of fantasies. And, although Thailand has been complicit in promoting tourism and Westernisation, there are consequences in that such promotion relies on a set of stereotypes rather than presenting a full and varied picture. Some texts, such as *The beach*, are not really about Thailand at all, but exploit it as a locale of descriptive convenience. Others use Thailand in order to rant against such perceived sins as polygamy and 'heathenism'.

§

This book has established that Thailand has been and still is presented in Western writing as a stereotypical erotic, exotic counterpoint to the Oriental fantasia of *The Arabian nights*. Sultry and languorous, yet seductive and even dangerous, it is a dreamlike location far removed from the responsibilities of the 'real world' in the West. The important question here, therefore, is how can Westerners write about Thailand without constructing it as alien, unreal, or vacuous? How can writing reveal Thailand as culturally different but equal in stature?

Clearly, more critical attention should be paid to writing by Thais themselves, such as Rattawut Lapcharoensap and Tew Bunnag. However, while more Thais are writing in English and more Thai works are being published in translation, the literature remains largely neglected in the West by anyone other than those who have a particular enthusiasm for it. Yet it has much to say about the nature of Westernisation, using the tropes of travel to point out the irony that, while Thailand has not been colonised, it is being virtually colonised by tourists. Thai writers such as Somtow and Pira search for a way to live with Westernisation while retaining the integrity of a Thai identity.

The answer in redressing the balance lies also in publishing work about Thailand by writers drawn from more divergent backgrounds than the authors of the large number of books about the sex industry. Otherwise, Thailand will continue to be presented in a two-dimensional way, as Iyer complains:

> Meet Thailand on the page—or on the screen—and you can be forgiven for not realizing that it's a largely rural country, with a complex history, daylight hours and a taste for shyness. The Bangkok of the imagination is heavily made up and dangerously close to underage (Iyer 2003).

Women travel writers such as Faith Adiele and Karen Connelly write about how they adapted to life in Thailand by casting themselves as the 'Other'. Novelists, including Lily Tuck and Robert Brunton, adopt a similar persona for their protagonists. Then there are writers who include the sex industry in their work but who confront the stereotypes. They include Andrew Hicks, who writes about the possibility of finding love outside the carnal exchange of the sex industry, and Angela Savage, who presents the sex industry without voyeurism or lasciviousness but uses it to drive a plot that condemns the underlying corruption of both Thailand and the West.

There is also the possibility that some writers will reflect on what they have written, will see beyond their stereotypical representations, as Iyer has done, and strive to construct a more rounded picture of Thailand. Rather than a 'paradise of earthly delights', featuring tourists who are 'not so much on the pulse as on the thighs of the Land of Smiles' (Iyer 2003), literature needs to reflect the diversity of Thailand in reality. 'What we need now is a Thailand not for export only and not confined to the shadows of Bangkok' (Iyer 2003). This new literature is emerging from the writing of independent travellers, particularly women, and from expatriates who learn Thai and make Thai friends, rather than restricting themselves to foreign enclaves. And, perhaps most importantly, it is emerging from Thais themselves, whose writing is becoming more accessible to English-speaking readers. By reflecting prejudices and preconceptions, they expose stereotypes as just that, in order to facilitate a greater understanding of the 'real' Thailand. It becomes, thereby, no longer the Thailand of Western imaginations, but a country of diverse expectation and experience, like any other country. Appropriately, Rattawut Lapcharoensap should have the last word, from his short story, 'Cockfighter', in which a mother talks to her daughter parodically about the time before Westernisation:

> Those were barbarous times, you know. We lived like monkeys. We didn't have television. We didn't have cars. We danced naked around bonfires at night…You should be thankful for the modern age (Rattawut 2005:169).

Notes

1   Written under my previous name, Caron Eastgate James (James 1999b).

2   Many writers maintain that Thailand's alliance with Japan during the Second World War constituted occupation. See Wimon Wiriyawit (1997) and Rong Syamananda (1990:173). E Bruce Reynolds (2004:9) says Japanese troops were 'uninvited' and that most Thais resented their arrival. David K Wyatt (2003:247) notes that the Thais at first resisted the Japanese invasion, but realised that to fight them 'would be suicide'.

3   See, for example, the *Bangkok Post* article 'Travel writer soldiers on' (Yvonne Bohwongprasert 2005), an interview with Harold Stephens, who has written many books and articles about Thailand. Bohwongprasert says Stephens is 'an explorer and adventurer in the truest sense of the word'. In a bizarre statement in the article, however, Stephens says a highlight of his career was travelling to the Australian Outback 'and meeting aborigines—who had yet to develop speech'! His current project is a book called *The Asian woman*.

4   This advertisement was published from as early as 20 February 2005, only seven weeks after the tsunami.

5   See also www.achr.net/000ACHRTsunami/Thailand%20TS/Tsunami%20Thailand. htm.

6   The first Baedeker guide to Thailand was not published until 1993, though a Bangkok city guide was published in 1981, according to a representative of the publisher, Martina Boehringer (personal email, 11 July 2005).

7   The Australian Department of Foreign Affairs and Trade advises travellers to Thailand not to visit the troubled south and to 'exercise a high degree of caution' when travelling to the rest of the country 'because of the high threat of terrorist attack. We continue to receive reports that terrorists may be planning attacks against a range of targets, including tourist areas and other places frequented by foreigners... Future terrorist attacks cannot be ruled out...The World Health Organisation (WHO) has confirmed human deaths from avian influenza in Thailand.' (www.smartraveller. gov.au, accessed 26.7.2008).

8   Until recent times in Thailand, locally-produced workable maps suitable for travellers were unavailable and even in the late 20th century, street maps to Bangkok were incomplete.

9   Fournereau's first description of Bangkok is not of its exotic appearance, but of his relief at finding the French flag flying outside the consulate and his joy at meeting fellow Europeans, 'especially one can speak French' [sic] (Fournereau 1998:17).

He later complains that it is difficult for the traveller in Bangkok as little French is spoken there.

10 Louis Leonowens returned to Siam as a young man and spent most of his life there.

11 See James McCarthy's memoirs, first published in 1900 (McCarthy 1994).

12 James Bond Island at Phang Nga Bay is known to Thais as Khao Phing Kan. Latest guides including Lonely Planet (Williams et al 2007) and Globetrotter (Hoskin 2006) play down James Bond Island—probably because the new generation of tourists is too young to remember the film. For more on film locations in Thailand, see James (1999a:32–7).

13 See *Tourists with typewriters* (Holland & Huggan 2003:197). Ironically, Evelyn's brother, Alec Waugh, was part of that flourishing: *Alec Waugh's Bangkok* (1970) has been reprinted many times.

14 See Christian Goodden 2001.

15 In 2007, Tony and Maureen Wheeler sold 75% of the company to the BBC, citing the demise of the print industry and rise of the digital age. Since then, changes have been made to take account of falling guide book sales: in June 2008, Lonely Planet and Telstra announced an internet site to provide access to the latest constantly updated travel information via mobile phone.

16 No author is named on the cover. Carl Parkes, the author of Moon Travel's budget *Bangkok handbook* (Parkes 2000), is revealed as co-author inside the book. Moon Travel has not produced a new Bangkok guide since 2000.

17 Publications include *Lonely Planet Thailand, Lonely Planet Bangkok* and *Bangkok Encounter*.

18 The 12th edition of the Lonely Planet guide (Williams et al 2007) is the first in which Cummings is not listed as an author.

19 Later guides included *A new guide to Bangkok* (Kim & Jaivid 1950); *Panorama of Thailand: a guide to the wonders and highlights of Thailand* (Thong-in 1966); *Thailand: a Siamese odyssey* (Davies 1970); *Bangkok!* (Poole & Wheeler 1970); *Discovering Thailand* (Clarac & Smithies 1971); *Student guide to Asia* (Jenkins 1973)—later editions published as *Asia traveller's guide*; *Hudson's guide to Chiang Mai and the North* (Hudson 1973); *Papineau's guide to Bangkok city of enchantment* (Papineau 1973).

20 Some royal and upper-class Thais learned English and some were educated in England at this time, but few ordinary working people would have been able to undertake such work.

21 Ziv and Sharett are graduates of the London School of Oriental and African Studies and have lived in Bangkok.

22 It is difficult to determine whether advertising takes its cue from editorial or whether it is the reverse situation. In some cases, advertising slogans inform editorial: in a post-tsunami report, journalist Seth Mydans says that in Thailand, 'people really do smile as advertised' (Mydans 2005).

23 Marco Polo claimed to have worked for Kublai Khan in China from 1271–1292. He returned to Europe and fought for the Venetians against the Genoese. Captured and imprisoned from 1296–98, he dictated his travels to another prisoner; copies were made and they were circulated. This quotation is from *The book of Ser Marco Polo the Venetian concerning the kingdoms and marvels of the East* (an important translation by Henry Yule in 1871, revised by H Cordier in 1903).

24 See Graham (1912). Ptolemy, who worked in Alexandria, got his information from the geographer, Marinus, who relied on the firsthand account of a sailor, Alexander. Hugh Clifford (1990) writes interestingly on early descriptions in *Further India*, first published in 1904.

25 'Tai' refers to people of Southeast Asia and China whose languages and racial background are related. They include the Thai, Lao, Shan and Lu.

26 Various writers have questioned the claims of Polo (1254–1324), some saying he might not have reached China at all. For a balanced examination, see Larner (1999).

27 See BJ Terwiel's foreword in *An Asian arcady* (May 1999). The ruler of Lanna at this time was King Mangrai.

28 In the 21st century, similar practices were popularly alleged regarding former Iraqi leader Saddam Hussein in public discussion in Australia on radio and in other media.

29 Ironically, some Western accounts were written by men who had never been to Siam, such as de l'Isle in 'The Grand Tour' (Paris, 1684, cited in Smithies 2001a:66) .

30 The translation was done by Alvaro Peres da Costa (translator, National Accreditation Authority for Translators and Interpreters), UNSW.

31 According to Lach and Flaumenhaft (1965:9), the term 'Siam' had been used since the 11th century. They mean used by Westerners, as Thais historically referred to themselves as 'Tai' (free). Loubère (1969:7) says the term 'Siam' was first used by the Portuguese and was probably derived from the language of Pegu (Myanmar).

32 Loubère (1969:6) accuses Pinto of making 'continual mistakes'. Congreve mentioned Pinto in *Love for Love* as a name synonymous with 'liar' (Pinto 1989:xxvii). Burton called him 'The Sinbad of Portugal though not so respectable', in a footnote to the third voyage of 'Sinbad the Seaman' in *The thousand nights and a night* (Wood 1926:26). Burton's translation and footnotes can be accessed at http://books.onelang. com/1001-Nights-Arabian-Nights-Vol-06/. Footnote 33 refers to a giant man-eating serpent described in the text, and Burton cites Pinto's description of snakes 'which slay men with their breath'—so on one hand, Burton is using Pinto to authenticate the existence of such creatures, yet on the other, he says Pinto is unreliable.

33 The play is set in 'Levo, a province of Siam', perhaps Louvo (Lopburi).

34 Paul Fussell does not mention Hakluyt in *The Norton book of travel* (1987), despite Hakluyt being the most important editor of travel narratives of his time.

35 In Act I, Scene 3 of *Macbeth* (c1605), the First Witch refers to someone as 'master o' the Tiger' and says he is 'to Aleppo gone'. As Smithies notes, she is referring to Fitch (Smithies 2001a: 66).

36 Moreland says Floris's original Dutch version has been lost and that only a flawed first English translation exists.

37 *Van Vliet's Siam* (Baker et al 2005) is the first English edition of the collected works.

38 Examples are Sir William Davenant's *The siege of Rhodes* (1656), Dryden's *The Indian Queen* (1663) and its sequel *The Indian Emperor* (1667).

39 Van Vliet in the 17th century and Leonowens in the 19th century are mentioned by Van der Cruysse (2002:68) as examples of Westerners who thought this way.

40 Much is still made in travel writing and guides today of how superstitious the Thais are. See, for example, the introduction to *Lonely Planet Thailand* (Cummings et al 2005:4).

41 The 2005 trial of Australian Schapelle Corby in Bali is a case in point, when much was made about the supposed shortfalls of Indonesia's justice system.

42 *The New Shorter Oxford English Dictionary* (1993) includes the following quotation from Gibbon to illustrate use of the word 'effeminate': 'Rome was...humbled beneath the effeminate luxury of Oriental despotism'.

43 Personal email, 15 August 2005, with Hoskin, an acquaintance from my time in Bangkok.

44 The location of Ban Wichayen is included in most guidebooks.

45 King Mongkut died after contracting malaria during the excursion.

46 Smithies writes an extensive note on Madame Constance, who was from a Portuguese-Japanese-Bengali background and who became a slave after Phaulkon was executed, until 1703, when she amazingly reclaimed a place in Ayutthayan society.

47 Biographical details of Hamilton are sketchy, but Smithies says he probably lived in or near Edinburgh. The book was reprinted in 1744, between 1808 and 1884 as part of a collection of volumes on travel, and in 1930, before its latest edition in 1997.

48 The comparison was tenuous: while Bangkok was a new city, Venice had been settled since the 5th century and united since 697.

49 Roberts was a special agent sent to negotiate a treaty of extraterritoriality for US citizens.

50 In the introduction to Buls's text, Tips notes that Buls was mayor from 1881–1899 and hosted King Chulalongkorn during his 1897 visit to Brussels (Buls 1994:vii).

51 This point is made by the translator, Erik Christian Haugaard, in his introduction to *The Penguin complete fairy tales and stories of Hans Andersen*. The Victorians, Haugaard says, 'had a tendency to make a kiss on the mouth, in translation, land on the cheek' (Andersen 1974).

52 *Kismet* was compiled by Robert Wright and George Forrest from a combination of music by 19th-century Russian composer Alexander Borodin and an earlier *Arabian Nights*-type tale. It employed a host of stock 'Eastern' characters (Maltin 2001:740). A film of *Kismet* was made in 1955 and is known also as *Oriental dream*.

53 Presumably, the merchant Robert Hunter, who is credited with 'discovering' conjoined twins Chang and Eng, from whom the term 'Siamese twins' is derived.

54 Ironically, McCarthy had come to Siam from a similar position with the Raj.

55 Feudge also wrote *Eastern side: or, missionary life in Siam* (1871) and many articles about her travels in Asia.

56 Feudge's description is reminiscent of, and might even have been the inspiration for, the depiction in *The King and I* of Anna Leonowens's arrangement of a grand dinner given by King Mongkut to impress English dignitaries and prove he is not a 'barbarian'. A similar scene appears in part in *Anna and the King of Siam* (Landon 2000).

57 The two were written 40 years apart, so perhaps the custom had changed. Today, many Thais still nap at lunchtime (customarily midday-1pm in offices), but there is no extended siesta.

58 In 1840 it took 42 days just to sail from Bangkok to Singapore whence a connecting line for Europe could be arranged (Neale 1999:11).

59 Hartzell's memoirs were not published until 2001, when they were edited by her granddaughter, Joan Acocella,who wrote an interesting biographical essay to accompany them.

60 The same—and real-life—sea captain of the *Chao Phraya* steamer is mentioned in many books, including Leonowens's *The English Governess*, (though she calls him only 'the captain') and my own novel, *The Occidentals* (James 1999b:14).

61 My own copy was purchased in 2006, after a long search, from Alibris in the US.

62 She mentions it and its long-term head mistress (1885–1923), Miss Cole, in *Never dies the dream*, though it was at a different campus and renamed Wattana Wittaya by the time Landon arrived in Bangkok. She is likely to have seen pictures of the old school, which she could have used in her description of Jasmine Hall in *Never dies the dream* (Landon 1949:15–6). In addition, she did much research on the life of Edna Cole, as revealed in the catalogue of her private papers at Wheaton College, Illinois (Margaret and Kenneth Landon papers, SC-38, Wheaton College Archives & Special Collections at http://www.wheaton.edu/learnres/ARCSC/collects/sc38/container.php)

63 Gutzlaff was a Prussian working for the Netherlands Missionary Society in Siam from 1828.

64 The journals of Tomlin, Gutzlaff and David Abeel have been recently published in one volume (Farrington 2001), without their original lengthy religious passages.

65 The cover announces her as 'Princess Ceril Birabongse', though the couple divorced long before he died in 1985. Birabongse was known in the West as the famous, charming racing-car driver B Bira. Ceril says she was devastated, after they were married, to discover monogamy was not in his plans.

66 I was first alerted to Landon's subconscious use of homoerotic images by Susan Fulop Kepner, University of California, Berkeley, in a personal email, 12 July 2004.

67 This does not seem to be the case today. In 2000 I went to Tak town (where Louis had lived for many years in the late 19th century) on a research trip and many elderly

people I talked to through an interpreter said they had never heard of him. He is better known among the wealthy and one businesswoman was able to show me the riverside site of Louis's house in Tak. The large teak house had been dismantled and removed. It is now at Pattaya, where in July 2008 it was listed for sale at 50,000,000 baht-plus.

68   Mrs McFarland's article was included in an 1884 book, *Siam and Laos as seen by our American missionaries*, edited by Mary Backus, also the wife of a missionary to Siam, Samuel House. Similar later volumes were published, including one in 1886 and one at the beginning of the 20th century, with added updated material. The books were intended for Americans contemplating taking up missionary work.

69   McFarland (1884:78) cites an instance of girls being paid a fuang a day (equal then in Britain to about threepence halfpenny, she says) for attending school, doing half a day's tuition and half a day's domestic work.

70   Reported in the *Bangkok Post*, 10 July 2005.

71   The picture is used on the cover of Klein's *Cold War Orientalism* (2003).

72   Owens was Anna's married name before she used the name Leonowens, the combination of two of her husband's names.

73   Estimates vary, but Loos says King Chulalongkorn was presented with 150 women during his 42-year reign, while King Mongkut was presented with 50 (in both cases, not all of them became 'wives') and previous kings with fewer (2006:115).

74   Thompson disappeared while on holiday in central Malaysia in 1967 and was never heard of again. (See Warren 1998.)

75   The film starred Marlon Brando and MR Kukrit Pramoj as the country's Prime Minister. Kukrit Pramoj actually went on to become Prime Minister of Thailand (1975-76).

76   She describes this trip in Leonowens (1988:300–13).

77   Kepner in personal email, 28 August 2006.

78   Chandler in personal email, 6 April 2008.

79   They are also mentioned in Cornwel-Smith (2007:16).

80   Surprisingly, the book has so far not been translated into English.

81   A picture of Leonowens's grave is available on the Find a Grave website (www.findagrave.com) where it is noted that the date of birth is erroneous.

82   New information about the Owenses' time in Western Australia, particularly about Thomas and his 'aggressive personality', was presented by Gerard Foley at the Royal Western Australian Historical Society on 19 March 2008 (Habegger & Foley 2009, forthcoming).

83   Compare Warren (2002:47) and Bristowe (1976:30-1).

84   This magnificent coffee-table book was commissioned to celebrate King Bhumipol's 60th birthday (text is in English and German). Surprisingly, there is a significant gaffe in the book—it says King Mongkut died in 1863 (he died in 1868). Not surprisingly, there is no mention of a classroom or a blackboard that once might have been used by Leonowens.

85 Kepner, in personal email, 31 October 2003 and 12 July 2004.

86 Kepner, in personal email, 31 October, 2003. Warren (2002:46) refers to Kepner again briefly in more recent work, naming her incorrectly as Susan *Fuller* Kepner. Obviously, the mistake is not deliberate, but underlines the fact that he does not take her work seriously. To be fair, Morgan (2008:245) also gets the name slightly wrong, referring to her once as Susan *Filop* Kepner.

87 See Tim Mackintosh-Smith's introduction in Burton (2004:xiii).

88 Seni Pramoj and Kukrit Pramoj wrote their book in 1948 to refute the portrait of King Mongkut shown in the 1946 film *Anna and the King of Siam* (not the 1956 film *The King and I*, as reported on the US Library of Congress Asian Collections website, www.loc.gov/rr/asian/guide/guide-southeast.html). AL Moffat used much of Seni and Kukrit's information for his biography of Mongkut (1961).

89 The guide also misspells Yul Brynner's name as 'Brunner'.

90 For example, Dea Birkett (1989) and Mary Russell (1986).

91 The address was given in conjunction with an exhibition of books from the collection of author and historian ML Manich Jumsai at the Siam Society in Bangkok.

92 Mongkut had 35 childbearing wives plus concubines. Many hundreds, perhaps thousands of women worked behind the *Nang Harm* walls and Western writers often mistook them as being all wives or romantic associates of the King.

93 Avis married an affluent banker, Tom Fyshe, and Anna lived with them in Canada for most of the rest of her life, indicating she did not make a fortune from her books or lectures; for more, see Dow (1991).

94 See NSCAD University's website at www.nscad.ns.ca. The University has named the Anna Leonowens Gallery after its founder.

95 Louis Leonowens in personal email correspondence, 2 January 2008.

96 Alfred Habegger in personal email, 8 February 2008. The book has the working title 'Anna: the life and legend of Mrs Leonowens' and will be published by Random House in 2009.

97 Lois K Yorke in personal email correspondence, 13 February 2008. She says she has finished researching the biography, which has the working title 'Getting to know you: the life and times of Anna Harriett Leonowens, 1831–1915'.

98 www.britannica.com, viewed 24.3.2008.

99 Samut Prakan is 30 kilometres south of Bangkok, an area known to tourists because of attractions such as the Ancient City and the Crocodile Farm.

100 I faced the same difficulty when researching the background for my historical novel, *The Occidentals*, set in 19th-century Siam just after Leonowens's time there. Writers of Thai history have varying versions of events, and dates often conflict. There is also confusion when converting Thai dates to the Gregorian calendar.

101 The illustration has the caption, 'Smâyâtee bought for 40 pieces of gold' (Leonowens 1953:86).

102 See, for example, Earle Goodenow's illustrations (Goodenow 2004).

103 It was also released by Trübner & Co in 1873 with the title *The romance of Siamese harem life.*

104 Leonowens told me this in personal correspondence, 11 October 2000.

105 For further information about the set visit the Rare Coin Wholesalers website at http://www.rcw1.com/m/KOSInfo.php?osCsid=52346cb51c2441dfb735ebbb05f2 27ec.

106 Kepner in personal email, 31 October 2003.

107 Kepner in personal email, 12 July 2004.

108 Kepner in personal email, 12 July 2004.

109 Kepner in personal email, 14 August 2006.

110 This film demonstrates how *The King and I*'s music has become an integral part of American culture not necessarily even connected in the psyche with Thailand.

111 These include *The Prince & I*, the memoirs of an English woman who married a Thai prince (Birabongse 1998) and *Katya and the Prince of Siam*, the story of Russian Katya Desnitsky, who married Prince Chakrabongse in 1906. (Hunter & Chakrabongse 1994). *King and I* was also the title of a 2006 book about Australian comedian Graham Kennedy by Rob Astbury.

112 For a detailed description of Leonowens's family life in Canada, see Dow (1991).

113 Even stranger is the article, 'Fibs on film'(*Bangkok Post* 1999) .

114 Thongbai makes the valid point that Thais have also been guilty of exaggerating or rewriting history in movies to suit their own ideals.

115 A *New York Times* article on 8 August 1970, about the documentary, notes that Grimble liked to shock—he had also asserted that Macbeth and Lady Macbeth were innocent of murder and that Joan of Arc belonged to a witchcraft cult.

116 This term is used to address some Western women in Thailand today. It could be partly explained by the fact that the equivalent polite Thai honorific, *khun*, is not gender-specific and is used for all adults without titles, regardless of their gender or marital status.

117 Louis's first wife was Caroline Knox, daughter of the British consul and his Thai wife, named only as 'Mrs Knox' in Western publications. Mrs Knox was descended from Thai nobility and had been a lady-in-waiting at the Second King's court (Minney 1962:22).

118 Chatri is a member of the Thai royal family and the film was funded mostly by Queen Sirikit. Released in Thailand in 2001, it was a popular success and was released internationally in 2003—shortened and repackaged in Hollywood style as *Francis Ford Coppola presents: The legend of Suriyothai.*

119 Also published in the UK in 1956 with the title *A Sort of Beauty.*

120 See, for example, Pira's novel *Shadowed country* (2004).

121 Both Supharb Lim (1997) and Ruengvuth Vuthrikrisan (1997) discuss the way the film appears to criticise Thai society for Aoi's predicament and Ruengvuth reveals that English speakers would miss the nuances of what is going on in Thai because they cannot be included in the subtitles.

122 This contribution to the collection is a transcript of the radio discussion. Although it was the women's choice not to be identified, the numbering of them as Voice 1, Voice 2, and so on, is reminiscent of Thai bar girls who are identified by the numbers on their bikinis.

123 The author says in personal email, 24 September 2006, that more than 10,000 copies have sold.

124 O'Rourke bought a rice farm for Aoi's family as a bonus for her participation in *The Good Woman of Bangkok* to encourage her to leave the sex industry; after a few months she opted to return to prostitution in Bangkok.

125 *The deer hunter* is set in Vietnam but was filmed in Thailand, with Patpong as Saigon's red-light district.

126 The guide, published in Hong Kong, was produced for guests at hotels such as the Indra Regent.

127 It would, however, have been unusual for a Thai who was wealthy enough to have such a car to drive it themselves. Thai journalist Ruengvuth Vuthikrisan (1997:204) repeats this myth in his review of *The good woman of Bangkok*.

128 Anyone who has been to Patpong will know the bars are definitely not suitable for children and that many adults would find the experience distasteful, too. They continue, however, to operate full of foreign, mainly male, customers.

129 Pirazzi and Vasant say sex workers make up only 0.1 to 0.5% of the population of Thailand, pointing out that not all prostitutes in Thailand are Thais.

130 Gerster is referring to Australian writing, but his comments are applicable to revisionist writing about Asia by other Westerners.

131 *Bangkok Hilton* was a vehicle for the young Nicole Kidman to capitalise on her success in Phillip Noyce's film *Dead calm,* also released in 1989.

132 Helen Fielding's 1999 novel and Beeban Kidron's 2004 film were sequels to the best-selling novel and film *Bridget Jones's Diary*

133 The novel won the Victorian Premier's Literary Award for an unpublished manuscript by an emerging Victorian author in 2004.

134 Arsan's real name is Marayat Rollet-Andriane. She was of Asian and European descent (though the countries are not specified) and born and bred in Bangkok. Rollet-Andriane married a diplomat at 16, but few details of her life seem to be known and she remains a mysterious figure. Several critics suggest the real author of *Emmanuelle* is a man, perhaps even her husband. William Warren for example, claims Rollet-Andriane is 'a Frenchman married to a ravishing Thai girl' (Warren 2000:219).

135 When the Hilton Hotel was built in 1983, the Lingam Shrine was incorporated, and still exists, as a fertility shrine and tourist attraction behind the hotel in what is now called Nai Lert Park. It was well known as a shrine in 1967; William Warren claims to have tidied it up from 1963 to make it accessible.

136 It was introduced to a new generation of readers when the excerpt 'Where the Footnotes Went' was reprinted in the popular *Travelers' tales guides Thailand* (O'Reilly & Habegger 1997).

137 For this study, I have used the 1999 collection of Parkin's works, *Ray Parkin's wartime trilogy*, which included *Out of the smoke*, *Into the smother*, and *The sword and the blossom*.

138 Rivett, a Melbourne journalist, is unusual in that he wrote his account as soon as the War ended.

139 While *Siam* has been critically acclaimed as a novel, Tuck does make mistakes, such as presenting characters eating Thai food with chopsticks (it is customary to use a fork and spoon) and describing women visiting the Grand Palace as being dressed in sleeveless blouses (this is considered immodest and they would have been required to cover their arms).

140 Claire would have been much more likely then to have read Landon's novel.

141 See Livesey (1999) for a review of Tuck's novel and Smith (2004) for more information about Tuck.

142 Tuck, born Lilian Solmsen in 1938 in France, was the daughter of German Jews who had fled when Hitler came to power. They lived in Peru and Uruguay, before moving to New York, where Tuck says that, as a foreigner, she was afraid to speak for a year. 'I was used to being the outsider and being lonely,' she told *Publishers Weekly* (Smith 2004, quoted in Downing 2006).

143 The article was also about *Anna and the King*, which was in production at the same time.

144 There are several biographies and plays about the twins and another recent novel (Strauss 2000).

145 William in real life was Brunton's brother David. About 90% of the story is true, according to Brunton in personal email correspondence, 31 July 2004. Brunton never returned to Thailand after working there in 1966.

146 *Monsoon country*, Book One of *Shadowed country*, was first published in 1981; Pira re-edited it for publication, with Book Two, *The force of karma*, together in the 2004 volume.

147 Like his character, Pira returned to the village of Napo to contribute to educating the region's children.

148 Rattawut says it is 'Koh Lukmak, the last in a long chain of Andaman Islands'—he should have used a lower case 'i', or 'islands in the Andaman Sea', as he doesn't appear to mean the Andaman Islands which are not in Thailand but are part of India.

149 Australian Government Department of Foreign Affairs and Trade travel advice is available at www.smartraveller.gov.au

glossary

farang	foreigner; traditionally a white foreigner but sometimes now used to refer to any non-Thai, particularly those from Western countries
khao manee	Thai cat, said to be the favourite of King Chulalongkorn and bred to have one blue eye and one yellow eye
klong	canal
Krung Thep	short form of the Thai name for Bangkok
maechi	Buddhist nun
mai pen rai	it doesn't matter; never mind; no worries
mamasan	supervisor of a 'girly' bar or brothel
nang harm	inner palace where the King's wives, concubines and attendants lived; often referred to as the 'harem' or 'seraglio'
panung	pleated, wrapped skirt, traditionally worn by Thais, both men and women
sanuk	fun
sawasdee	hello
soi	laneway

Adiele, Faith 2001, 'Passing through bandit country' in Conlon, Faith, Ingrid Emerick and Christina Henry de Tessan (eds), *A woman alone: travel tales from around the globe*, Seal Press, Emeryville.

—— 2005, *Meeting Faith: the forest journals of a black Buddhist nun*, WW Norton, New York.

Adirex, Paul 2004, *Rattanakosin: the birth of Bangkok*, Aries Books, Bangkok.

Adul Tinaphong 2005, *Patpong Road untold story*, Ghaomai Publications, Bangkok.

Anake Nawigamune 2000, *A century of Thai graphic design*, David Smythe (ed & trans), River Books, Bangkok.

Andersen, Hans Christian 1974, *The Penguin complete fairy tales and stories of Hans Andersen*, Erik Christian Haugaard (trans), Penguin, Middlesex.

Anderson, Benedict 1978, 'Studies of the Thai state: the state of Thai studies' in Ayal, Eliezar B (ed) *The study of Thailand*, Ohio University Centre for International Studies, Athens.

Anderson, Benedict ROG, and Ruchira Mendiones (eds) 1985, *In the mirror: literature and politics in Siam in the American era*, Editions Duang Kamol, Bangkok.

Anderson, Monica 2006, *Women and the politics of travel, 1870–1914*, Fairleigh Dickinson University Press, Cranbury.

Anggraeni, Dewi 2003, *Who did this to our Bali?*, Indra Publications, Sydney.

Anonymous 1871, Review of Leonowens's *The English Governess at the Siamese Court* 1870, Francis Bret Harte (ed), *Overland Monthly*, (6)3, March.

Anonymous 1873, Review of Leonowens's *The romance of the harem*, Charles Hodge and Lyman H Atwater (eds), *The Presbyterian Quarterly and Princeton Review*, (6), April.

Anonymous 1698, *The unnatural mother: the scene in the Kingdom of Siam as it is now accommodated at the new theatre in Lincolns-Inn-Fields by His Majesty's Servants*, 'written by a young lady', R Buffet, London.

Anson, Robert Sam 1997, 'Sixth sense' in O'Reilly, James, and Larry Habegger (eds), *Travelers' tales guides Thailand*, Travelers' Tales Inc, San Francisco.

Antonio, J 1997 [1904], *The 1904 traveller's guide to Bangkok and Siam*, White Lotus, Bangkok.

AOA Bangkok guidebook c1975, AOA, Hong Kong.

Arabian nights entertainments: consisting of one thousand and one stories, 1736, told by the Sultaness of the Indies, Translated into French from the Arabian MSS by M Galland, and now done into English from the last Paris edition, T Longman, London.

Arsan, Emmanuelle 1971 [1967], *Emmanuelle*, Lowell Bair (trans), Grove Press, New York.

Atkinson, Frances 2006, 'Crime with a conscience', *The Age*, 11 June.

Augustin, Andreas, and Andrew Williamson 2006, *The Oriental Bangkok*, The Most Famous Hotels in the World, Vienna.

Australian and New Zealand Women's Group 2005, *The Bangkok guide*, 16th ed, ANZWG, Bangkok.

Aylwen, Axel 1988, *The Falcon of Siam*, Methuen, London.

—— 1991, *The Falcon takes wing*, Methuen, London.

—— 2006, *The Falcon's last flight*, Falcon Books, Bangkok.

Backus, Mary (ed) 1884, *Siam and Laos as seen by our American missionaries*, Presbyterian Board of Publication, Philadelphia.

Bacon, George B 2005[1881], *Siam: the land of the white elephant as it was and is*, revised by Frederick Wells Williams, Elibron Classics.

Bahr, Lucy Leonowens 2001, 'Letter from abroad', *5163: the magazine of the Nova Scotia College of Art and Design for alumni & friends*, 1(1), www.nscad.ns.ca/info/5163-W01.pdf, viewed 1.7.2008.

Baker, Chris, and Pasuk Phongpaichit 2005, *A history of Thailand*, Cambridge University Press, Cambridge.

Baker, Chris, Dhiravat Na Pombejra, Alfons van der Kraan, and David K Wyatt 2005, *Van Vliet's Siam*, Silkworm Books, Chiang Mai.

Bangkok Post 1998, 'Write a new script, film studio told', 12 November.

Bangkok Post 1999, 'Fibs on film', 28 March.

Bangkok Women's Writers Group 2007, *Bangkok blondes*, Bangkok Book House, Bangkok.

Barmé, Scot 2002, *Woman, man, Bangkok*, Rowman and Littlefield, Lanham, Maryland.

Barrett, Dean 2003, *Skytrain to murder,* Village East Books, Vero Beach.

—— 2004 [2001], *Thailand:land of beautiful women*, Village East Books, Vero Beach.

Barwise, JM, and NJ White 2002, *A traveller's history of South East Asia*, Cassell & Co, London.

Bassenne, Marthe 1995 [1912], *In Laos and Siam*, Walter EJ Tips (ed & trans), White Lotus, Bangkok. Originally published in 1912 as 'Au Laos et au Siam', *Le tour du monde*, 18 NS.

Bassnett, Susan 2002, 'Travel writing and gender' in Hulme, Peter, and Tim Youngs (eds), *A Cambridge companion to travel writing*, Cambridge University Press, Cambridge.

Beauvoir, L, marquis de 1986 [1870], *A week in Siam January 1867*, Siam Society, Bangkok. Reprint of an extract, in its original English translation, from *Voyage autour du monde*, first published in 1870.

Beek, Steve van 1999, *Bangkok then and now*, AB Publications, Nonthaburi.

Behdad, Ali 1994, *Belated travelers: Orientalism in the age of colonial dissolution*, Duke University Press, Durham.

Bennetts, Anna 2007, 'Extra', in Bangkok Women's Writers Group, *Bangkok blondes*, Bangkok Book House, Bangkok.

Bernstein, Matthew, and Gaylyn Studlar 1997, *Visions of the East: Orientalism in film*, Rutgers University Press, New Brunswick.

Berry, Chris 1997, 'Dennis O'Rourke's original sin, *The good woman of Bangkok*, or 'Is this what they mean by "Australia in Asia?"' in Berry, Chris, Annette Hamilton and Laleen Jayamanne, *The filmmaker and the prostitute: Dennis O'Rourke's The good woman of Bangkok*, Power Publications, Sydney.

Berry, Chris, Annette Hamilton and Laleen Jayamanne (eds) 1997, *The filmmaker and the prostitute: Dennis O'Rourke's The good woman of Bangkok*, Power Publications, Sydney.

Betron, Myra 2007, 'Hovering in between', in Bangkok Women's Writers Group, *Bangkok blondes*, Bangkok Book House, Bangkok.

Birabongse, Ceril 1992, *The Prince and I: life with Prince Bira of Siam*, Veloce Publishing, Dorset.

Birkett, Dea 1989, *Spinsters abroad: Victorian lady explorers*, Basil Blackwell, London.

Bishop, Ryan, and Lillian S Robinson 1998, *Night market: sexual cultures and the Thai economic miracle*, Routledge, New York.

Blanc, Marcel le 2003 [1692], *History of Siam in 1688*, Michael Smithies (ed & trans), Silkworm Books, Chiang Mai.

Blofeld, John 1987 [1972], *King Maha Mongkut of Siam*, Michael Smithies (intro), The Siam Society, Bangkok.

Bok, Hilary 2003, 'Baron de Montesquieu, Charles-Louis de Secondat', *The Stanford Encyclopedia of Philosophy (Fall 2003 Edition)*, Edward N Zalta (ed) plato. stanford.edu/archives/fall2003/entries/montesquieu/, viewed 1.7.2008.

Borthwick, John 2004, 'Land of smiles' and 'Not so secret island business' in 'Destination Thailand: welcome to the land of smiles', supplement to *The Weekend Australian*, 14–15 February.

Botan 1982, *Letters from Thailand*, Susan Fulop (trans), Editions Duang Kamol, Bangkok.

—— 1996, 'From *That woman's name is Boonrawd'* in *The Lioness in bloom: modern Thai fiction about women*, Susan Fulop Kepner (ed & trans), University of California Press, Berkeley.

Boulle, Pierre 1958, *Walt Disney's Siam*, Nouvelles Éditions SA, Lausanne.

—— 2002 [1952], *The bridge on the River Kwai*, Vintage, London.

Bowring, John 1857, *The Kingdom and people of Siam; with a narrative of the mission to that country in 1855*, (2), John W Parker and Son, London.

Bradley, Dan F 1899, *Simo: the story of a boy of Siam*, The Ram's Horn Co, Chicago.

Bradley, William L 1981, *Siam then: the foreign colony in Bangkok before and after Anna*, William Carey Library, Pasadena.

Bristowe, WS 1976, *Louis and the King of Siam*, Thai-American Publishers, New York.

Broinowski, Alison 1991, *The yellow lady: Australian impressions of Asia*, Oxford University Press, Melbourne.

Brown, Susan 1995, 'Alternatives to the missionary position: Anna Leonowens as Victorian travel writer', *Feminist Studies*, 21(3).

Brunton, Robert 2004, *Golden pavilions*, Pandanus Books, Canberra.

Buls, Charles 1994 [1901], *Siamese sketches*, White Lotus, Bangkok.

Bunbury, Stephanie 2003, 'No need to be ashamed', *The Sunday Age*, 22 June.

Brundrett, Ross 2005, 'Paradise Lost', Travel, *Herald Sun*, 14 January.

Burdett, John 2003, *Bangkok 8*, Bantam, London.

—— 2005, *Bangkok tattoo*, Bantam, London.

—— 2007, *Bangkok haunts*, Bantam, London.

Burton, Richard F (ed & trans) 1885, *The book of a thousand nights and a night*, Kamashastra Society, Benares.

—— 2004 [1855/1856], *A secret pilgrimage to Mecca and Medina*, Folio Society, London.

Butler, Danny 2004, 'Holiday playground turns to hell on earth', *Herald Sun*, 28 December.

Buzard, James 1993, *The beaten track: European tourism, literature, and the ways to 'culture' 1800–1918*, Clarendon Press, Oxford.

Caddy, Florence 1992 [1889] *To Siam and Malaya in the Duke of Sutherland's yacht, 'Sans Peur'*, Oxford University Press, Singapore.

Campbell, JGD 1902, *Siam in the twentieth century*, Edward Arnold, London.

—— 1985 [1897], *Siam in the twentieth century: being the experiences and impressions of a British official*, White Lotus, Bangkok.

Campbell, Reginald 1937 [1935], *Teak-wallah*, Hodder and Stoughton, London.

Campos, Joaquim de 1940, 'Early Portuguese accounts of Thailand', *Journal of the Thailand Research Society*, 32(1).

Carbone, Suzanne, and Lawrence Money 2005, 'Against the tide', Diary, *The Age*, 14 March.

Carter, A Cecil (ed) 1988 [1904], *The Kingdom of Siam 1904*, Siam Society, Bangkok.

Carter, Helen 2004, 'Holiday dream turns to scenes of horror', *Guardian Unlimited*, 27 December.

Cartland, Barbara 1988, *Sapphires in Siam*, Jove Books, New York.

Catz, Rebecca 1904, *Subsidios para a sua biographia e para o estudo da sua obra*, Christovam Ayres (ed), Typographia da Academia, Lisbon, Documento B.

Chalermsri Chantasingh 1998, 'Musical not an accurate portrayal of Siam', *Topeka Capital-Journal*, 29 November, www.cjonline.com/stories/112998/fea_ kingandimain.shtml, viewed 1.7.2008.

—— 1999, 'The Americanisation of *The King and I*: the transformation of the English governess to an American legend', PhD thesis, University of Kansas.

—— 2000, 'Renewals of American idealism: the motif of American imperialism in *The King and I*, its progenitors and progeny', Eighth Maple Leaf and Eagle Conference on North American Studies, University of Helsinki, September 11–14.

Chambers, Erve 2000, *Native tours: the anthropology of travel and tourism*, Waveland Press, Long Grove.

Chami Jotisalikorn and Annette Tan 2006, *thailandchic: hotels restaurants shops spas*, Archipelago Press, Singapore.

Chandler, David P 2000 *A history of Cambodia*, Westview Press, Boulder.

Chataway, Lynette 2005, *Noble Sindhu horses*, Pandanus, Canberra.

Choisy, Abbé de 1993, *Journal of a voyage to Siam 1685–1686*, Michael Smithies (intro), Oxford University Press, Kuala Lumpur. Originally published in French in 1687 as *Journal du voyage de Siam fait en 1685 et 1686*, Mabre-Cramoisy, Paris.

Chu-Chueh Cheng 2004, 'Frances Trollope's America and Anna Leonowens's Siam: questionable travel and problematic writing' in Siegel, Kristi (ed), *Gender, genre, and identity in women's travel writing*, Peter Lang, New York.

Clarac, Achille, and Michael Smithies 1971, *Discovering Thailand*, Siam Publications, Bangkok.

Clark, Steve (ed) 1999, *Travel writing and Empire: postcolonial theory in transit,* Zed Books, London.

Clifford, Hugh 1990 [1904], *Further India:the story of exploration,* White Lotus, Bangkok.

Collis, Maurice 1936, *Siamese white,* Faber and Faber, London.

—— 1990 [1949], *The grand peregrination: being the life and adventures of Fernão Mendes Pinto,* Carcanet, Manchester.

Conlon, Faith, Ingrid Emerick and Christina Henry de Tessan (eds) 2001, *A woman alone: travel tales from around the globe,* Seal Press, Emeryville, California.

Connelly, Karen 2001, *Dream of a thousand lives: a sojourn in Thailand,* Seal Press, Seattle. Originally published as *Touch the dragon: a Thai journal,* 1993.

Conrad, Joseph 1986 [1917], 'The shadow-line' in Ingram, Allan (ed), *Joseph Conrad: selected literary criticism and* The shadow-line, Methuen, London.

Considine, Austin, and Newley Purnell 2006, 'Thailand tourists: "Coup? what coup?"', *New York Times,* 8 October.

Conway, Susan 1992, *Thai textiles,* Asia Books, Bangkok.

Conyers-Keynes, S 1950, *A white man in Thailand,* Robert Hale, London.

Cooper, Robert, and Nanthapa Cooper 2005, *Culture shock: a survival guide to customs and etiquette: Thailand,* Marshall Cavendish, Singapore.

Cornwel-Smith, Philip (ed) 2005a, *Time Out Bangkok,* Time Out, London.

—— 2005b, *Very Thai,* River Books, Bangkok.

—— 2007, *Time Out Bangkok and beaches,* Time Out, London.

Courval, Louise de 2001, *Papaya salad (make it spicy, please!): fond memories of Thailand and beyond,* Post Books, Bangkok.

Crawfurd, John 1967 [1828], *Journal of an embassy from the Governor-General of India to the Courts of Siam and Cochin China,* David K Wyatt (ed), Oxford University Press, Kuala Lumpur.

Cribb, TJ 1999, 'Writing up the log: the legacy of Hakluyt', in Clark, Steve (ed) 1999, *Travel writing and Empire: postcolonial theory in transit,* Zed Books, London.

Cruysse, Dirk van der 2002 [1991], *Siam and the West 1500–1700,* Michael Smithies (trans), Silkworm Books, Chiang Mai.

Cruysse, Dirk van der, and Michael Smithies (eds) 2002, *The diary of Kosa Pan, Thai Ambassador to France June–July 1686,* Visudh Busayakul (trans), Silkworm Books, Chiang Mai.

Cummings, Joe 1990, *Thailand—a travel survival kit,* 4th ed, Lonely Planet, Melbourne.

—— 2001, 'The Joe Cummings interview', *Khao San Road*, www.khaosanroad.com/joecummingsp1.htm, viewed 1.7.2008.

Cummings, Joe, and China Williams 2004, *Lonely Planet Bangkok city guide*, Lonely Planet, Melbourne.

Cummings, Joe, Becca Blond, Morgan Konn, Matt Warren and China Williams 2005, *Lonely Planet Thailand*, 11th ed, Lonely Planet, Melbourne.

Cummings, Joe, Sandra Bao, Steven Martin and China Williams 2003, *Lonely Planet Thailand*, 10th ed, Lonely Planet, Melbourne.

Curtis, Lillian Johnson 1998 [1903], *The Laos of North Siam*, White Lotus, Bangkok.

Dale, Leigh 2002, 'Imperial Traveler, Colonial Observer: Humanity and Difference in *Five Years in Kaffirland*', Helen Gilbert and Anna Johnston (eds) 2002, *In transit: travel, text, empire*, Peter Lang, New York.

Dalton, William 1862, *Phaulcon the adventurer: or The Europeans in the East: a romantic biography*, SO Beeton, London.

Dann, Caron 2007, 'Freewheeling', *goodreading*, October.

Dapin, Mark 2004, 'Thai breakers', *Good Weekend (The Age)*, 9–11 April.

Davies, David 1973 [1967], *Thailand: the rice bowl of Asia*, Frederick Muller, London.

Davies, Derek AC 1970, *Thailand: a Siamese odyssey*, Kodansha International Ltd, Tokyo.

Davis, Bonnie 1989, 'A mid-19th century Christmas celebration in Siam', *Living in Thailand*, December.

Dawson, Alan 1999, 'New "Anna" revives decades-old debate', *Bangkok Post*, 7 December.

Deviah, MA 1997, 'Controversy over "Good Woman"' in Berry, Chris, Annette Hamilton and Laleen Jayamanne, *The filmmaker and the prostitute: Dennis O'Rourke's The good woman of Bangkok*, Power Publications, Sydney.

D'Cruz, JV, and William Steele 2003, *Australia's ambivalence towards Asia*, Monash Asia Institute, Clayton.

Dhanit Yupho 1963, *The Khon and Lakon dance dramas presented by the Department of Fine Arts*, Department of Fine Arts, Bangkok.

Donaldson, Laura E 1992, *Decolonizing feminisms: race, gender and empire building*, University of North Carolina Press, Chapel Hill.

Dow, Leslie Smith 1991, *Anna Leonowens: a life beyond* The King and I, Pottersfield Press, Porters Lake.

Downing, George 2006, 'Lily Tuck: a biographical essay', The Novel Club of Cleveland, May 2, www.thenovelclub.org, viewed 1.7.2008

Dunlop, EE 1986, *The war diaries of Weary Dunlop: Java and the Burma-Thailand Railway 1942–1945*, Nelson Publications, Melbourne.

Eckardt, James 1999, *Bangkok people*, Asia Books, Bangkok.

Edwards, Paul 2005, 'After the tsunami', Travel, *The Age*, 23 January.

Emery, Edith 1969, *Encounter with Asia*, Ward Lock, Sydney.

Exell, FK 1963 *Siamese tapestry*, Robert Hale, London.

—— 1976, *In Siamese service*, Cassell, London.

Farrington, Anthony (ed) 2001, *Early missionaries in Bangkok: the journals of Tomlin, Gutzlaff and Abeel 1828–1832*, White Lotus, Bangkok.

Feeser, Andrea 2002, 'Constance Fredericka Gordon Cumming's "picturesque" vision: a Christian, Westernized Hawai'i' in Siegel, Kristi (ed), *Issues in travel writing: empire, spectacle, and displacement,* Peter Lang, New York.

Fellows, Warren 1997, *The damage done: twelve years of hell in a Bangkok prison*, Macmillan, Sydney.

Feudge, Fannie Roper 1871, *Eastern side: or, missionary life in Siam,* Bible and Publishing Society.

—— 1876, 'Christmas in the Far East', *St Nicholas Magazine*, January.

Fielding, Helen 2004 [1999], *Bridget Jones: the edge of reason*, Picador, London.

Finlayson, George 1826, *The Mission to Siam and Hue the Capital of Cochin China in the years 1821–2*, John Murray, London.

Fleet, Greg 2002, *Thai die*, Random House, Sydney.

Floris, Pieter 1934, *Pieter Floris; his voyage to the East Indies in the Globe 1611–1615*, WH Moreland (ed), Hakluyt Society, London.

Foster, David 1983, *Plumbum*, Penguin, Ringwood.

Fournereau, Lucien 1998 [1894], *Bangkok in 1892*, White Lotus, Bangkok.

Fraser, Keath (ed) 1993, *Worst journeys: the Picador book of travel,* Picador, London.

Friend, Tad 2005, 'The parachute artist: have Tony Wheeler's guidebooks traveled too far?', *The New Yorker*, 18 April, www.newyorker.com/archive/2005/04/18/050418fa_fact_friend, viewed 1.7.2008. Reprinted as 'He's been everywhere, man', *Good Weekend* (*The Age*), 13 August.

Furze, Carey 2003, *Held*, McMillan, Rozelle.

Fussell, Paul (ed) 1987, *The Norton book of travel*, WW Norton and Co, New York.

Gagliardi, Jason 2004, 'Glittering golden temples', *South China Morning Post*, 23 December. Also on www.equinoxpublishing.com/bio/default.htm, viewed 1.7.2008.

—— 2006, 'Coup in Asia, no one dead', *The First Post*, 20 September, www.thefirstpost.co.uk/1583,features,coup-in-asia-no-one-dead, viewed 1.7.2008.

Gailert Nana and Pramin Kreuathong 2004, *Palace spy, or, the world of illusion of Anna Leonowens*, Matichon, Bangkok. Thai language.

Garland, Alex 1997 [1996], *The beach*, Penguin, London,

Gebicki, Michael 2005, 'After the tsunami: return to paradise', *Royal Auto*, March.

Geldof, Bob 1986, *Is that it?* Penguin Books, London.

—— 1993, 'Is that it?' in Fraser, Keath (ed), *Worst journeys: The Picador book of travel*, Picador, London.

Gerster, Robin 1992 [1987], *Big-noting: the heroic theme in Australian war writing*, Melbourne University Press, Carlton.

—— (ed) 1995, *Hotel Asia*, Penguin, Ringwood.

Gerster, Robin, and Peter Pierce (eds) 2004, *On the war-path: an anthology of Australian military travel*, Melbourne University Press, Melbourne.

Gilbert, Helen and Anna Johnston (eds) 2002, *In transit: travel, text, empire*, Peter Lang, New York.

Gluckman, Ron c1999, 'Big bucks in backpacking', interview with Tony Wheeler, gluckman.com/LonelyPlanet.htm, viewed 1.7.08.

Gollin, Rita K 2002, *Annie Adams Fields: woman of letters*, University of Massachusetts Press, Amherst.

Goodden, Christian 2001, *Hinterlands: sixteen new do-it-yourself jungle treks in Thailand's Nan and Mae Hong Son provinces*, Jungle Books, London.

Goodenow, Earle (illus) 2004 [1946], *The Arabian Nights*, Grosset and Dunlap, New York.

Gordon, Ernest 1963, *Miracle on the River Kwai*, Quality Book Club, London.

Graham, AW 1912, *Siam: a handbook of practical, commercial, and political information*, Alexander Moring Ltd, London.

Gray, Paul and Lucy Ridout 2007 *The Rough Guide to Bangkok*, 4th ed, Rough Guides, New York.

Gregory, Sandra, and Michael Tierney 2003, *Forget you had a daughter: doing time in the 'Bangkok Hilton'*, Vision, London.

Grewal, Inderpal 1996, *Home and harem: nation, gender, empire and the cultures of travel*, Duke University Press, Durham.

Griswold, Alexander B 1961, *King Mongkut of Siam*, Asia Society, New York.

Groen, Rick 1997, 'Has director abused the power of film?' in Berry, Chris, Annette Hamilton and Laleen Jayamanne, *The filmmaker and the prostitute: Dennis O'Rourke's* The good woman of Bangkok, Power Publications, Sydney.

A guide to Kanchanaburi, Thailand c1992, no publisher named. In Thai and English. Purchased on location at the 'bridge on the River Kwai', 1992.

Habegger, Alfred, and Gerard Foley 2009 (forthcoming), 'Thomas and Anna Leonowens in Western Australia', *Early Days: Journal of the Royal Western Australian History Society.*

Hakluyt, Richard 1589, *The principal navigations, voyages, and discoveries of the English nation*, George Bishop and Ralph Newberie, London.

Hamilton, Alexander 1997 [1727], *A Scottish sea captain in South East Asia 1689–1723*, Michael Smithies (ed), Silkworm Books, Chiang Mai.

Hamilton, Annette 1997, 'Mistaken identities: art, truth and dare' in Berry, Chris, Annette Hamilton and Laleen Jayamanne, *The filmmaker and the prostitute: Dennis O'Rourke's The good woman of Bangkok*, Power Publications, Sydney.

Hámori, László 1966, *Adventure in Bangkok*, Annabelle MacMillan (trans), Robert Frankenberg (illus), Harcourt, Brace & World, New York.

Hand, Elizabeth 1999, *Anna and the King*, HarperEntertainment, New York.

Handley, Paul M 2006, *The King never smiles: a biography of Thailand's Bhumibol Adulyadej*, Yale University Press, New Haven.

Hartzell, Jessie MacKinnon 2001, *Mission to Siam: the memoirs of Jessie MacKinnon Hartzell*, Joan Acocella (ed), University of Hawai'i Press, Honolulu.

Harvey World Travel advertisement 2005, Escape, *Sunday Herald Sun*, 8 May.

Heeres, JE, and CH Coote (eds) 1965 [1898]), *Abel Jansz Tasman's journal of his discovery of Van Diemens Land & New Zealand in 1642, with documents relating to his exploration of Australia in 1644*, NA Kovich, Los Angeles.

Hicks, Andrew 2004a, *Thai girl*, TYS Books, Bangkok.

—— 2004b 'Readers forum' *Thai girl* website, www.thaigirl2004.com/reader%20 Forum.html, viewed 1.7.2008.

—— 2004c 'Why I wrote *Thai girl*', *Thai girl* website, www.thaigirl2004.com/ why%20i%20wrote.html, viewed 1.7.2008.

Higham, Charles FW 2004, *Encyclopedia of ancient Asian civilizations*, Facts on File, New York.

Hodgson, Barbara 2005, *Dreaming of East: Western women and the exotic allure of the Orient*, Greystone Books, Vancouver.

Holland, Cecilia 1999, *The Story of Anna and the King*, HarperEntertainment, New York.

Holland, Patrick, and Graham Huggan 2003 [1998], *Tourists with typewriters: critical reflections on contemporary travel writing*, University of Michigan Press, Ann Arbor.

Hollinger, Carol 1977 [1965], *Mai pen rai means never mind: an American housewife's honest love affair with the irrepressible people of Thailand*, Asia Book Co, Bangkok.

—— 1997, 'Where the footnotes went' in O'Reilly, James, and Larry Habegger (eds), *Travelers' tales guides Thailand: true stories of life on the road*, Travelers' Tales Inc, San Francisco.

Hong Lysa 1999, 'Palace women at the margins of social change: an aspect of the politics of social history in the reign of King Chulalongkorn', *Journal of Southeast Asian Studies*, (30).

—— 2002, 'Extraterritoriality in semi-colonial Bangkok during the reign of King Chulalongkorn', lecture at Monash University, Melbourne, 15 August.

Hopkins, Jerry 2005, *Bangkok Babylon: the real-life exploits of Bangkok's legendary expatriates are often stranger than fiction*, Periplus, Singapore.

Hoskin, John 2002, *Falcon at the Court of Siam*, Asia Books, Bangkok.

—— 2006, *Globetrotter travel guide Thailand*, 6th ed, New Holland Publishers, London.

Houellebecq, Michel 2002, *Platform*, Frank Wynne (trans), William Heinemann, London. Originally published 1999 in French with the title *Plateforme*.

Hudak, Thomas John 1994, 'Thailand' in *Traveller's literary companion: South-East Asia*, Alistair Dingwall (ed), In Print Publishing, Brighton.

Hudson, Roy 1973, *Hudson's guide to Chiang Mai and the north*, 5th ed, Hudson Enterprises, Chiang Mai.

Hunter, Eileen, and Narissa Chakrabongse 1994, *Katya and the Prince of Siam*, River Books, Thailand.

Hunter, Melanie R 2002, 'British travel writing and imperial authority' in Siegel, Kristi (ed), *Issues in travel writing: empire, spectacle, and displacement*, Peter Lang, New York.

Ishiguro, Kazuo 2000, *When we were orphans*, Faber and Faber, London.

Iyer, Pico 1997, 'Paradise found, paradise lost', in O'Reilly, James and Larry Habegger (eds) *Travelers' Tales Guides Thailand*, Travelers' Tales Inc, San Francisco. Originally published as 'Indian summer of love' in *Islands*, January/Februrary 1991.

—— 2001 [1998], *Video night in Kathmandu and other reports from the not-so-Far East*, Bloomsbury, London.

—— 2003, 'The art of titillation: cheap sex. cheap drugs. sordid foreigners. Books about Thailand rarely escape the tawdry clichés', *Time Asia*, 9 June.

Jackson, Peter A 2008, 'Thai semicolonial hybridities: Bhabha and Garcia Canclini in dialogue on power and cultural blending' *Asian Studies Review*, 32(2), June.

—— 2004, 'The performative state: semi-coloniality and the tyranny of images in modern Thailand', *Sojourn: Journal of Social Issues in Southeast Asia*, 19(2).

James, Caron 1999a, 'Blockbusters—Starring Thailand', *Thailand and Indochina traveller*, February–March.

—— 1999b, *The Occidentals*, Asia Books, Bangkok.

—— 2001, 'Take Tak, too: Caron James braves the wild, wild east of Thailand's Tak', Future Lifestyles, *The Sunday Age*, 21 October.

—— 2006, 'Constructing Thailand: a literary history of western representation', PhD thesis, Monash University, Clayton.

Jenkins, David 1973, *Student guide to Asia*, Australian Union of Students, Acme Books, East Brunswick.

Jenkins, Ruth Y 2004, 'The gaze of the Victorian woman traveler: spectacles and phenomena' in Siegel, Kristi (ed), *Gender, genre, and identity in women's travel writing*, Peter Lang, New York.

Kabbani, Rana 1994, *Imperial fictions: Europe's myths of Orient*, Pandora, London.

Kaempfer, Engelbert 2003 [1727], *A description of the Kingdom of Siam*, Orchid Press, Bangkok. First published 1906 as *The history of Japan...together with a description of the Kingdom of Siam*, JG Scheuchzer and J MacLehose (trans), Glasgow.

Kampoon Boontawee 1988, *A child of the northeast*, Susan Fulop Kepner (trans), Editions Duangkamol, Bangkok.

Kanok Abhiradee 2005, 'President's message', *Sawasdee*, March.

Kaplan, Robert D 1996, *The ends of the earth: a journey at the dawn of the 21st century*, Random House, New York.

Kehm, Michelle 2001, 'Redeye to Thai' in Conlon, Faith, Ingrid Emerick and Christina Henry de Tessan (eds), *A woman alone: travel tales from around the globe*, Seal Press, Emeryville.

Kepner, Susan Fulop 1996a, 'Anna and Margaret and the King of Siam', *Crossroads: An Interdisciplinary Journal of Southeast Asian Studies*, 10(2).

—— (ed) 1996b, *The Lioness in bloom: modern Thai fiction about women*, University of California Press, Berkeley.

Khammaan Khonkhai 1982, *The teachers of Mad Dog Swamp*, Gehan Wijeyewardene (trans), University of Queensland Press, St Lucia.

Kim Korwong and Jaivid Rangthong 1950, *A new guide to Bangkok*, 2nd ed, Hatha Dhip, Bangkok.

'King Mongkut's letters to Anna: when madame teacher plays political negotiator' 2003, *Art and Culture* magazine. Thai language.

Kipling, Rudyard 1915 [1892], 'The ballad of East and West' in *Departmental ditties and ballads and barrack-room ballads*, Doubleday, New York.

Klein, Christina 2003, *Cold War Orientalism: Asia in the middlebrow imagination, 1945–1961*, University of California Press, Berkeley.

Klein, Naomi 2005, 'Profit$[sic] of doom', in *Good Weekend* (*The Age*), 14 May.

Knight, Mark 2004, 'Paradise Lost' (cartoon), *Herald Sun*, December 29.

Kon Krailat 1985, 'In the mirror' in Anderson, Benedict ROG, and Ruchira Mendiones, *In the mirror: literature and politics in Siam in the American era*, Editions Duang Kamol, Bangkok.

Kornerup, Ebbe 1999 [1928], *Thailand in the 1920s*, M Guiterman (trans), White Lotus, Bangkok.

Kosa Pan 2002, *The diary of Kosa Pan, Thai Ambassador to France June–July 1686*, Michael Smithies (ed), Silkworm Books, Chiang Mai.

Krull, Germaine, and Dorothea Melchers 1964, *Bangkok: Siam's City of Angels*, Robert Hale, London.

—— 1966, *Tales from Siam*, Robert Hale, London.

Kukrit Pramoj 1998 [1953], *Four reigns*, Silkworm Books, Chiang Mai.

Kurosawa, Susan (ed) 2004, 'Destination Thailand: welcome to the Land of Smiles', supplement, *The Weekend Australian*, 14–15 February.

Lach, Donald F, and Carol Flaumenhaft 1965, *Asia on the eve of Europe's expansion*, Prentice-Hall, Englewood Cliffs.

Lach, F, and Theodore Nicholas Foss 1990, 'Images of Asia and Asians in European fiction, 1500–1800' in Winks, Robin W, and James R Rush (eds), *Asia in Western fiction*, University of Hawai'i Press.

Landon, Margaret 1949, *Never dies the dream*, Doubleday and Co, New York.

—— 2000 [1943], *Anna and the King of Siam*, HarperPerennial, New York.

Langton, Marcia 1997, 'Some comments on *The good woman of Bangkok*' in Berry, Chris, Annette Hamilton and Laleen Jayamanne, *The filmmaker and the prostitute: Dennis O'Rourke's* The good woman of Bangkok, Power Publications, Sydney.

Larner, John 1999, *Marco Polo and the discovery of the world*, Yale University Press, New Haven.

Lawrence, Karen R 1994, *Penelope voyages: women and travel in the British literary tradition*, Cornell University Press, Ithaca.

Lederer, William J, and Eugene Burdick 1958, *The ugly American*, WW Norton, New York.

Leonowens, Anna 1873, *The romance of Siamese harem life*, Trübner and Co , London.

—— 1884, *Life and travel in India: being recollections of a journey before the days of railroads*, Trübner and Co, London.

—— 1953 [1873], *Siamese harem life* Freya Stark (intro), Arthur Baker Ltd, London.

—— 1988 [1870], *The English Governess at the Siamese Court*, Oxford University Press, New York.

—— 1991 [1873], *The romance of the harem*, Susan Morgan (ed), University Press of Virginia, Charlottesville. Originally published 1873 by James R Osgood, 1873.

Lewis, CS 2004, Letter to Margaret Landon, *The collected letters of CS Lewis vol II: Books, broadcasts, and the War 1931–1949*, Walter Hooper (ed), HarperSanFrancisco, New York.

Lightwood, Teresa 1960, *Teresa of Siam*, Cassell and Company, London.

Linschoten, Jan Huygen van 1885, *The Voyage of John Huygen van Linschoten to the East Indies in 1598*, Hakluyt Society, London.

Little, Alison, and Ann Pukas 2005, 'Tsunami: 2,000 British dead? Fears of cover up as toll suddenly rises', *International Express*, Australian edition, 11–17 January.

Livesey, Margot 1999, 'An innocent abroad', *New York Times*, 12 December.

Loos, Tamara 2006, *Subject Siam: family, law, and colonial modernity in Thailand*, Cornell University Press, Ithaca.

Loria, Peter 2002, *Soldiers in Siam*, Writers Club Press, Lincoln, 2002.

Loubère, Simon de la 1969 [1693], *A new historical relation of the Kingdom of Siam*, Oxford University Press, Kuala Lumpur.

Lyall, Kimina 2006, *Out of the blue: facing the tsunami*, ABC Books, Sydney.

Macdonald, Phil, and Carl Parkes 2001, *The National Geographic Traveler Thailand*, National Geographic Society, Washington DC.

Maier, Joseph 2006a, 'Easter letter', Mercy Centre, www.mercycentre.org, April.

——2006b, *Welcome to the Bangkok slaughterhouse: the battle for human dignity in Bangkok's bleakest slums*, Periplus, Singapore.

Maltin, Leonard (ed) 2001, *Leonard Maltin's movie and video guide*, Signet, New York.

Manich Jumsai, ML 1991, *King Mongkut of Thailand and the British: the model of a great friendship*, 3rd ed, Chalermnit, Bangkok.

Marchetti, Gina 1993, *Romance and the 'Yellow Peril': race, sex, and discursive strategies in Hollywood fictions*, University of California Press, Berkeley.

Martin, Fiona, et al 1997, 'Coming out show: china dolls, bar girls and dragon ladies' in Berry, Chris, Annette Hamilton and Laleen Jayamanne, *The filmmaker and the prostitute: Dennis O'Rourke's* The good woman of Bangkok, Power Publications, Sydney.

Martin, Jeannie 1997, 'Missionary positions' in Berry, Chris, Annette Hamilton and Laleen Jayamanne, *The filmmaker and the prostitute: Dennis O'Rourke's* The good woman of Bangkok, Power Publications, Sydney.

Masters, Catherine, and Brett Phibbs 2005, 'On this shattered island, the dead pile up on luggage trolleys', *NZ Herald*, 3 January.

Matheson, Veronica (ed) 2005, Escape, *Sunday Herald Sun*, 20 February.

Maugham, W Somerset 2001 [1930], *The Gentleman in the parlour*, Vintage, London.

May, Reginald le 1999 [1926], *An Asian arcady: the land and peoples of Northern Siam*, White Lotus, Bangkok.

McCarthy, James 1994 [1900], *Surveying and exploring in Siam with descriptions of Lao dependencies and of battles against the Chinese Haws*, White Lotus, Bangkok.

McDonell, Nick 2005, *The third brother*, Text, Melbourne.

McFarland, Mrs SG 1884, 'The schools of Siam' in Backus, Mary (ed), *Siam and Laos as seen by our American missionaries*, Presbyterian Board of Publication, Philadelphia.

McGilvary, Daniel 2002 [1912], *A half century among the Siamese and the Lao: an autobiography*, White Lotus, Bangkok.

Minney, RJ 1962, *Fanny and the Regent of Siam*, Collins, London.

Moffat, AL 1961, *Mongkut the King of Siam*, Cornell University Press, Ithaca.

Moore, Christopher G 2000, *Chairs,* Heaven Lake Press, Bangkok.

Morga, Antonio de 1868 [1609], *The Philippine Islands, Moluccas, Siam, Cambodia, Japan and China at the close of the sixteenth century*, Henry EJ Stanley (trans), Hakluyt Society, London.

Morgan, Susan (ed) 1996, *Place matters: gendered geography in Victorian women's travel books about South East Asia*, Rutgers University Press, New Brunswick.

—— 2008, *Bombay Anna: the real story and remarkable adventures of The King and I governess,* University of California Press, Berkeley.

Morison, Alan 2004, 'Tourists tell of hell in paradise', *The Age*, 27 December.

Moseley, CWRD (ed) 1983, *The travels of Sir John Mandeville*, Chaucer Press, Suffolk.

Mouhot, Henri 1989 [1860], *Travels in Siam, Cambodia and Laos, 1858–1860*, Oxford in Asia, Singapore.

Musgrove, Brian 1999, 'Travel and unsettlement: Freud on vacation' in Clark, Steve (ed), *Travel writing and empire: postcolonial theory in transit*, Zed Books, London.

Mydans, Seth 2005, 'After the tsunami, rebuilding paradise', *New York Times*, 24 April.

Myers, Robin, and Michael Harris (eds) 1999, *Journeys through the market: travel, travellers and the book trade*, Oak Knoll Press, Delaware.

Neale, FA 1999 [1852], *Narrative of a residence at the capital of the Kingdom of Siam*, White Lotus, Bangkok.

Neis, P 1997 [1884], *Travels in Upper Laos and Siam: with an account of the Chinese Haw invasion and Puan resistance*, White Lotus, Bangkok.

Nichols, Fiona 1985, *Phuket*, Times Editions, Singapore.

Nicoll, Allardyce 1923, *A history of restoration drama 1600–1700*, Cambridge University Press, Cambridge.

Nine Network 2007, Media Release for *Sunday*, 'Sunday, November 18 at the special time of 8am–10am', 16 November.

Nithi Sthapitanonda and Brian Mertens 2006, *Architecture of Thailand: a guide to traditional and contemporary forms*, Thames & Hudson, London.

Noy Thrupkaew 2003, 'The King and Thai: a contested history gets the royal treatment', *The American Prospect*, 8, August 31, www.prospect.org/cs/ articles?article=the_king_and_thai, viewed 1.7.2008.

Oaten, Edward Farley 1973 [1909], *European travellers in India during the fifteenth, sixteenth and seventeenth centuries*, Pustak Kendra, Lucknow.

Oates, Carlie 2007, 'Phuket: if poolside foot scrubs, cocktails and canoeing through secluded lagoons sound like paradise, this island may just be your heaven on earth', *Sunday Magazine* (*Sunday Herald Sun*), 16 September.

Odzer, Cleo 1997, *Patpong sisters: an American woman's view of the Bangkok sex world*, Arcade Publishing, New York.

Olearius, Adam 1662, *The voyages and travels of the ambassadors sent by Frederick Duke of Holstein, to the great Duke of Muscovy, and the King of Persia*, Thomas Dring and John Starkey, London.

O'Neill, Thomas 1997, 'The Mekong', in O'Reilly, James, and Larry Habegger (eds), *Travelers' tales guides Thailand: true stories of life on the road*, Travelers' Tales Inc, San Francisco.

Onnucha Hutasingh 2006, 'King's exhibit poorly prepared', *Bangkok Post*, 17 September.

O'Reilly, James, and Larry Habegger (eds) 1997, *Travelers' tales guides Thailand: true stories of life on the road*, Travelers' Tales Inc, San Francisco.

O'Rourke, Dennis 1996,'Documentary fictions: bibliography, truth and moral Lies', *Documenting a life*, seminar, National Library of Australia, Canberra, October 26, www.nla.gov.au/events/doclife/orourke.html, viewed 1.7.2008.

—— 'Afterword: *The filmmaker and the prostitute*—the controversy over *The good woman of Bangkok*' in Berry, Chris, Annette Hamilton and Laleen Jayamanne, *The filmmaker and the prostitute: Dennis O'Rourke's* The good woman of Bangkok, Power Publications, Sydney.

Osterhammel, Jürgen 1997, *Colonialism: a theoretical overview*, Marcus Wiener Publishers, Princeton.

Palling Bruce 2006, 'The billionaire who lost his country', *The First Post*, 20 September, www.thefirstpost.co.uk/1966,features,the-billionaire-who-lost-his-country, viewed 1.7.2008.

Papineau, Aristide JG 1973, *Papineau's guide to Bangkok city of enchantment*, 7th ed, André Publications, Singapore.

Parkes, Carl 2000, *Bangkok handbook*, 3rd ed, Moon Travel Handbooks, Avalon Travel Publishing, Emeryville.

Parkin, Ray 1963 *Into the smother*, Hogarth, London.

—— 1999, *Ray Parkin's wartime trilogy*, Melbourne University Press, Melbourne.

Peek, Ian Denys 2003, *One fourteenth of an elephant: a memoir of life and death on the Burma-Thailand Railway*, Pan, Sydney.

Pinto, Fernão Mendes 1904, *Subsidios para a sua biographia e para o estudo da sua obra*, Christovam Ayres (ed), Typographia da Academia, Lisbon.

——1983, *Cartas de Fernão Mendes Pinto e outros documentos*, Rebecca Catz (ed), Biblioteca National/Editorial Presença, Lisbon.

—— 1989 [1614], *The travels of Mendes Pinto*, Rebecca D Catz (ed and trans), University of Chicago Press, Chicago.

Piprell, Colin 2001, *Bangkok knights*, Asia Books, Bangkok.

Pira Sudham 1991 [1983], *Pira Sudham's best: Siamese drama and other stories from Thailand*, Shire Books, Bangkok.

—— 2004, *Shadowed country*, Asiashire, Bangkok.

Pirazzi, Chris, and Vitida Vasant 2004, *Thailand fever: a road map for Thai-Western relationships*, Paiboon Poomsan Publishing, Bangkok.

Polo, Marco 1975 [1298], *The book of Ser Marco Polo the Venetian concerning the kingdoms and marvels of the East*, John Murray, London. Translated by Henry Yule in 1871 and edited for publication by H Cordier in 1903.

Poole, Frederick King 1970, *Bangkok!*, photographs and guide by Nik Wheeler, Asia Pacific Press, Singapore.

Pornsawan Tripasai 2003, 'Simulating Siam: case studies in the imaginative colonisation of Thailand', MA thesis, Monash University, Clayton.

—— 2004, 'Debating Anna: the textual politics of English literature teaching in Thailand', Australian Association for Research in Education conference, Melbourne, November.

—— 2006, 'Anna Leonowens and the imaginative colonisation of Thailand', 16th Biennial Conference of the Asian Studies Association of Australia, Wollongong, June 26–29.

Powers, John 1997, 'An unreliable memoir' in Berry, Chris, Annette Hamilton and Laleen Jayamanne, *The filmmaker and the prostitute: Dennis O'Rourke's The good woman of Bangkok*, Power Publications, Sydney.

Prasso, Sheridan 2006, *The Asian mystique: dragon ladies, geisha girls and our fantasies of the exotic Orient*, Public Affairs, New York.

Pratt, Mary Louise 1992, *Imperial eyes: travel writing and transculturation*, Routledge, London.

Quartermaine, Ian 2005, *Sleepless in Bangkok*, IQ Inc, Bangkok.

Rattawut Lapcharoensap 2005, *Sightseeing*, Picador, Sydney.

Reed, Thomas E 1999, *Anna and the King* user comments, 28 May, www.imdb.com/title/tt0068039/maindetails#comment, viewed 1.7.2008.

Regan, Tom 1999, 'The life and times of Anna…and the film: The King and a lie', *Bangkok Post*, 24 December.

Reid, Daniel 1990, *Our world in colour: Bangkok*, The Guidebook Company, Hong Kong.

Renard, Ronald D 2001, Review, *The Journal of the Siam Society*, 89(1&2).

Reynolds, Craig J 2006, *Seditious histories: contesting Thai and Southeast Asian pasts*, University of Washington Press, Seattle.

Reynolds, E Bruce 2004, *Thailand's secret war: the free Thai, OSS, and SOE during World War II*, Cambridge University Press, Cambridge.

Reynolds, Jack 1956, *A woman of Bangkok*, Ballantine, New York.

Richardson, D 2004, *Dr Richardson's missions to Siam 1829–1839*, Anthony Farrington (ed), White Lotus, Bangkok.

Riding, Alan 2004, 'Globe-trotting Englishwomen who helped map the world', *NY Times*, August 19.

Rivett, Rohan D 1957 [1946], *Behind Bamboo: an inside story of the Japanese prison Camps*, Angus and Robertson, London.

Roberts, Edmund 1972 [1837], *Embassy to the Eastern Courts of Cochin-China, Siam, and Muscat; in the U.S. Sloop-of-War Peacock, David Geisinger, Commander, during the years 1832–3–4*, Scholarly Resources, Delaware.

Robinson, Jane 1990, *Wayward women: a guide to women travellers*, Oxford University Press, Oxford.

Rong Syamananda 1990 [1971], *A history of Thailand*, 7th ed, Chulalongkorn University, Bangkok.

Ruengvuth Vuthrikrisan 1997, 'The good woman of Bangkok: looking back and forth' in Berry, Chris, Annette Hamilton and Laleen Jayamanne, *The filmmaker and the prostitute: Dennis O'Rourke's The good woman of Bangkok*, Power Publications, Sydney.

Rushdie, Salman 1988, *The Satanic verses*, Viking, London.

Russell, Mary 1986, *The blessings of a good thick skirt: women travellers and their families*, Collins, London.

Said, Edward W 1994 [1993], *Culture and imperialism*, Vintage, London.

—— 2000, 'Orientalism reconsidered' in Macfie, AL (ed), *Orientalism: a reader*, Edinburgh University Press, Edinburgh.

—— 2003 [1978], *Orientalism: Western conceptions of the Orient*, Penguin, London.

Savage, Angela 2006, *Behind the night bazaar*, Text, Melbourne.

Seabrook, Jeremy 2004, 'In death, imperialism lives on', *The Guardian*, 31 December, www.guardian.co.uk/world/2004/dec/31/tsunami2004.pressandpublishing, viewed 1.7.2008.

Seidenfaden, Eric 1958 [1928], *Guide to Bangkok with notes on Siam*, Siam Society, Bangkok.

Seni Pramoj and Kukrit Pramoj 1987 [1948], *A King of Siam speaks*, Siam Society, Bangkok.

Shearer, Alistair 1989, *Thailand the Lotus Kingdom*, John Murray, London.

Sheehan, Sean 2002, *The magic of Bangkok*, New Holland Publishers, London.

Sheward, Tamara 2003, *bad karma: confessions of a reckless traveller in Southeast Asia*, Penguin, Camberwell.

Siam and the Siamese as described by American missionaries, 1886, T Woolmer, London.

Siegel, Kristi 2002 (ed), *Issues in travel writing: empire, spectacle, and Displacement*, Peter Lang, New York.

—— (ed) 2004, *Gender, genre, and identity in women's travel writing*, Peter Lang, New York.

Siegel, Kristi and Toni B Wulff 2002, 'Travel as spectacle: the illusion of knowledge and sight', in Siegel, *Issues in travel writing: empire, spectacle, and displacement*, Peter Lang, New York.

Sioris, George A 1998, *Phaulkon, the Greek First Counsellor at the Court of Siam: an appraisal*, Siam Society, Bangkok.

Slouka, Mark 2003, *God's fool*, Picador, London.

Smith, Malcolm, 1947, *A physician at the Court of Siam*, Country Life, London.

Smith, Wendy 2004, 'Lily Tuck: at home as a foreigner', *Publishers Weekly*, 7 June.

Smithies, Michael 1995, 'Anna Leonowens', in Gullick, John (ed), *Adventurous women in South-East Asia: six lives*, Oxford University Press, Kuala Lumpur.

—— (ed) 1997a, *Aspects of the Embassy to Siam 1685*, Silkworm Books, Chiang Mai

—— 1997b, *The Siamese memories of the Count Claude de Forbin 1685–1688*, Silkworm, Chiang Mai.

—— 2001a, 'On books for the Ayutthayan Era', *The Journal of the Siam Society*, 89(1/2).

—— 2001b, 'On books from the nineteenth century: address by Michael Smithies, 11 October 2001', *The Journal of the Siam Society*, 89(1/2).

Smyth, H Warrington 1994 [1898], *Five years in Siam from 1891–1896*, 2v, White Lotus, Bangkok.

Somtow, SP 2002 [1994], *Jasmine nights*, Asia Books.

Sparrow, Gerald 1955, *Land of the moon flower*, Elek Books, London.

Spurr, David 2001 [1993], *The rhetoric of empire: colonial discourse in journalism, travel writing, and imperial administration*, Duke University Press, Durham.

Sriwittayapaknam School (1999), *Anna and* The King and I: *a historical look at* The King and I, Samut Pakran, www.thaistudents.com/kingandi/, viewed 1.7.2008.

Stanton, Mary Bulkley (ed) 2003, *Siam was our home: a narrative memoir of Edna Bruner Bulkley's years in Thailand in the early 1900s, with added memories from her children*, Hara Publishing, Seattle.

Stephens, Harold 2005, 'The mighty oriental jungle of Southeast Asia, exploring the world's oldest rainforest', *ROH Weekly Travel Feature*, www.thaiair.com/Royal_Orchid_Holidays/Roh_travel_feature/rohweekly-69tharticle-1.htm, viewed 1.7.2008.

Stevenson, William 2001, *The revolutionary King: the true-life sequel to* The King and I, Robinson, London.

Strach, Walter 2000, 'Constance Phaulkon: myth or reality?', *Explorations in Southeast Asian Studies* (4).

Strandberg, Olle 1953, *Tigerland and South Sea*, Michael Joseph, London.

Strauss, Darin 2000, *Chang and Eng*, Plume, New York.

Suárez, Thomas 1999, *Early mapping of Southeast Asia*, Periplus, Hong Kong.

Summers, Julie 2005, *The Colonel of Tamarkan: Philip Toosey and the Bridge on the River Kwai*, Simon and Schuster, London.

The Sunday Age 2005, 'World unites in mercy', 2 January.

Supharb Lim 1997, 'The good woman of Bangkok' in Berry, Chris, Annette Hamilton and Laleen Jayamanne, *The filmmaker and the prostitute: Dennis O'Rourke's* The good woman of Bangkok, Power Publications, Sydney.

Swinglehurst, Edmund 1982, *Cook's tours: the story of popular travel*, Blandford Press, Poole.

Tang, Alisa 2005, 'Tsunami wipes out overdeveloped tourist spots', *Honolulu Advertiser*, 7 January.

Terwiel, BJ 1989, *Through travellers' eyes: an approach to early nineteenth-century Thai history*, Editions Duang Kamol, Bangkok.

—— 2005, *Thailand's political history from the fall of Ayutthaya to recent times*, River Books, Bangkok.

Tew Bunnag 2003, *Fragile days: tales from Bangkok*, SNP International, Singapore.

Thai Airways advertisement 2005, Escape, *Sunday Herald Sun*, 6 March.

Thiro, Rosalyn (ed) 2004, *Eyewitness travel guides Thailand*, 6th ed, Dorling Kindersley, London.

Thongbai Thongpao 2001, 'Movies are not so precious as friends', *Bangkok Post*, 24 June.

Thongchai Winichakul 1997 [1994], *Siam mapped: a history of the geo-body of a nation*, University of Hawai'i Press, Honolulu.

Thong-in Soonsawad 1966 [1965], *Panorama of Thailand: a guide to the wonders and highlights of Thailand*, 2nd ed, Printing Incorporated, Wichita.

Time Australia 2005, 'Special Report, January 10.

Tips, Walter EJ (ed and intro) 1996, *The 1894 directory for Bangkok and Siam*, White Lotus, Bangkok. Original edited by Charles Thorne (1894).

Torney-Parlicki, Prue 2000, *Somewhere in Asia: war, journalism and Australia's neighbours 1941-1975*, University of New South Wales Press, Sydney.

Tourism Authority of Thailand 2005, *Andaman today* brochure.

Travel Indochina 2004/2005, *Handmade holidays Thailand*.

Tuck, Lily 1999, *Siam or the woman who shot a man: a novel*, Plume, New York.

Uamdao Noikorn 1999, 'Film Board to get third script of *Anna and the King'*, *Bangkok Post*, 8 December.

Uchtomskij, Prince Esper Esperovitch 1999 [1894], *Csarevitch Nicolas of Russia in Siam and Saigon*, Walter EJ Tips (ed and trans), White Lotus, Bangkok.

Urry, John 2002 [1991], *The tourist gaze*, Sage Publications, London.

Varthema, Ludovico di 1970 [1510], *Itinerary of Ludovico di Varthema of Bologna from 1502 to 1508*, Richard Carnac Temple (ed), N Israel, Amsterdam and Da Capo Press, New York.

Vickers, Adrian 1989, *Bali: a paradise created*, Periplus, Hong Kong.

Vincent, Frank 1988 [1874], *The land of the white elephant*, White Lotus, Bangkok.

Vries, Clare de 2002, *Of cats and kings*, Bloomsbury, London.

Walker, Dave, and Richard S Ehrlich (eds) 1995 [1992], *"Hello my big big honey!": love letters to Bangkok bar girls and their revealing interviews*, Dragon Dance, Bangkok.

Wanit Jarungkit-anan 1985, 'Michigan test' in Anderson, Benedict ROG, and Ruchira Mendiones, *In the mirror: literature and politics in Siam in the American Era*, Editions Duang Kamol, Bangkok.

Warren, William 1988, *The Grand Palace*, with pictures by Manop Boonyavatana, The Office of His Majesty's Private Secretary, Bangkok.

—— 1992, 'Who was Anna Leonowens?', *Sawasdee*, Thai Airways, Hong Kong, February.

—— 'Who Was Anna Leonowens?' in O'Reilly, James and Larry Habegger (eds), *Travelers' tales guides Thailand: true stories of life on the road*, Travelers' Tales Inc, San Francisco.

—— 1998, *Jim Thompson: the unsolved mystery*, Archipelago Press, Singapore.

—— 1999, 'King ranks among the country's greats', Postbag, *Bangkok Post*, 9 December.

—— 2000, *The truth About Anna...and other stories*, Archipelago Press, Singapore.

—— 2002, *Bangkok*, Reaktion Books, London.

Waterson, Steve (ed) 2005, 'Special report', *Time Australia*, 10 January.

Waugh, Alec 1990 [1970], *Alec Waugh's Bangkok: story of a city*, Orientations, Bangkok.

Waugh, Evelyn 1959 [1946], *When the going was good*, Penguin, Harmondsworth.

Wells, Kenneth E 1958, *History of Protestant work in Thailand 1828–1958*, Church of Christ in Thailand, Bangkok.

Westerhausen, Klaus 2002, *Beyond the beach: an ethnography of modern travellers in Asia*, White Lotus, Bangkok.

Wheaton College Archives and Special Collections *Margaret and Kenneth Landon Papers*, Wheaton, www.wheaton.edu/learnres/ARCSC/collects/sc38/, viewed 1.7.2008.

Wheeler, Tony 1975, *South East Asia on a shoestring*, Lonely Planet, South Yarra.

Wheeler, Tony, and Maureen Wheeler 2005, *Once while travelling: The Lonely Planet story*, Viking, Camberwell.

Williams, China 2007, *Lonely Planet Bangkok encounter*, Lonely Planet, Melbourne.

Williams, China, Aaron Anderson, Brett Atkinson, Tim Bewer, Becca Blond, Virginia Jealous, and Lisa Steer 2007, *Lonely Planet Thailand*, 12th ed, Lonely Planet, Melbourne.

—— 2006, *Lonely Planet Thailand's Islands and Beaches*, 5th ed, Lonely Planet, Melbourne.

—— 2008, *South East Asia on a Shoestring*, 13th ed, Lonely Planet, Melbourne.

Wilmington, Michael 1997, '"Bangkok": powerful, unsettling' in Berry, Chris, Annette Hamilton and Laleen Jayamanne, *The filmmaker and the prostitute: Dennis O'Rourke's* The good woman of Bangkok, Power Publications, Sydney.

Wimon Wiriyawit 1997, *Free Thai: personal recollections and official documents*, White Lotus, Bangkok.

Winks, Robin W, and James R Rush, (eds) 1990, *Asia in Western fiction*, University of Hawai'i Press.

Wood, WAR 1926, 'Fernao Mendez Pinto's account of events in Siam', *Journal of the Siam Society*, 20(1).

—— 1991 [1965], *Consul in paradise: sixty-nine years in Siam*, Trasvin, Bangkok.

Wraps of the World advertisement 2005, *Fresh* magazine and others, Pillsbury.

Wright, Arnold, and Oliver Breakspear 1994 [1903], *Twentieth century impressions of Siam*, White Lotus, Bangkok.

Wyatt, David K, and Aroonrut Wichienkeeo (eds) 1998, *The Chiang Mai chronicle*, 2nd ed, Silkworm, Chiang Mai.

Wyatt, David K (ed) 2000, *The Royal chronicles of Ayutthaya: a synoptic translation*, Siam Society, Bangkok.

—— 2002, *Siam in Mind*, Silkworm, Chiang Mai.

—— (ed) 2003, *Thailand: a short history*, 2nd ed, Yale University Press, New Haven.

Young, Ernest 1986 [1898], *The Kingdom of the yellow robe: a description of Old Siam*, Oxford University Press, Singapore.

Yvonne Bohwongprasert 2005, 'Travel writer soldiers on', *Bangkok Post*, 5 May.

Ziv, Daniel, and Guy Sharett 2005, *Bangkok inside out*, Equinox, Bangkok.

Stage & Screen productions

Films listed under directors' names

Andersson, Benny, Bjorn Ulvaeus and Tim Rice 1984, 'One night in Bangkok', song performed by Murray Head, from the musical, *Chess*.

Boyle, Danny, *The beach*, film, US, 2000.

Cameron, Ken 1989, *Bangkok Hilton*, TV mini-series, Australia.

Chatri Chalerm Yukol 2001, *The legend of Suriyothai*, film, Thailand, foreign release 2003.

Chelsom 2004, Peter, *Shall we dance?*, film, US.

Cromwell, John 1946, *Anna and the King of Siam*, film, US.

Englund, George 1963, *The ugly American*, film, US.

Jaeckin, Just 1974, *Emmanuelle*, film, France.

Kaplan, Jonathan 1999, *Brokedown palace*, film, US.

Kidron, Beeban 2004, *Bridget Jones: the edge of reason*, film, US-UK-France.

Lang, Walter 1956, *The King and I*, film, US.

Lean, David 1957, *The bridge on the River Kwai*, film, UK.

Mitchell, Mike 1999, *Deuce Bigalow: male gigolo*, film, US.

O'Rourke, Dennis 1991, *The good woman of Bangkok*, film, Australia and UK.

Rich, Richard 1999, *The King and I*, animated film, US-Australia.

Rogers, Richard and Hammerstein II, Oscar 1951, *The King and I*, stage show, Broadway, US.

Smith, Steven 1999 *Anna and the King: the real story of Anna Leonowens*, documentary, US.

Tennant, Andy 1999, *Anna and the King*, film, US.

Trecartin, F Whitman, and Karen Whiteside 2000, *Anna Leonowens: getting to know you*, documentary, UK and Canada.

Twentieth Century Fox TV 1972, *Anna and the King*, TV series, US.